The Secret Lives
of Sports Fans

ALSO BY ERIC SIMONS

Darwin Slept Here

The Secret Lives of Sports Fans

THE SCIENCE OF SPORTS OBSESSION

Eric Simons

OVERLOOK DUCKWORTH
NEW YORK • LONDON

For Dad and Nick,
There's always next year
And for Mom and Hari,
There's always the off season

This edition first published in hardcover in the United States and the
United Kingdom in 2013 by Overlook Duckworth, Peter Mayer Publishers, Inc.

NEW YORK
141 Wooster Street
New York, NY 10012
www.overlookpress.com
For bulk and special sales, please contact sales@overlookny.com,
or write us at the above address

LONDON
90-93 Cowcross Street
London EC1M 6BF
inquiries@duckworth-publishers.co.uk
www.ducknet.co.uk

Cataloging-in-Publication Data is available from the Library of Congress

Book design and typeformatting by Bernard Schleifer
Manufactured in the United States of America
ISBN US: 978-1-59020-864-9
ISBN UK: 978-0-7156-4527-7

Contents

Introduction: Fan Nature

FROM THE BREAK OF THE HUDDLE TO THE BREAK OF THE heart takes about ten seconds.* Ten: The twenty-year-old University of California quarterback Kevin Riley, our champion and savior in just his first collegiate game, emerges from amid his teammates and strides confidently to the line of scrimmage. Down by three points, fourteen seconds to go, no time-outs, twelve yards away from a glorious victory. Riley has played brilliantly in the debut performance of a lifetime. In the stands we are in love, swooning with expectant joy.

Nine: Fifty rows high in California Memorial Stadium I stand with my father, my companion at Cal football games since he hauled me out on his shoulders when I was four months old. My dad has been going to Cal games since his first year at Berkeley in 1971, when he went to watch a high

---

*Thank you, Michael Lewis.

school acquaintance play wide receiver. For thirty years he's had the same seats, section TT row 50, and now we're looking almost directly down on the action.

Eight: Riley snaps the ball and drops back to pass. Everyone is standing. Every*thing*: the hairs on my arms and neck are standing. It is absolutely *crackling* in the stadium, the greatest electrical storm any of us have ever experienced. My heart is pounding. It is a foggy, atmospheric October night in Berkeley. Sweat drips down my arms.

Seven: Riley scans the end zone, looking for the game-winning touchdown pass that will blow this crumbling old structure off its foundation. He may not know it, but up in the gallery we're aware that he's probably looking at the greatest array of Cal offensive talent any of us will ever see, with seven future pros on offense alone.

Six: None of the big names appears to be open. Riley moves to his left. A low murmur rumbles forth from the fans. *Throw the ball away.*

Five: Even if we don't get the touchdown here, it's okay. Riley will throw the ball away; we'll go to overtime. Surely, we cannot lose at home in overtime when we are the number-two-ranked team in the country and Oregon State is unranked. It's homecoming. The crowd is delirious after an inspired comeback. Number-one-ranked LSU has already lost. We will win—we will be fans of the number one team in college football—if we just get it to OT. None of us alive in this stadium has ever seen Cal ranked at the top in college football. Only a handful of us alive in this stadium have ever seen Cal win the Pacific-10 Conference and go to the hallowed Rose Bowl, which last happened in 1959. The school's last Rose Bowl victory was in 1938. We want this to happen so, so badly. It is a desire beyond longing, beyond lust, beyond addictive craving. *Throw the ball away, Kevin. Let's go.*

Four: Riley runs forward. He does not throw the ball away. I gasp. Seventy thousand people gasp. The Rubicon looms, beyond which he will either run for the winning touchdown or get tackled and force us to watch helplessly as time runs out. *Throw the ball away!*

Three: The die is cast. Riley is running. The collective inhalation of seventy thousand souls freezes the moment forever in our brains. None of us will ever forget this exact second of hopeless, helpless terror.

Two: Oregon State defenders swarm to Riley. He thrashes forward eight yards from the goal line. His knee hits the turf. The clock rolls.

One: Final score Oregon State 31, California 28.

Zero: The coach winds up and slams his headset into the grass. Seventy thousand stunned spectators stand silent. I teeter with hands on my head, my mouth agape, my soul on the rack.

An hour later I'm riding the train from Berkeley back to my home in San Francisco. It's Saturday night and the train is full of people going out to the city, people dressed in sophisticated theater clothes, people headed to pleasant restaurants with linen tablecloths and Napa cabernet, people headed for swanky cocktails and cheery friends. I'm slumping by myself, crammed defensively in the corner, feeling like absolute shit. My clothes are sweat-stained and reeking. My head aches from the constricting grasp of my faded Cal hat. For dinner I had a six-dollar steamed hot dog and a three-dollar bottle of water.

I describe this carefully because I think this sports experience was one of the most emotionally complicated moments of my life and it makes me more than a little curious about human biology to admit it. I think I had more of my brain active simultaneously in those ten seconds than I ever have in any other non-sporting circumstance. I say this, six years later and as soberly as I can, without judgment and certainly without pride. I loved my wedding. I loved being there for the birth of my daughter. Both were wonderful, rich, emotional occasions that I'll always cherish. I'm just saying that diversity-of-feelings-wise, neither one held a candle to the raging pep-rally bonfire inside me on the night of October 13, 2007. And when you know that more than a billion people around the world can all say, *Oh, dude, I've sure been* there *before*, you're no longer talking about some little quirk of human nature. Sports fandom appears to be a species-level design flaw.

In those ten seconds my hormone system blew up. My brain blew up. Neurons fired away like gangbusters in the brain centers for empathy, action, language, pride, identity, self, reward, relationships, love, addiction, perception, pain, and happiness. If you've seen those images at the end of heartbreaking games, where the fan is standing there with his hands on his head and his mouth yawning—or if you've been that fan—you know that it feels like all this stuff is frothing around on the inside trying to beat its way out of your body like an alien chest-burster.

This book seeks to explain the science behind what actually happened to me in those few moments, and to explain why we feel the way we do about sports and why so many rational people follow them with such seemingly irrational passion. As human beings we come equipped with reflex responses to watching competition. But we also make a cultural choice to be sports fans, and from that choice a host of other related personal and societal consequences follows. Drawing from science—mainly from fields far outside of sports psychology—as well as a bit of philosophy and sociology, the book answers the question of why we continue to make that choice even when the rewards often seem dubious. Watching sports is insanely complicated—and very personal—but underneath the layers of personality and culture lie the biological and psychological roots of a universal obsession.

WE TALK ABOUT SPORTS IN METAPHORS: AS WAR, AS LOVE, AS poetry, as ritual, as beastliness, as religion. It turns out that the quest to better understand those metaphors takes us to some delightful places. A lab in Portugal constructed a fish boxing-ring to learn about what happens to the testosterone of spectator fish. A researcher at Princeton created an elaborate ruse to get Yankees and Red Sox fans to lie in a brain scanner and revel in each other's misery. Two endocrinologists in British Columbia designed their own game of competitive Tetris to see how aggressive people get when they win a video game. A relationship scientist in New York brought loving couples into his lab to test how much a lifetime of romance had made their brains think alike. A social psychologist in Scotland applied the lessons of soccer crowds to improve modern policing. A sociologist in the 1950s taught pigeons to lift their heads for a treat so that he could see how long it takes an animal to stop doing something when it stops getting a reward. Almost anything can help explain sports fandom, so that's what this book is about: weird creatures and strange behaviors found in the lab and in the bleachers. And I surely do not want to discount in any way the rare crossovers, like the man who has dressed in a gorilla suit for every Oakland Raiders game for the last sixteen years.

It's not just the emotional component of sports fandom that's puzzling. Rationally, we know that we're often enabling athletes to destroy their minds and bodies for our amusement. Our spending at least lets our concussion-addled heroes jet to Vegas to make it rain in strip clubs. Our devotion leads to universities taking money from academics and prioritizing athletics, lowering standards to admit donor-inspiring athletes, and covering up any number of abuses. Our loyalty leads us to turn rival fans into inhuman enemies because they're wearing the wrong colors. Our gatherings can turn into crowd violence and destructive riots.

It's some small comfort to a defensive modern sports fan that the human race has managed to survive for thousands of years with the same problems. A fragment from the writings of the sixth-century BC Greek philosopher Xenophanes shows him complaining about his fellow citizens preferring athletes to philosophers and rewarding athletes with riches, acclaim, and public commemoration for useless skills like running or wrestling. "He would get all these things although he did not deserve them, as I deserve them, for our wisdom is better than the strength of men or of horses," Xenophanes wrote. "This is indeed a very wrong custom, nor is it right to prefer strength to excellent wisdom."

Upton Sinclair, the journalist and author of *The Jungle*, visited UC Berkeley for his 1922 book *The Goose-step* to watch what he called "the little barbarians at play." He related with disgust that Strawberry Canyon had been taken over for a million-dollar stadium, which he labeled an act of "vandalism." Sinclair was in his most withering form and saved the best for the students. "In other parts of the world, when you hear of the 'classics,' you think of Homer and Virgil; but in California the 'classics' are the annual Stanford-California foot-ball game, and the intercollegiate track-meet, and the Pacific Coast tennis doubles," he wrote. He visited a fraternity, where the "well-groomed young gladiators did not know quite how to talk to a Socialist author, so between courses of the dinner they relieved their embarrassment by singing, or rather shouting in very loud tones—and I observed that their songs invariably dealt with fighting somebody. I asked a student about to graduate what he thought of his classmates, and his answer was, 'They are a mob of little haters. They hate the Germans, they hate the Russians, they hate the Socialists, they hate the Japs. They are ready to hate the French or the English any time they are told to; and always they hate Stanford.'"

That philosophers and muckrakers have criticized sports fans for more than two thousand years indicates something about the universal nature of the way humans behave in the presence of competition. Certainly there are universal elements to our reaction, from the hormonal and neuronal reflexes that underlie our understanding of the world to the instantaneous groups that we construct to explain it. But what surprises me is how much control we have over those reflexes. Our predisposition to enjoy sports and to attach emotionally to teams is not a one-way track to mob violence, to warped priorities, or even to treating philosophers poorly. The more science reveals about those predispositions and those attachments, the clearer it is that sports fandom is a uniquely human endeavor that offers a surprising window into the emotional, rational, and irrational behaviors that have always made us what we are.

PART ONE
Reflex

1
The Edge of Your Seat: The Physical Experience of Fandom

IT IS DARK AND A LITTLE BIT STALE IN OUR CORNER OF KILO-watt, a bar in San Francisco. I am sitting on the edge of a maroon vinyl booth into which, if we were really drunk and friendly, we could squeeze probably six people. Tonight, for our special occasion, it's just the three of us, and we feel like we'd rather have the space. Ashwin slouches to my right in a checked shirt and fashionable hipster beard. Patrick sits across from me in a *Radiolab* T-shirt that shows off just a bit of tattooed bicep. On the other side of the room a bartender stands on a stepladder and changes the channel on the magnificent HD big-screen hanging on the wall. My beloved San Jose Sharks appear, skating warm-up circles on the blazing white ice. One or two Sharks fans hang around the bar, but back in our corner it's just the three of us in the booth and a few guys playing pool who barely glance up from the table. We have a pitcher of amber Great White Shark beer on the table and hockey on the television. It's game time.

I reach into my jacket pocket, pull out three test tubes, and spread them out on the table in front of me. They glint in the dim bar light, blue caps almost black. I hand Ashwin and Patrick each a plastic straw and a black marker to ID their samples. It's time for us to learn what's happening inside of us when we watch sports.

EARLY IN THE SPRING OF 1991, A POST-BACCALAUREATE STUDENT at Georgia State University named Paul Bernhardt went on a prison visit with a faculty mentor. The mentor, a well-known testosterone researcher named James Dabbs, was studying the roots of aggression in men and was looking for a link between high levels of the hormone testosterone and violent crime. Bernhardt was there to help by collecting spit samples from the inmates, from which they could measure the testosterone.

Bernhardt doesn't remember much about the prison visit, but he remembers stopping for lunch on the way back. He and Dabbs started tossing around ideas, considering all the splendid ways testosterone might manifest itself in aggressive behavior. It's trickier than you might think; the obvious experiment of injecting people with testosterone doesn't really seem to make them any more aggressive at all. But there is an enormous scientific literature on this subject showing males—not just men, you see, because this is true in birds and monkeys and rats and, well, pretty much every species that has testosterone and females around to have sex with—behaving belligerently in the presence of high testosterone. Dabbs (who died in 2004) had always pushed for a more reasoned approach to the oft-maligned hormone, although his work had generally shown links between it and aggression in a wide variety of places. But at some point in their lunch, for Bernhardt, one obvious and unexplored place popped up.

"You know," Bernhardt remembers saying, "it would be interesting to do this with sports fans."

If you are a sports fan and care about a particular team, this is probably the first thing you notice about a game: butt-in-seat appearances to the contrary, it is a physical experience. Things are happening in your body. Your heart races. Your palms get sweaty. You *feel* the outcome: conquest often comes with a kind of triumphant, energetic bloodlust; defeat can deliver a kind of restless exhaustion, cheek-burning frustration, and anger. The mood swing can feel surreal, out-of-body, like you've been possessed. One friend of mine, a New England sports fan who runs a Buddhist meditation center in western Massachusetts and has spent close to thirty years focusing on being present in the moment and self-aware, calls the emotional power of live sports humbling. All the meditation has served to do, he says, is make him more aware of the anger, the frustration, and the pain when the Patriots lose. "Like Saint Augustine said, the thing about anger when you're paying attention to it is it's like passing a knife through yourself before you pass it through another person," he told me once. We were chatting on the phone while he drove out to the Zen center. "It's not a metaphor at all. That's really how it feels when you can't get away from it, when you actually feel it."

Your body is constantly undergoing little, reflex-like hormonal changes that in some way affect the way you feel.

Someone's riding my tail on the freeway and I probably have a little testosterone increase that makes me more aggressive in response to the perceived challenge. (There is most tantalizing evidence now that, in fact, you can predict the level of my testosterone increase and the aggressiveness of my response by the shape of my face.) I kiss my wife good night and a little bit of oxytocin makes me more loving (and also possibly more likely to act defensively toward people different than me). I'm editing a story on a deadline and my adrenal glands secrete stress-hormone cortisol that makes me more alert and more irritable.

But driving, kissing, typing: these are all actions that I'm undertaking directly. Here's the big question about sports fans: What if just watching a game sets off all these unconscious reflex hormonal changes—aggression and stress ones in particular—and they're affecting not just the way you feel but the way you act? What if the malignant force that possesses you during the game is actually your own endocrine system?

Watching sports, the major theories of hormones and competition suggest, could be in some sense changing your personality without any conscious agreement on your part. It's not all negative; you might be more aggressive or more cooperative, more trusting or more selfish. You might even be furiously angry or furiously pleased with your team and have no hormonal change at all. What's known as neuroendocrinology—that's the study of brain and hormones together—is a rapidly changing science at the moment, and exciting stuff is flying out of the labs at a pretty high velocity. But there's already a surprising amount of research that suggests you are changed by the experience of watching a sports team you care about and mostly helpless to defy that change. To be a sports fan, first of all, is to seriously under-mine your free will.

TESTING YOUR OWN HORMONES BASED ON SALIVA SAMPLES, IT turns out, isn't particularly difficult. You have to drool into a test tube, which is the hard part—three to five minutes of drool, and it's not exactly the most dignified thing you'll do all week—but then you just seal the test tube, freeze it, and mail it off to the lab packed in dry ice. In my case, when I decided to see what was happening in my body when I watched sports, the Yerkes National Primate Research Center Core Laboratory at Emory University cheerfully agreed to provide me with a progress report.

My goal was to work up to testing in a social occasion, but I started by simply testing myself while at home. My favorite hockey team is the San Jose Sharks and I planned the tests around several late-season games. The first occasion was a Sharks loss against archrival Anaheim that seemed at the time to sound the death knell on their season. I was angry and frustrated, although not exceptionally so—possibly I had already adjusted to the season being over and had lowered my expectations correspondingly. Still, when the game ended I slumped back and swore mildly, and my wife, absorbed in a magazine and ever sympathetic to my sporting plight, looked over and chuckled and said, "Aww, are you *angry* now?" I gazed back sort of blankly, and she continued to giggle and said, "Shouldn't you be drooling?" So I went over and stood over the sink, with my head tilted, and let the anger and the spit ooze out. (For the next test, I decided, I would use a straw.)

When I got the results back some months later, I noticed a few things from the first test. One was that I had started with relatively low testosterone levels. It had been a long day; I'd actually played pickup hockey myself at lunch. By the time I started drooling at 6:45 p.m., I was physically exhausted. My testosterone hadn't reached its low point, though. Around 8:20, ten minutes after Anaheim had scored the first goal of the game, I was down 15 percent from the game start. Then came a curious rebound. Drooling crankily over the sink at 9:30 p.m., my testosterone had risen more than 25 percent from where it had started the game. It appeared to be surging with the loss and underlying my irritation. Could there be a connection?

IN THE PARLANCE OF SOCIOLOGY, WHAT WE'RE WATCHING WHEN we watch sports is a dominance competition. Two animals (or two packs of animals) are fighting it out for some evolutionarily important benefit—mates, food, social glory, stuff like that. There's some debate about how closely sports mimics these old-school evolutionary conditions, but the consensus is that competition awakens some pretty old instincts. Hormonal changes in spectators appear to come from something buried deep in our genetic code because they go way back down the evolutionary tree. The best way I can think of to explain this is to tell the story of what happened when Rui Oliveira, a researcher at the University of Applied Psychology in Lisbon, set up an utterly ingenious experiment to see what happened in the hormones of spectator fish.

Oliveira works with the Mozambique tilapia, a medium-size bluish-gray cichlid native to southern Africa. These fish are fighters and they have two forms of male sex hormone, 11-ketotestosterone and testosterone, which is the major player in competition-related hormonal changes. Cichlids are belligerent enough that you can rely on them to attack their own reflection in the mirror. But Oliveira has shown in other research that a fish attacking its reflection doesn't have a hormonal change, which he suggests means it is actually the competition with another animal that matters and not just the fight.* So what happens to the hormones of a cichlid watching two other cichlids fight?

Basically, Oliveira found a way to establish a fish boxing-ring. There was a three-day introductory period, in which the bystander fish was able to see both competitors through a one-way mirror, but an opaque partition prevented the fighters from seeing (or getting at) each other. Then, on the third day, researchers raised the partition for one hour. The fish went fin-to-fin.

Oliveira took urine samples from the bystander two hours before the fight, thirty minutes after the fight, two hours after the fight, and six hours after the fight. He then measured the amount of testosterone in the fish pee. He found exactly what he'd predicted: a surge in testosterone in the spectator fish. "Our results," Oliveira wrote in a 2001 paper in *Nature*, "indicate that the endocrine system of spectators responds to social interactions in which they themselves do not participate."

Even in fish there are a few other hormones at work, too, including the stress hormone cortisol. But testosterone

---

*Like many results in neuroendocrinology, this finding has been challenged. Other labs that let fish fight their own reflections in the mirror have found testosterone increases.

is of such particular interest because of the way it's been shown to make both animals and people act. Remember where Dabbs and Bernhardt were looking for high testosterone: among violent criminals in Georgia prisons. We don't necessarily mind if our sports fans are stressed out on cortisol, but it's pretty interesting if they're getting aggressive or violent on testosterone. It would be even more interesting—this is one of the grails of modern testosterone research—if any sports-mediated changes turned out to have long-lasting effects.

Testosterone turns out to be quite the mysterious and complicated little bundle of carbon rings. One of the things it does, researchers say, is help regulate social interaction. Testosterone does raise your physical power by promoting muscle growth, but it also raises your brainpower and situational awareness. It can make you more aggressive, but Allan Mazur, a Syracuse sociologist and engineer who has done some of the most widely cited work on testosterone and competition, argues that it's much more a dominance hormone than an aggression one. High-testosterone people or monkeys who dominate a group can do so just as well by consensus building and subtle conversational tools, Mazur says, as by force. Dominance doesn't have to involve frat house bluster and chest thumping.

The important thing to know is that when confronted with a challenge, your testosterone often (but not always) goes up. That's generally true whether you're a monkey or a human; it's been studied up and down the mammal order and even further afield. The so-called challenge hypothesis actually comes from University of California– Davis neurobiologist John Wingfield, who proposed it to account for testosterone changes he'd observed in several kinds of bird species. The evolutionary idea is that strutting about the place with elevated testosterone—stepping high, wide, and plentiful on a hormone high—is quite costly since you're spending a lot of extra time and energy on aggression and combat. Much better would be, as is the case in, for example, the male superb fairy wren, to keep your testosterone low until you're in the presence of male challengers or mates.

The challenge hypothesis predicts you'll see an increase in testosterone at the start of a competition and has a great deal of empirical support. But there's probably more to the hormone story than that. Testosterone might also respond to the outcome of the competition and, most important, influence what you do next. Allan Mazur's idea, which carries the slightly unwieldy moniker "biosocial model of dominance," is that winners should have increased testosterone and losers should have decreased testosterone as a way of maintaining social order. The winners, with their ensuing testosterone high, will go on and compete again and win again, Mazur says, while the losers won't waste energy on subsequent challenges.

This is Mazur's theory in a nutshell: In any kind of grouping, in primates as well as humans, there tends to be ranking of individuals. It's extremely subtle and often there's easy agreement on how everyone ranks out. But sometimes you don't agree and then there are little challenges over rank. Like, for example, Mazur says, "You're at a cocktail party and you're having a conversation and this guy seems like an asshole to you. You say something about where you went and he says something about where he went. It may not go anywhere, but on the other hand it might."

At some point, in other words, you and the asshole having the conversation about all the places he's been and things he's done will decide where his accomplishments rank him. Is he a name-dropper who found himself on third base and thought he hit a triple? Or is he actually understating the hardships of his efforts to play Prometheus for third-world urchins? This happens all the time in human society, Mazur told me, and in fact the most interesting thing of all is how *quiet* humans manage to make these high-stress struggles for dominance. "We sort," Mazur said, "in a very gentle manner."

Mazur's theory has been applied widely in the animal kingdom and generally but not entirely supported by the evidence. Mazur himself worked with monkeys and found consistent winner and loser effects in fights. Still, he proposed his idea in the late 1970s and popularized it with a major paper in 1985, before anyone had really figured out how to test it on humans. It's harder, after all, to have people battle for social glory in a lab. (Running a real-life fight club would be a tough sell to academic committees that oversee human subjects testing.)

But you can ask them to play sports against each other. That's what Mazur did in the 1990s, and that's where he found most of the evidence to support this theory in humans. He found winners with increased testosterone and losers with decreased testosterone after playing tennis, judo, and even chess. Others have since found it consistently in all sorts of tasks: soccer, basketball, even video games. It's significant to find the same effect in competitive Tetris that you find in judo, since physical activity also changes the hormone balance in the body. Video games and chess confirm that a winner effect isn't just something that happens when you exercise.

The question for our purposes is whether a sports team winning—again, a random collection of dudes competing for dominance for themselves—also hooks into a fan's own dominance feelings. Back in the language of psychology, we're making this a *vicarious* dominance competition—the critical bit there being that we are not participating, and at least as it appears, our own status or position in the social hierarchy is not at stake. Are we really like Rui Oliveira's spectator fish? Or are my hormones while watching the Sharks just doing their own thing, totally unconnected to the game?

When Paul Bernhardt suggested over lunch to James Dabbs that they could measure testosterone in winning and losing fans, this was still a purely theoretical question. Mazur's work suggested that maybe you *should* see a winner and loser effect. But no one had ever actually looked to see what would happen.

Dabbs agreed almost immediately that it would be very interesting. "Can you do it?" he asked.

Bernhardt, still essentially an undergraduate student, remembers saying something like, "Uhhhhh . . . yes."

He suggested an upcoming Georgia–Georgia Tech basketball game, an in-state rivalry game with high-flying passions. Bernhardt could approach random undergraduate fans a few times during the game and ask them for spit samples ("You'll do anything to get into grad school," he now jokes with his students), and then they could measure the testosterone in the spit.

During the game, Bernhardt went up to fifteen young men and asked them if they'd fill out a questionnaire, chew some gum, and conscientiously spit into a test tube twice, once during the game and once afterward. Four said no; three more said yes and forgot to leave a postgame sample. That left eight participants—enough to show a significant increase in testosterone in winning fans and a decrease in losing fans—but not nearly enough to establish a reliable conclusion. Intrigued by the successful result, Bernhardt and Dabbs waited for an opportunity to test it out with a larger group. In 1994, the Brazil–Italy World Cup final provided that opportunity.

"IF YOU ARE A BOY IN BRAZIL, YOU ARE BORN ALREADY WITH A soccer ball," says Carlos Carvalho. "You *have* to play soccer."

Carlos was not good at soccer.

"I could not make a good soccer player," he says. He was good at swimming. Growing up on Rio de Janeiro's Ilha do Governador, in the middle of the massive, glittering Guanabara Bay, Carlos always liked the water. He made a good swimmer.

It mattered little. He played and followed soccer anyway.

"It's a religion," he says.

Carlos's journey as religious devotee of the beautiful game—from early apostasy to a fundamentalist revival far from home—ends, for us, in a single testosterone data point. But if you want to understand the way testosterone works in the body, I've learned, it helps to know whom it's working in.

In the early 1980s, just after he graduated from college, Carlos wanted to move to the United States to learn English. He found a college in Los Angeles, filled out the paperwork, and sent it and $20 to cover the application fee along with a friend, who was a pilot for Brazil's Varig Airlines. The pilot dropped off the paperwork but used the cash for a taxi. A few weeks later Carlos received a letter in the mail informing him that the college hadn't received his fee. He says it was almost impossible to send money out of Brazil at that time, so his L.A. dreams had vanished in that cab ride. A few days later, at the bank where he worked, a coworker saw him with a stack of American papers, asked about Carlos's ESL intentions, and finally said, "My sister lives in Atlanta. Why don't you just go there?"

It was a coincidence that would shape the rest of Carlos's life—and, oddly enough, have a direct bearing on the future of sports fan hormone research.

Carlos arrived in Atlanta in 1986 and enrolled in an ESL certification at Georgia State University. Shortly after his arrival, someone introduced him to another Brazilian woman, Lucia Jennings, and her American husband, Jeff. Carlos met Lucia and Jeff at a Brazilian nightclub called Club Rio (owned by Lucia's brother-in-law), and Carlos and Lucia clicked almost immediately. They became friends and social partners. Twenty-five years later they sat across from me in a pizza parlor in Atlanta's Buckhead neighborhood, giggling, finishing each other's sentences, and describing the way that from that first meeting in Club Rio they decided to strike up a business partnership to expand Brazilian cultural reach in Atlanta.

At the time, they said, there were maybe five thousand

Brazilians in Atlanta. To two Cariocas from twelve-million-person Rio, the city of four hundred thousand felt sleepy. The Olympics hadn't happened yet. Delta Airlines hadn't made a hub of the Atlanta airport. The Brazilian American Society became their missionary project, and Brazilian-style Carnival parties the chief method of their evangelism. For nine years, from the time they met in 1987 to 1996, Lucia and Carlos organized parties of all kinds. As part of their outreach—student groups, international organizations—they'd get requests of all sorts to mention various other causes.

"People always came to us to say, 'Can we use your party for this?'" Lucia said.

Those people, it turned out, included psychology researchers.

LIKE A LOT OF SOCCER-PLAYING AMERICAN KIDS, I REMEMBER wearing a USA SOCCER T-shirt around for a few weeks during the 1994 World Cup. I was mildly interested that games were taking place at Stanford Stadium just down the road from where I lived, and mildly proud when the men's national team managed to emerge from the group stage. I remember Colombia's yellow-blue-and-red uniforms, and later the Andrés Escobar shooting. I remember where I was on July 4 when the USA played Brazil (at an ice rink), and that I was proud again that we hadn't embarrassed ourselves against the most intimidating team in the world. These must have been fairly typical thoughts for a teenage neophyte to the international game (if not the sport itself, which I'd been playing at a relatively competitive level since I was a child).

But what impresses me now is that after that July 4 game I must have lost interest because I remember almost nothing. Five days later Brazil beat the Netherlands in a scintillating 3–2 game in which all five goals were scored in a thirty-minute stretch of the second half. I recently went and watched the highlights from that game on YouTube, and found everything the score line promised. In 1994 I didn't notice. Nor do I remember five days later when Brazil downed Sweden to head to the finals.

Carlos Carvalho, though, noticed. His evangelism was receiving a boost on the national stage; the project he and Lucia had started a decade earlier to carve out some idea that *hey, there are Brazilians here* was suddenly in its Constantine-at-the-Milvian-Bridge moment. The famed blue-and-yellow of Brazil was front-page news in America; victory against the equally historic Italians promised the spoils of mass conversion. The stakes were enormous personally and professionally. Carlos and Lucia had been hosting World Cup parties the entire time for his Brazilian friends and for the grand finale they wanted to go big. They found an Atlanta tavern called the Beer Mug with a huge TV and room for a few extra people. On July 17, 1994, two hundred fans followed them there.

When someone arrived at the bar, Carlos remembers, there was a procedure. First they would look for him or Lucia. Salutations conducted, they'd go for face paint, yellow and blue stripes. Then they'd go visit the small research table at the bar entrance and spit in a cup for science. Then, Carlos says, they'd wrap themselves in the flag, climb up on one of the bar's high tables, and get ready to party.

The researcher, of course, was Paul Bernhardt, collecting

data for his second study of sports fans. Another pair of assistants was across town at a pizza place, where fans of Italy had gathered. Bernhardt and his colleagues repeated the spit sample process, personally collecting one test tube from just before the game and one from just after, and asking participants to self-administer the gum-chewing and spitting the following morning and mail a sample back to the researchers.

The Brazil-Italy final was the first zero-zero result in World Cup history. After a scoreless overtime the game went to penalty kicks, another first for a World Cup final. Lucia remembers it mainly with a chorus of tension. "Tense, tense, tense, tense," she said as Carlos tried to describe the scene. He mainly remembers people standing on tables. At the end, Carlos said, he was shocked into silence, just standing there, looking at the big screen. "Tense, tense, tense," Lucia said again. Carlos remembers each kick, he says. The atmosphere was unbearable. People had been jumping up and down, dancing on the bar, pleading with the television for two hours. "We were sweating so much," Carlos said.

The first Brazilian missed his penalty kick. The first Italian missed his kick. The second Brazilian (the legendary Romário) made his penalty kick. The second Italian did likewise. So on through the third. Tied at two, each team had two shooters left. Italy first: Daniele Massaro shot weakly to the right and the Brazilian goalie Cláudio Taffarel knocked it away. Massaro walked away and shouted a curse. Taffarel rolled up and raised one finger into the air.

Brazil's Dunga, the occasional captain who would go on to coach the 2010 Brazilian national team, came next and didn't waver—didn't even stop over the ball, just backed up, rocked on his heels, and pushed off forward at a run before opening up and placing the ball in the right corner. The TV feed showed him walking away without cracking a smile— just a kind of massive relief as his deeply corrugated forehead relaxed. The players on the Brazilian sideline jumped up and down, arms linked. Brazil up 3–2 and one shooter left for Italy.

The Italian shooter, though, happened to be Roberto Baggio. Baggio was the winner the year before of both FIFA's* World Footballer of the Year Award and the Ballon d'Or, twenty-eight years old, and at the absolute peak of his form in a career that would leave him among the greatest strikers of all time.

Baggio looks down as he backs up. His lips are pressed together. In the television close-up you can see the tension in his face, see his ponytail flip just a bit as he glances over at the referee, see the harsh Pasadena sun on his cheek. Baggio rocks, just like Dunga, not pausing at the back. He takes a stutter step, his stride lengthens, and then suddenly as he approaches the ball the form goes off and he leans back too much and the ball comes flying off his foot in an utterly, shockingly, catastrophically wrong direction. The ball sails over the crossbar by a few feet as the Brazilian goalie falls to the turf in the other direction. As jubilant Brazilians scream onto the field behind him, Baggio stands frozen and just stares. His hands fall to his sides. He drops his head. On the Italian-language television broadcast I found the announcer says in horrified monotone, "*Alto. E il campeonato del mundo es finito. Brazile.*" Roberto Baggio, in that moment, looks like the loneliest, lowest-testosterone person in the world.

---

*Fédération Internationale de Football Association.

The Italian fans at the Atlanta pizzeria, no doubt wanting the entire nightmare to end, dropped out of participation in Bernhardt's study so precipitously the following morning that the day-after sample couldn't be used in the final results.* In the article he later wrote for the journal *Physiology and Behavior*, Bernhardt noted that after the game the Italian fans were "despondent" and that "the greater failure of Italian fans to provide samples the next day suggests that mood changes after a contest is much more than just a fleeting change."

In the Beer Mug tavern in Atlanta, though, there were no tears shed for Roberto Baggio. Delirium reigned. People were screaming, waving flags, pouring onto the street to celebrate.

"The adrenaline, the hormones, testosterone, I don't know what it was, but everyone was extremely high," Carvalho remembers. "At the end there was, when Brazil won, there was . . ."

He paused, chewing on the *s* as he tried to sort out the aftermath. "I don't know," he said, finally. "I don't even know how to describe it. Yelling, jumping."

Jennings, ever the party organizer, interrupted.

"I wonder," she said, "if everybody paid their bills!"

That was an easier metric.

"Nobody could pay their bills," Carvalho said. "I'm serious. Oh my God."

Fans screaming in the street ran afoul of the Atlanta police, who had little context for understanding the World

---

*One of the Italian samples that was mailed back was contaminated with blood, which is both gross and utterly sympathetic. You can just imagine: "Man, it was such a horrible stomach-crushing loss that I was spitting up blood the next morning."

Cup. (In the *Atlanta Journal-Constitution* the morning of the final, the lead sports column was a mocking takedown of soccer as a sport and the World Cup as an event.) Seeing dozens of apparently crazed radicals descending into the roadway, the police ordered everyone back to the sidewalk and then started to make arrests. Carlos and Lucia recall this part almost fondly as evidence of the closed nature of pre-Olympics Atlanta. That night, Lucia made the rounds on the talk shows, explaining to curious television reporters that they were celebrating in the streets because Brazil had won the World Cup, a very important event in their home country, and the way one celebrates something like that is by waving flags in the streets. The conversion had begun. A decade later Americans reacting to the World Cup final with puzzled concern seems like an anachronism from a century ago.

Paul Bernhardt, meanwhile, went home with data. Ultimately, he had usable samples from twenty-six men (whose higher baseline testosterone would make tracking changes easier). That's still not enough to satisfy scientists, but the results were consistent: a testosterone rise for the Brazilian fans, a testosterone drop for the Italians. These groups, sitting in sports bars more than two thousand miles from the site of the game, watching twenty-two soccer players that none of them knew personally, were so invested in the outcome that they had essentially the same testosterone response that the players themselves did. Whether the competition was direct or vicarious didn't appear to matter.

I TESTED MY OWN TESTOSTERONE FOR THE SECOND TIME IN THE first Sharks game of the 2012 Stanley Cup playoffs. The first result, from a disappointing Sharks loss, had seemed to show me defying Bernhardt's pattern of winners going up and losers going down. It was time to see what would happen when they won.* At this point, a week after my first test, the Sharks had miraculously turned their season around and won their final four games to make the playoffs. Although the playoff matchup looked pretty grim, there was at least some optimism that an underperforming group had finally figured out how to play to its talent. The playoff opener was an exciting one; the Sharks scored first, the Blues tied it late, and then Marty Havlat scored on a wrist shot in overtime to win the game for the Sharks. This time I had a real emotional outburst. This time I danced over to the sink to drool, and I had trouble aiming the drool (I had forgotten to buy straws) because I kept interrupting myself to chant triumphantly at my dog. Surely, I thought, this time the testosterone would be tracking my triumphalism.

Once again the hormone refused to play ball. Or at least there was no clear story. My highest level came at the game's start. It was also much higher this time around—exactly twice what it had been at the start of the first test. Much like in the first test, my testosterone plunged early, dropping almost 40 percent when I tested after the first goal of the game—but this time the Sharks had scored the goal. Maybe the goal relaxed me—or maybe I'd just hit a natural decline. Testosterone in men follows a roughly ninety-minute cycle

---

*Obviously, I couldn't ask my sports teams to win or lose at my convenience for personal hormone testing. The solution was to just keep collecting drool samples over multiple games, and then only analyze the appropriate games. (Finally, a use for the Sharks' legendary inconsistency.) It didn't take too long.

of pulses and can vary considerably, which is why researchers rely on large sample sizes that allow for averaging out little biological fluctuations.

Whatever the cause, though, my hormonal troops had rallied after the overtime winner. When the game ended I was still down from the puck drop five hours earlier, but I was back up 37 percent from my low point. And my testosterone stayed there. An hour and a half after the game had ended, my testosterone was still within a picogram per milliliter of where it had been a few seconds after Havlat's game-winner. My 10:00 p.m. testosterone this time around was also higher than the 10:00 p.m. testosterone from the first test—I appeared to have just had a more hormonal day.

I'd done two tests and neither had conformed to the Bernhardt results. Reading work by other researchers that cite Bernhardt, I saw that because of the sample size of his two papers and the slightly uneven testing times, his work isn't considered the most methodologically robust research. Some researchers, noting how few people Bernhardt was able to test, have dismissed the entire idea of a winner effect as an anomaly that can't be reproduced. Since I wasn't exactly able to counter their claims with my own evidence, it was time to look elsewhere.

BERNHARDT PUBLISHED HIS RESULTS IN 1998 AND THEN . . . NOT much really happened. Bernhardt moved on, to a postdoctoral position at the University of Utah and then a teaching position in the Psychology Department at Frostburg State University in western Maryland. He doesn't have time for research these days, and his study languished—that is, until an explosion of interest in the topic in the last decade that came too late for his career as a researcher. "If I'd been able to garner funding and institutional support . . ." Bernhardt told me, before trailing off. "But who's where they thought they'd be ten years ago?"

In the last few years, though, the study of hormones and behavior has blown up again. Inspired by the ideas of Allan Mazur, a number of young researchers in North America and Europe started to pursue more sophisticated ways of looking for competition-related hormonal changes. One of these was Steven Stanton, who in 2008 decided it was time to try to replicate Bernhardt's results. Stanton was a post-doctoral researcher at Duke at the time, focusing on the biological basis of social behavior, and he wanted to revisit Bernhardt's experiment with a year-appropriate twist: there was an obvious, enormous vicarious dominance competition taking place in 2008 that involved more than one hundred million Americans. If you've ever complained (or just wondered) about how people treat political elections like sporting contests, well, Stanton was right with you.

On November 3, 2008, Stanton at Duke and his colleagues at Michigan opened their laboratories to close to two hundred men and women, sixty-nine in Durham and ninety-four in Ann Arbor. They had each participant fill out a questionnaire and gave them all take-home spit collection kits. Then they asked them to go home and on the following day, to spit into the test tube for sample number one just as the polls closed on the East Coast in the Obama-McCain presidential election.

At 8:00 p.m. Eastern Time the participants started spitting. Their next instruction was to spit into the tube again the minute they heard the results of the election, and every twenty minutes for the next hour. They refrigerated the samples overnight, then brought them back to the lab in the morning, where the spit was frozen for analysis.

When Stanton ran the testosterone analysis on his frozen saliva samples, the result was a resounding confirmation of Bernhardt's sports fan finding. Men who voted for John McCain or Libertarian candidate Robert Barr saw significantly decreased testosterone levels after the election results were announced. Men who voted for Barack Obama had stable testosterone, resisting, Stanton suggests, a natural decline in the body's testosterone that would have otherwise showed up. Stanton tried several different methods to find another explanation for the changing testosterone: alcohol use (which depresses testosterone), where the voter viewed the election (could be a group effect that influences the presence of such a social hormone), and who was there with the voter. None of them seemed to make a difference. The single biggest predictor of change in testosterone level that night was whom the man had voted for. "While voting involves direct participation in the electoral process, voters don't personally win or lose the election," Stanton wrote. "In this regard, the present results are similar to the study by Bernhardt and colleagues which showed that male sports fans' testosterone levels changed according to whether their team won or lost."

He also found one other fascinating result: women showed nothing at all.

In the questionnaire he had participants fill out before the election, Stanton asked all sorts of questions about how much the voters liked the candidates, how intensely they felt about them, their political values, and how conservative

they were. On these questions there were no differences
between the sexes. Women had the same range of political
values, were just as conservative (or not), and identified just
as intensely with the candidates (or not). The women, in
other words, wanted their candidates to win just as badly.
Female McCain supporters and Obama supporters were just
as irritated or elated at the result. When Stanton looked at
cortisol levels, he found that women and men McCain voters
in North Carolina had similar cortisol surges after the results
were announced, meaning the election was similarly stressful. But in testosterone levels, only the men responded to the
outcome.

This gender difference turns out to be pretty consistent
in dominance competition studies, even the direct ones.
Stanton's explanation is in part that where the hormone is
made in the body affects how quickly it can be pumped out
in response to a social situation and also how quickly it can
be measured. The testes in men are the short-order cooks of
the hormone world: You need a lot of that there testosterone
scrambled up real quick? Here it comes, with sauce. The
adrenal glands, meanwhile, are like pastry chefs: small
amounts made a little bit more to order. They dab out a bit
of testosterone in both men and women, but for women,
that's pretty much all you get. The ovaries, meanwhile,
aren't in the kitchen at all. They will make and contribute
testosterone, but only on a small scale. And this turns out to
be the other weird thing about the testes that separates them
from the ovaries: they respond to social situations. Not like
you should sit and converse with them or anything, but for
some reason they activate after a dominance competition.
Not so the ovaries; not in that quantity the adrenal glands.

What bugs me about all this is that it seems that if you come factory-equipped with a male reproductive system, you can't opt out. My teams lose a lot, which according to the theory means I'm getting jerked around with low testosterone all the time. I do like the other stuff about being a sports fan. I like the aesthetics of the game. It's a nice community feeling, sometimes, when I watch with other people. Why can't I chose to just enjoy the good times and ignore the bad times? Why do I have to cede the keys to my endocrine system to these guys I don't even know?

I pressed this question particularly on Allan Mazur, who sounded almost amused.

"You tell me," he said, when I asked him why I cared so much.

Mazur is self-effacing about his own biosocial model of dominance. When I called him to talk about his theory and the modern evidence in support of it, he started by telling me, "The first thing is you shouldn't believe any of this stuff too literally. It's really hard to do research on this and everybody's kind of biased. You can't really expect to have the last word on anything."

We chatted generally for a few minutes, and then he returned to the theme.

"I'll tell you something funny," he said. "I've studied testosterone for years, my testosterone is appropriate for my age, but I talked my proctologist into prescribing it for me. He's very sympathetic to my research. Well, I'll tell you the truth. Nothing has happened. The fact of the matter is, it's not budged my T-levels at all and I've felt no behavioral effects at all. I'm not convinced myself this stuff is real."

In the end, it felt almost like I was trying to convince

him. I know how I feel after watching my teams win or lose.
Look, I will swear to you that I'm really, really not the type
to laugh gloatingly and scream "Suck it asshole!" at a television without something weird taking place inside of me. I
don't just *feel* more aggressive after my team wins; I *display*
more aggression. I know equally well that following a lot of
losses I feel surly and peevish. I am more likely to sulk, to be
easily irritable, to throw things. Surely, surely, there must be
something happening there.

"You're talking to a guy who doesn't give a fig, so probably you can explain it better than I can," Mazur said. "It's
always a mystery to me why people pay so much attention."

At which point it was time for my grand finale hormone
test. My results so far hadn't backed up Mazur's biosocial
model—or really showed anything clearly at all except to
suggest to me that I'm an angry loser. But so much of
Mazur's work suggests that testosterone is an extroverted
hormone. It needs some other people around before it comes
out to play. Fortunately, I had a few in mind.

IN OCTOBER 2004 I SET OFF INTO THE WILDERNESS OF SOUTH-
ern Chile for a weeklong backpacking trip.* I remember particularly the first night and the last. The first night I camped
in the shade of the park's famous natural monument, a trident of granite towers that clawed into the gray sky. A furious
wind flayed the surface of the shallow lake near my camp-
site and by early afternoon it started to snow. I retreated into

---

*I left with the Yankees leading the Red Sox 3–0 in the baseball playoffs.
I returned a week later, went to ESPN.com, and saw a preview of the Red
Sox–Cardinals World Series. It utterly blew my mind.

my small tent, feeling utterly alone in the universe, and spent several hours staring blankly at the flapping yellow canvas while the wind screeched and whistled through my tent poles. That night I had the first and only nightmare of my life: The Mordor-like granite towers had inspired a *Lord of the Rings* meditation that ended when I jerked out of a restless sleep at 3:00 a.m. to stare into the glowing yellow eyes of a fully fleshed-out and vivid Gollum perched on my legs.

I spent the next few days hiking in what you might call a vulnerable frame of mind, with the park's otherworldly beauty reinforcing my loneliness. The last night I pitched my tent in a designated camping area on the shores of a sapphire lake and late in the afternoon wandered into a small wooden gazebo that the park had set up in the middle of the campground. It was off-season but there was another camper there, a young guy, about my age, with a bit of scruff emerging from his wool scarf. He turned out to be American —a relative rarity on the hiking trails of South America— and he turned out, like me, to be almost out of food. As a way of lightening my load for the trip, I had decided against carrying a stove or hot food. By the last day, I was living off a bag of peanuts. Patrick had done almost the same thing; he sat across the gazebo peering curiously at me from behind a jar of peanut butter. I don't necessarily recommend this as a method of backpacking, but it turns out to be an okay way of establishing a friendship.

I don't have a lot of close guy friends, and the handful that I do have aren't sports fans. (We're going to talk more about alienation and marketing in chapter 7.) I almost always watch games at home on my own. Sometimes my wife—not only not a fan but pretty much opposed to the entire enterprise of sports—leaves me alone to my emotional turmoil and sometimes she watches patiently and asks that I struggle to suppress my feeling rebellion. Either way, games are something I generally watch on my own, process on my own, and feel on my own. I guess that makes me a lonely sports fan, and maybe, oddly enough, that's one of the things driving my testosterone response. It's low to start because there's no one around, just me and my thoughts, and then it's high at the end because I'm looking for someone to fight, something to release the tension from the game, and don't have the right outlet.

Patrick's orbit and mine have somehow crossed infrequently but at odd and lonely times in our lives. He's also a sports fan but not a hockey fan. When I thought about measuring my own testosterone while watching sports, I thought for some reason that Patrick would be the right social foil for me. Ashwin, a moderate Sharks fan, childhood friend of mine, and by incredible coincidence a close friend of Patrick's, would join us as a calming influence and the middle orbit between my fanaticism and Patrick's relative indifference. We had a methodology, we had subjects, and we had a research question: When we parked ourselves in front of a hockey game—an important one, at that, that would leave me in a vulnerable mood yet again, what would you see in our testosterone? What would you see in us?

The challenge hypothesis and the biosocial model suggest that we'd all have slightly elevated levels of testosterone, since we're also sorting our own dominance hierarchy. The work of Bernhardt and Stanton suggests that since I'm the one most invested, I should see the biggest hormonal change linked to the game while Patrick would change the least. But this was based on the idea that you couldn't feel the change. Because in terms of caring, we actually also proposed that Patrick would care the most. Ashwin and I would be happy, after all, to have good company, and so would probably care less about the game than usual. Patrick, meanwhile, would be concerned about his two friends and so would respond to the game more than he ordinarily would. Does that make sense? It did to us.

The three of us, in any case, would watch the Sharks in the playoffs, and we'd pause at intervals to spit into test tubes, and we'd see if it was different when you took our friendship and added in a hockey game that we all cared about to some variable degree.

The day we picked was Ashwin's turn for a day of personal crisis; he'd just published one of his first major long-form stories in the *Atlantic* and was getting mixed feedback. At the time Patrick was crashing on the couch in the small Oakland apartment that Ashwin shared with his brother, and the first thing Patrick said when I sat down at the Monk's Kettle gastropub was how much better Ashwin was looking than he had looked in the morning. I handed them both straws, test tubes, and sugar-free gum.*

---

*There is utterly amazing scientific literature on the collection, storage, and mailing of testosterone samples. Included in this literature are discussions of the types of gum a researcher can offer subjects in order to induce drooling without changing the sample; some research suggests that sugar-free Trident is okay while sugared is not, but new research challenges that and says that all gum raises testosterone, and in any case the act of chewing appears to increase testosterone if done for more than two minutes. Which is the second note I would add: it takes a surprisingly long time to fill a 5-mL test tube with drool. Much longer than you would think. The literature suggests a range from three to ten minutes. Picture yourself holding a test tube to your lip, trying to fill it with drool, and you can imagine how long that ten minutes feels.

We looked like we were all sitting there with milk shakes.

Since we have a fairly easy familiarity, nothing felt all that different. But already, something was showing up in the hormones. Mine was elevated from where it had been on previous days at this time. Patrick's, although we didn't have anything to compare it to, was ever so slightly higher than the average level for male testosterone in the Stanton politics study. And Ashwin, who had been having his self-esteem and professional reputation challenged all day—holy shit. Ashwin's testosterone was blowing the roof off the bar. He clocked in at something like 50 percent higher than the Stanton average. In raw terms, for that night, at least, his anxiety seemed to make it so that he was literally twice the man that I was. (The testosterone researcher Justin Carré, when I mentioned this to him, said that Ashwin's level was actually just high normal—Carré regularly sees men who are *twice* that.)

I asked Steven Stanton what he thought. Could Ashwin's testosterone be responding to the challenge? Stanton, like all the researchers, was fairly uncomfortable with the question, since, you know, a single test from an individual does not equal science (or really anything at all). "Again," he said, "whenever you're asking these 'could it?' questions, of course the answer is, yes it could. Does it fit theoretically? Yes it does."

In other words it would at least be reasonable to propose that if you took one hundred random people and then challenged them on a professional accomplishment, you would see on average elevated testosterone. "But," Stanton said, "you only have samples from him on one day. He could just be a high testosterone guy."

We had dinner and beer. This was another research variable, since alcohol depresses testosterone and we might be biasing our own samples downward. On the other hand, I didn't necessarily want to contribute to the scientific literature—I just wanted to see what our hormones were doing while we watched a game under normal conditions.

A few minutes before the opening face-off we wandered across Sixteenth Street to Kilowatt, which Ashwin, our local food-and-drink expert, said was one of San Francisco's better hockey bars. We grabbed a booth in the back by the pool tables with a clear view, and I spread out the test tubes. The thing I found quickly was that it was probably the least I had ever cared about a Sharks playoff game played in my presence. I feel so powerfully addicted to this team that I'll track regular season games by refreshing the browser on my phone every fifteen seconds at a wedding until my wife confiscates the phone. If they're on television while we're out to dinner with family, I'll have to be reminded to pay attention to the people sitting in front of me. I have a regular habit of excusing myself from the dinner table in restaurants and wandering to the bathroom so I can check the score on my phone.

I don't see Ashwin and Patrick all that often. Still, I was actually quite surprised to find that it was more interesting to talk over all the various things we had in common but hadn't had a chance to discuss yet than it was to watch the game. I also started to realize that our friendship has never been particularly sports-based. I am closer to my brother than I am to these two friends, but my brother would amplify my feeling about the game because a lot of what we do together is watch hockey. My brother, seeing me excuse myself in a fancy restaurant to go to the bathroom, would ask me what the score was when I returned.

We had spent the run-up to the game explaining to Patrick that what St. Louis would do was score first and then protect the 1–0 lead for the rest of the game, and so it was unsurprising when the Blues scored early in the first period and when it was still 1–0 at the start of the third. It also made for a boring game—not a lot of chances to score for either team—and sapped some of the drama. I wondered if that corresponded to a sapping of testosterone. We tested at the first goal and everything seemed to support that idea: Ashwin's and my testosterone hit our nightly lows. Mine had dropped 25 percent, Ashwin's 17 percent—even the magnitude of the drop seemed to back up our predictions about the hormone tracking our investment in the team. Patrick, unfortunately, did not cap his second sample properly. When I reached into my jacket pocket to get a test tube for the third test, it was to find my hand covered in Patrick's drool. This hormone testing is hazardous stuff.

THE BIGGEST LESSON I'D LEARNED TO THIS POINT WAS THAT hormones are just mysterious things. You think of what we've said about testosterone so far: you have no reliable ability at all to tell whether it's high or low, you can't control whether you make more or less of it. You can't even feel it. In my first home test I would have sworn I had low testosterone at the exact moment when it had peaked for the night. My friends and I sitting in a bar having a conversation and watching sports were blissfully ignorant of what was happening in our bodies. My friend Ashwin, feeling anxious and uncertain over the publication of a magazine article, was actually oozing testosterone out his ears. Sitting at home on the couch feeling depressed and angry after a team I'm deeply invested in had lost, my testosterone was secretly confounding theory by rising. One study out of the Netherlands actually dosed half its participants with testosterone and half with a placebo before having them do a competitive task, then asked at the end whether participants thought they got the placebo or the real juice. The participants showed absolutely no ability to tell. The whole thing feels silent: your lurking hormones. The conscious brain, the psychology of the individual—none of that seems to be involved at all.

But that is not how humans work. The hormonal response is not just unadulterated reflex. What we humans *do* is adulterate our reflexes. Whether you have an outcome-related testosterone increase depends entirely, researchers say, on that individual psychology. It depends on how you think, how you care about the team, how your personality responds to life. As it so happens, that's what we're going to spend the rest of this book talking about. But let's linger for a moment with our hormone researchers. It seems like this places an impossible burden on them: they have to control the experiment but also know what's happening in the subjects' brains, not just in the moment but for hours at a time, and not just for those hours but all the preconceptions and biases and thoughts that make up those people that could contribute to their hormonal shifts on the day of the competition.

Neuroendocrinology is an active field, and researchers already are identifying some of the things that play into winner, loser, and challenge effects. One definite marker appears to be stress. Although, as with everything, the interaction is complicated, the stress hormone cortisol seems to inhibit testosterone production, possibly as part of an evolutionary mechanism to prevent stressful situations from turning into Darwin Award ones because we decided to act with testosterone-fueled belligerence in the face of bears. Running with this, Samuele Zilioli and Neil Watson, researchers at Simon Fraser University in British Columbia, had an idea that you might predict the strength of the winner and loser effect by the level of cortisol and testosterone in the body before a competition. They decided to test this, naturally, with Tetris.

Zilioli and Watson actually went out and had a game designer make a custom version of Tetris for them that allowed it to appear as if players were playing head-to-head. The two competitors would sit in the same room but without being able to see each other's screens, and the game was rigged so that one would have a very easy time of it and one would have an impossibly difficult time of it. The games were also rigged to start and end at the same time to preserve the appearance of direct competition. The results looked very much like Stanton's election results: losers' testosterone went down and winners' testosterone held stable but increased relative to the losers'. Zilioli and Watson then split the winners out by their preliminary cortisol level and found a significant effect. Winners with low starting stress had larger testosterone increases than winners with high starting stress. The effect was even more pronounced in competitors with high starting testosterone. Not only does testosterone respond to winning and losing; how much it does (and, competitively speaking, how much of an advantage you receive) depends on how stressed you are. For the first time, the researchers declared in the journal *Psychoneuroendocrinology*, there was empirical evidence that the hormone system was actually, in essence, talking to itself during competitions.

MEANWHILE, BACK IN THE HOCKEY BAR: THE BLUES SCORED again early in the third period to take a 2–0 lead, an utterly insurmountable gap for a team with as little resilience as the Sharks. That was the depressing moment; it was early in the third period and we had just drooled ten minutes earlier, but as we slumped back Ashwin and I agreed that the game was over. "Shit," Ashwin said. He thought about it for a few seconds. "We should be spitting now," he said.

That point felt like the nightly low for me. It was the first time I'd thought and cared about the game. After the delightful diversion of my friends, it was a sudden recall to this other Thing happening, this Thing that I remembered I cared way too much about. The game was a critical one, a must-win for the Sharks. Losing meant a 3–1 series deficit heading back to St. Louis for the next game and almost assured their playoff demise. Faced with the prospect that this was likely a season-ending goal, I would have bet a considerable sum that this would be my testosterone low.

I would have lost my money. My testosterone, defying prediction, had jumped back up 15 percent from the start of the third period. I was angry again; my testosterone, it seems, pairs with angry. This time it was Ashwin and Patrick who were down hormonally. After the first goal, Ashwin had rebounded slightly to the start of the third period, at which point he was down only about 7 percent from his starting point. Patrick, too, had had his testosterone increase at the start of the third period. But now, Ashwin was back down 5 percent and Patrick was down 13 percent from the third-period levels of just ten minutes earlier.

That was where we all stayed. The Sharks scored with a minute left in the game to make it 2–1, but it was little consolation. With six seconds to go Ashwin and I declared it over and started drooling. "You can't spit before it's over!" Patrick insisted, but we just explained to him that he comes from a team with a winning tradition and so cannot possibly understand. "It's over," I said.

That second St. Louis goal, it seemed, really had ended the night. Since it happened our testosterone had barely changed. We were all within a percentage point of where we'd been half an hour before.

The game ended and we weren't quite ready to go home, so Patrick disappeared and then came back from the bar with three shots of whiskey and three beers. We sat there for another hour, and I'm honestly not sure if it was the whiskey or the conversation, but the game receded quickly into the background. At midnight, when we stumbled out of the bar and over to La Oaxaqueña for tacos al pastor, it felt like it had happened weeks ago. I had some triumphant epiphany: This is what it's like to be a sports fan with friends. Losing doesn't have to matter as much.

That's what I felt, at least. I was most curious to see whether the testosterone would agree. So now here's the question. I was far less angry than usual after a loss, almost certainly because the distraction of the spit test made it more fun—there was always this element of wonder about the evening, this idea that *finally* I would get a chance to look at the bodily functions underlying my behavior and, win or lose, be able to show off to everyone else.

But it was also the chance to hang out with these friends who I don't get to see often enough. As I walked home, feeling almost cheerful, I felt the power of that friendship. I'm in my midthirties now, with a wife, a kid, a house, and pretty regular work. We live within an hour's drive of both my family and my wife's family and have family commitments; many of my close friends from college have moved to the Bay Area and I try to see them as often as possible. When I first met Patrick, I was twenty-four and on the run from the first and worst job I'd ever had. The world seemed a huge, glorious place, and there could never be enough new things to try, new people to meet, new places to see. It's different now, and not in a way that I mind. I struggle to figure out how to maintain existing friendships while staying home on a Friday night to make faces at my infant daughter. But sometimes it's nice to hang out for a long time with friends that I don't see regularly because it reminds me of that craving for new experiences, and I feel, well, ten years younger again.

That perspective, I think, is what made the game feel almost irrelevant. It was a reminder of the arc of my own life, the places I'd been and the person I'd been, and a reminder that even as a die-hard Sharks fan the team isn't the only thing that defines me. This new midthirties life can feel isolating even with its wonderful moments, and I felt strongly that the universe, even the benighted hostile universe that year after year toys contemptuously with my hockey team, seemed to have shrunk just a tiny bit around me. The Sharks had lost, but I was . . . yeah. I was happy.

Mellow and content is an emotional state you rarely hear associated with testosterone. So then. Depressing loss with a zero-anger finish: low testosterone?

Not exactly. At the end of the night I had just hit my second-highest hormone level of the night. I was back to within 7 percent of my starting point six hours earlier. Ashwin was not only back to his pregame level, he had exceeded it. He'd dropped a bit during the game and then, somehow unwinding at midnight in a small Mexican restaurant, he had more testosterone than he'd had at 6:00 p.m. Patrick, meanwhile, when viewed in sum, looked almost exactly like a person who'd not watched any game at all. He'd increased a little at the start of the game and then been declining slowly throughout the night, every sample just a bit down from the previous one, in what I imagined was an almost archetypal circadian rhythm. Hormonally, it seemed, he might as well have been sitting at home alone.

What to make of all this? My testosterone had gone up every time I'd watched hockey, win or lose, social setting or home on the couch, alcohol or Hetch Hetchy tap water. Ashwin's had gone up after a dispiriting Sharks loss. Patrick, our friend who didn't *really* care, looked hormonally just like a person who didn't really care.

I put all this to Carré, a researcher at Wayne State University. His take was: this is just further proof that you can't really tell. The ultimate goal of a lot of testosterone research is to be able to predict an individual's testosterone level from their mood, or their facial structure, or even their answers to a series of questions about aggression, but the science just isn't there yet. The winner effect shows up often enough to be more than just background noise, but not so often that you can say with certainty that it will be there. I would have sworn, again, that I had a testosterone drop after the Sharks lost, and I would have been wrong.

WHEN HE DID HIS 1994 EXPERIMENT, PAUL BERNHARDT WAS the only researcher ever to look at World Cup soccer fans. But in 2010, a team of Dutch and Spanish researchers had had the idea to repeat the experiment for the Spain-Holland World Cup final. This was another exhilarating matchup. Neither team had ever won the World Cup before, so there was a strong element of novelty. As an American, I'm used to picking other teams to follow in international soccer (since we're always eliminated early), and even though Landon Donovan's last-minute heroism had stirred the patriotism within me to probably an all-time high, once we were out I was strongly rooting for Spain–Holland.

By now, the design of Leander van der Meij's experiment should sound pretty familiar. He and his team found fifty Spanish soccer fans—twenty-five men and twenty-five women—and had them drool into test tubes during the game. Each participant gave three samples, one just before the match, one at halftime, one after. But van der Meij added a nice twist: he also had each participant give three samples at the same time of day on a nongame control day.

The game, like the 1994 final, was yet another 0–0 tie that went to overtime. But this time it didn't go to penalty kicks. Andrés Iniesta buried a rocket in the corner on a sweet half-volley in the 116th minute to give Spain a 1–0 championship. The Spanish went crazy; my favorite moment of the postgame celebration was the Spanish goalie Iker

Casillas crying on air and then swooping in on his TV-reporter girlfriend for an emotional on-air kiss. There was a lot of commenting about this afterward, about whether it was professional and whether it was overly macho (or typically Spaniard-y) and what it meant for the reporter's career and whatnot, but I mean, what more anecdotal proof could you possibly have that Casillas was on a testosterone high than responding to a reporter's question with a cinema-quality emotional kiss?

Based on everything I knew, then, I expected the Spanish fans to see testosterone increases, too. And they did—but not related to the outcome. In fact, van der Meij's paper says, on the day of the game, the testosterone peaked at the start. Compared to the control day, though, it was consistently up in the male—but not the female—participants. Van der Meij suggests that his work confirms the challenge hypothesis but offers a critique of Mazur's biosocial dominance model. He noted that Bernhardt's 1994 study had a very small sample size and that there was no control-day testing. Maybe, he seems to suggest, you can just toss that one out as a small-sample anomaly and subscribe to challenge-related testosterone increases as the real thing going on in sports fans. We exchanged a few e-mails and van der Meij told me he doesn't really believe there's a strong winner effect—that maybe you might find it in a very careful situation but the challenge and anticipation rise in testosterone is much more important.

Carré and Stanton disagree with that assessment, obviously. Van der Meij is right that the results are still inconsistent, but it's not just Bernhardt that has found a vicarious winner effect. Stanton found it in a well-controlled study with hundreds of participants. Carré has found outcome-related testosterone increases in a variety of situations, including one clever test in which he had ice hockey players watch video replays of their own games.

Tests on fans are much more rare than tests of people competing directly against each other. Maybe one of the most intriguing things about the winner/loser effect in fans is that it would be proof that the fans are essentially reacting the same way the competitors are. Based on everything we're going to learn about how we view our teams, I believe that's likely to be the case, meaning the lessons learned in direct experiments should apply whether you're competing or watching. But that doesn't help us if we don't know what happens in direct competition. So I want to bring up one more study completed recently by Justin Carré: the first start-to-finish test of the biosocial model of dominance.

Carré's lab found more than two hundred participants and split them first into two main groups. Everyone was asked to play a video game on the Xbox Kinect—a game console that requires the players to move around to make actions happen on the screen—with half assigned to play volleyball and half assigned to boxing. Each group was then split again, half into a winners' bracket in which the artificial intelligence of their computer opponent was set extremely low and half into a losers' bracket in which the AI of the opponent was impossibly high. For fifteen minutes the winners beat the crap out of their boxing or volleyball opponent, and the losers got the crap beat out of them by the computer. The reason for the volleyball/boxing split was to check whether the aggressive or violent quality of the game itself might increase testosterone. But in the men, the first analysis he'd run, it didn't seem to matter.

Whether they won at volleyball or boxing, their testosterone went up. Not only that, in postgame assessments of aggression—"there's a nice lab-based measure of reactive aggression," Carré said—winners were more aggressive than losers. When he controlled the thing for testosterone, the effect disappeared, indicating that the testosterone response really did underlie the aggression. What it all suggests, Carré told me, is that "changes in testosterone might be the cause of heightened aggression among winners." He hasn't run further tests yet, but "I think," he said, "we have a pretty clean story on testosterone."

How much is testosterone really *causing* the aggression? Let's check in with our rodent friends. In a series of experiments run by the lab of Catherine Marler at the University of Wisconsin–Madison mice injected with testosterone were far more likely to engage in and win territorial fights than mice injected with a saline solution. To control the experiment better, Marler's lab castrated the mice so that the injected testosterone was the only testosterone they had access to. For what it's worth, other labs have found similar results with fish. But again, along the lines of difficulty originally encountered by Allan Mazur, there's no real way to sneak physical castration of humans by a human subjects committee. (And if you did, Carré points out, few men would line up to undergo it.)

Carré's lab has turned, instead, to "chemical castration" to study testosterone and aggression. Basically, he's been giving volunteers a shot that knocks out their testosterone completely for forty-eight hours. Half the subjects then get a testosterone gel while the other half get a placebo, and he puts everyone in a brain scanner to check responses to threatening and rewarding cues. They're looking for a connection between testosterone and brain areas known to play a role in aggression, and if they find it they've got several more studies lined up to go.

These things proceed slowly, Carré said, but he's convinced there's a winner effect. What's actually amazing, he said, is that even with all the uncontrolled variables, there are still several studies that have found one. We were talking about Patrick's testosterone declining over the night while Ashwin's and mine went up, and I was speculating about all the hundreds of combinations of things that had happened to the three of us that might be affecting our hormonal state that night.

"It's messy, right?" Carré agreed. But this was his positive spin on the strength of the response he's seen in his work: "The fact that we find these effects so consistently is pretty exciting."

THERE'S ONE FINAL, OBVIOUS, SIMPLE CONTROL ON YOUR HORmonal response to a game: how the winner and loser interpret the result. Underlying everything we've talked about in this chapter is the major point that you have to care first. Carlos Carvalho probably had a testosterone surge because Brazilian victory in the World Cup meant a personal and professional confirmation. Ashwin, Patrick, and I set out to see what was happening in our bodies, only to realize that ultimately what happened—or had already happened—in our brains mattered just as much. From the incredible mess of the results, you can see how hard it is for hormone researchers to really get a handle on this stuff.

Alicia Salvador, a researcher at the University of Valencia, has identified a whole host of things that might change your testosterone response: Do you expect to win or lose? Anticipation could activate brain structures that we'll talk more about later, setting up a testosterone response that's much more related to the fulfillment of an expectation than to the actual outcome of the competition. Does the competition matter to you? How much do you think you can control the outcome? Salvador suggests that athletes who think they played an important role in winning the game for their team will show a winner effect, but those who played a minor role won't.

Researchers in neuroendocrinology started out thinking they could follow the evolutionary predictions and just account for everything with observations of winners and losers, Salvador wrote in a 2009 paper in *Neuroscience and Biobehavioral Reviews*. That didn't turn out to be the case, and now researchers have begun to understand that perception, appraisal, control, and importance are just as significant to understanding the hormone response as who won and who lost. "Only when we started to ask about motivation to win, causal attribution of outcome and satisfaction did we start to explain part of the hormonal response variance," Salvador wrote. "This need to take into account the individual's cognitive processes has been increasingly considered in the studies on this topic, but when their findings are analyzed, a puzzle with a lot of missing pieces still appears."

That nature gave us hormonal reflexes and then we found a way to exert control over them without even knowing it is powerful idea. It is one of those things that seems fundamental to our species. It is one of those things contributing to the seething, frothing cauldron of feedback loops that makes fall Saturdays in Berkeley the most emotional moments in my life. It is also the exact same thing, it appears, that's happening in the brain.

2
Sports as Empathy: Mirror Neurons

IF THERE'S ANY SINGLE INCIDENT THAT INSPIRED THIS BOOK, it's the night of May 4, 2008. A Sunday night, cold and dreary in the foggy Bay Area, almost exactly forty-eight hours before my final master's thesis (a long magazine article about ecology) was due in graduate school. I had mostly written the thesis, but there are always odds and ends to take care of—making the edits suggested by reviewers, getting the paper right, getting the cover sheets signed, getting everything printed and turned in. Instead of doing any of that, or having a restful evening so as to prepare to do that, I sat at home and watched Game Six of the NHL Western Conference Semifinals live from Dallas. The game started at 6:00 p.m. and for the next five hours and fourteen minutes I slowly fused into my couch. Out the big windows of my living room the sun faded into the fog and the lights of San Francisco came on—the checkered windows of the Transamerica Pyramid, the domed rotunda of city hall, the glow of the new federal building on Mission Street. The game was tied 1–1 after regulation and went to overtime. The red line of brake lights on Highway 101 drifted into the night as traffic slackened. The game went to a second overtime, and a third. My wife went to bed. My dog went to bed. I just sat there.

Somewhere in the fourth overtime—that's past two full games played—one of the Sharks players was called for a penalty. On the ensuing power play, Dallas was able to control the puck inside the Sharks defensive zone. Two players passed it back and forth at the point, and then there was a long pass through the middle to the face-off dot, and then the Dallas player with the puck faked a shot and my brain leaped out of my skull because I saw the same thing that he did, which was a wide-open Stars player right in front of the net. He passed and Brenden Morrow tipped the puck into the gaping net and the Sharks goalie crumpled to the ice and, well, dammit, *that* was a waste of five hours.

Years later, what I remember most about that game is the sinking feeling a split second before the goal was scored. From start to finish that play I just described took about four seconds, but that *moment* is frozen in time in my head. Most sports fans know that feeling, the one where you see something happening before you can even articulate it, and so you just get a flash of dread as the guillotine drops. It's the feeling in baseball when you know the ball is gone the second it hits the bat, or in football when you see the defensive back about to jump a pass route, or in soccer when you're watching your lionhearted hero standing nervously over a decisive penalty kick and just know from his body language that it's sailing high.

It is not, the research seems to say, just hindsight bias covering for your gloomy pessimism. There is some of that, of course, in every thigh-slapping expectorated *I knew it!* But there is more. There is also something happening in the brain, something about perception and action and anticipation, and that's what I wanted to explore.

IN THE SHERLOCK HOLMES STORY "A SCANDAL IN BOHEMIA," the famous detective, to impress Watson, offers up a variety of deductions about his friend. When he then explains what led to his deductions, Watson laughs at the simplicity of the observations.

"When I hear you give your reasons," Watson says, "the thing always appears to me to be so ridiculously simple that I could easily do it myself, though at each successive instance of your reasoning I am baffled until you explain your process. And yet I believe my eyes are as good as yours."

Holmes lights a cigarette, sits in his chair, and then utters his famous rebuke, "You see, but you do not observe." He suggests that Watson has often seen the steps leading into their formerly shared rooms; he challenges Watson to say how many there are. Watson, of course, has no idea. Holmes pounces: "Quite so. You have not observed. And yet you have seen."

Let us take a brief moment to defend Watson: Seeing the world is something of a monumentally complicated task in the brain. The eyes, as Holmes suggests, record everything— a constant stream of information coming in. But all that information doesn't mean anything at all unless you then *do* something to it in the brain. You have to *observe*. Philosophers through the ages have taken different angles on the meaning of the eye-brain interface; it gets at the core of some of the greatest questions in human history. Who am I and how do I know? What's the relation between the mental and the physical? How do you prove that something is real when the only way you have of proving it is your own perception? Here's my own rephrasing: Why is it that of all the things coming in through my eyes on the night of May 4, 2008— all the objects and colors and shapes and textures of the room, the flickering light of the television, all the different things displayed on that television screen—my brain chose the Dallas Stars forward standing expectantly in front of the net to observe and commit to memory?

One of the reasons I noticed Brenden Morrow has to do with a remarkable bit of circuitry in the brain, discovered and labeled only in the last twenty years, that's known as the mirror neuron system. This is the critical idea of mirror neurons: scientists used to think that perception and action were processed in different parts of the brain. You had one part over here that saw the world, and then if you needed to actually *do* something about it, you'd go to this other part over here with all the motor neurons. And then a group of Italian researchers found these certain brain cells that went off whether you were doing the action or just watching. "To think," as Ralph Waldo Emerson wrote, "is to act." Or, to take an example from neuroscientist Marco Iacoboni's *Mirroring People*, whether you kick a soccer ball, or see a soccer ball get kicked, or just say the word *kick*, the mirror neurons in your brain will fire. The more familiar you are with the action, the more intense the mirroring. For actions that you've both done and watched a lot—like ice hockey for me—you run essentially a full-scale simulation of the motion that you see.

The discovery story for mirror neurons is a bit of a mystery, but, as with hormones, the early work was done in monkeys. Vittorio Gallese, Luciano Fadiga, Leonardo Fogassi, and Giacomo Rizzolatti were mapping monkey brains, recording electrical signals from neurons in what's known as the neocortex—the relatively new part of the brain in humans and monkeys that controls a lot of the advanced stuff we do. The researchers were working on motor neurons, which activate to control action, and at some point they noticed that some neurons fired both when the monkey made the action and when the monkey just saw a researcher make the same action.

From this relatively simple observation, and the much more complex deductions the researchers made about it, has come a massive new leap in neuroscience that some scientists now think explains much of what makes us human. It is still a very new field, and the claims in the media can often sound hyperbolic, but this is in some sense the science of our understanding of the world—the science of empathy. Language, they say, probably originated here. Autism could be a lack of functioning in the mirror neuron system. Serial killers could have broken mirror neuron systems. Sports fans are so invested in athletes because they are mirroring them the entire time, running active simulations as if it were the fan out there on the field. In the next few chapters we're going to talk about identity, relationships, love, addiction, and conflict. All of these complicated human traits and behaviors, Iacoboni says, will probably eventually have as their underlying component an explanation in the mirror neuron system.

"The way I was taught is that the best scientific theories should explain a lot of things with very few principles," he told me. "All these things, they all go together. They remind us that the way we understand the states of others is by simulating that state onto our own body. It goes back to the notion of closeness, there's no way of understanding the state of other people except by getting them so close to us that we mimic what they do."

IN 1976, EMPATHY RESEARCHERS DOLF ZILLMANN AND JOANNE Cantor proposed something they called "disposition of mirth." Basically the assumption and question were: All jokes are at the expense of someone, all drama is at the expense of someone, so when is it okay to laugh or enjoy the outcome? Twenty years before the discovery of mirror neurons, Zillmann had collected data on empathy by making six different versions of a short film—three different beginnings and three different endings. The three beginnings set the audience up to like, dislike, or not care about the boy in the film by having him interact with his brother in a bratty, pleasant, or neutral kind of way. The three endings then set the audience up to have a reaction by having the boy either receive a shiny new bike, suffer a painful bike accident, or have nothing happen at all. The test, of course, was to see how the people watching reacted to the boy falling down on his bike if, say, they already had been primed to like or dislike or not care about him. The data, Zillmann argued, were conclusive.

"A recent investigation of empathy," he wrote, "has revealed that mishaps are, in fact, only appreciated when they happen to resented people."

The reverse was true as well, and in short, Zillmann concluded, when you like someone and he succeeds or you dislike someone and he fails, you rejoice; when you like someone and he fails or you dislike someone and he succeeds, you feel miserable.

Disposition of mirth has since been cited often to explain the behavior of sports fans, particularly by sports psychologist Daniel Wann at Murray State and those who have worked with him. There's an entire literature devoted to what we do after games: beginning with basking in reflected glory (BIRG) and cutting off reflected failure (CORF). Cody Havard, a professor of sports psychology at the University of Memphis, has applied disposition of mirth to explain college football rivalries and added new terms to the mix like glory out of reflected failure (GORF).

We'll get more into rivalry and schadenfreude later, but what's fun for now is that all this vast literature on how people act with empathy and what kinds of things make us happy seems to be explained by mirror neurons. We intuitively understand the way the boy has behaved and what he deserves for his actions because we instantly, unconsciously put ourselves in his shoes, and then the brain talks to itself and comes up with emotion to match the action. We do the same for our sports heroes, mirroring their joy in victory and basking in glory that, on a neural level, is felt more personally than Zillmann and Cantor probably imagined. Marco Iacoboni has shown this in experiments using brain imaging: When people view a face, for example, the mirror neuron areas of the brain activate to simulate the expression, and a pathway called the insula lights up to carry the simulation from the mirror neuron areas to the limbic system, which handles (among many other things) emotion and memory. "It seems," Iacoboni writes in *Mirroring People*, "as if our brain is *built* for mirroring, and that only through mirroring—through the simulation in our brain of the felt experience of other minds—do we deeply understand what other people are feeling."

As with the hormones, though, we shouldn't get too carried away. The studies that support mirror neuron theories of emotion and action interpretation are small-scale, carefully controlled, and different from real life. The difference between a monkey watching another monkey grab a teacup and me reading a hockey play from the body language and positioning of several NHL players is immense. Although no one questions the existence of mirror neurons, there are certainly critics who point out that for all the overarching claims of the new research, the evidence still lags a bit behind. But pretty much all psychology and neuroscience is about extrapolation.

"Experiments in the lab are always controlled," Iacoboni said. "Real life is not controlled."

So we're going to extrapolate a little to try to get further into what happened in my brain—and what might happen in the brain of a more expert watcher—as the San Jose Sharks season died.

WE ALL KNOW, SALVATORE AGLIOTI WRITES IN THE OPENING to his 2008 paper in the journal *Nature Neuroscience*, that pro athletes have better motor and sensory skills than novices. But we also don't really understand what's going on in their brains that makes them better. Nor do we understand why can't-miss physical freaks, the people with more talent than everyone else, can still lose to lesser athletes at the pro level. This is not an argument about hard work, which is the bromide of choice for columnists and old-school TV announcers trying to explain why someone who's taller doesn't get a rebound over someone shorter. This is an argument, actually, about natural talents that you can't measure in workouts.

Wayne Gretzky famously said, "A good hockey player plays where the puck is. A great hockey player plays where the puck is going to be." Pretty much everyone who watched or played with Gretzky knew his anticipation was better than everyone else's, and that it was so good it allowed him to almost easily overcome his physical limitations. He was, as at least one sports journalist labeled him, "the Einstein of hockey." But how did he know where the puck was going to be? Since he has not (like Einstein) donated his brain to science, we are going to have to make an educated guess. Gretzky's own explanation is that he worked hard in practice and learned his smarts beginning with training under his dad, Wally. "Some say I have a 'sixth sense.' . . Baloney," he said in the autobiography he cowrote with Rick Reilly.* "I've just learned to guess what's going to happen next. It's anticipation. It's not God-given, it's Wally-given. He used to stand on the blue line and say to me, 'Watch, this is how everybody else does it.' Then he'd shoot a puck along the boards and into the corner and then go chasing after it. Then he'd come back and say, 'Now, this is how the smart player

---

*From the same paragraph: "Some scientist even theorized that my motor neutrons fire faster than most people—and we all know how painful that can be—and I'm therefore a fraction of a second ahead of everybody else on the ice." Maybe that is why the Great One wasn't a great coach.

does it.' He'd shoot it into the corner again, only this time he cut across to the other side and picked it up over there. Who says anticipation can't be taught?"

Still, the vast majority of professional hockey players work hard in practice and have worked hard in practice since they were kids. That's why they're in the NHL. Many of them even had dads who played in the backyard rink with them, teaching them secrets of the game. Some of them must have tried to learn better anticipation. And yet none of them are Wayne Gretzky.

Aglioti, a neuroscientist at the University of Rome, wanted to see if he could apply the insights from mirror neurons to understand why some elite athletes are so much better at predicting and anticipating action than others—or rather, to make it easier to design an experiment, why elite athletes are better at predicting and anticipating than novice athletes. He ran two experiments, the first with basketball players and fans and a second with basketball and soccer players and fans. For the first test he brought ten professional players, ten "expert watchers"—a combination of sports journalists and coaches who watched a lot but hadn't played the game in years—and ten novices who'd never played basketball into his lab. He then asked each participant to judge the success of a free throw at one of ten freeze frames in a two-second video of the shot. The participants were asked whether the shot was going to go in and were given a choice of "yes," "no," and "uncertain."

He found that both elite athletes and expert watchers were considerably more certain about where the ball was going than novices. The novices rarely would make a judgment until the ball had clearly left the shooter's hand and they could assess its trajectory; athletes and expert watchers tended to make predictions based on the body language of the shooter alone. And here's the great thing (particularly if you feel the way I do about sports journalists): there was no significant difference in uncertainty between elite athletes and expert watchers—they all thought they knew where the ball was going. But the elite athletes were correct way more often.

Okay, but this is probably what you'd predict. What makes Aglioti's study special is that he then essentially repeated the experiment, but this time with everyone hooked up to the brain-scanning device known as transcranial magnetic stimulation. TMS measures electrical activity in the brain at a particular time, and although it's not great for figuring out precisely where in the brain things happen, you can position the scanner to look at particular parts of the brain. So Aglioti and his team were able to place the TMS coil in a spot to check for activation in the left primary motor cortex—an area rich with mirror neurons that should, in theory, fire on the sight of another human in action.

They found a few interesting things. This time around, the expert watchers were more on par with the elite athletes; both showed significant activation in the motor cortex when they saw video of the basketball player shooting. (Aglioti also did the same experiment with both a still photo of a basketball shot and a video of a soccer player kicking a ball, but the results were less clear.) The difference was that the neurons of elite athletes activated in particular and with special ferocity only when the shot was a miss. This is why Aglioti says that's important: In basketball, of course, if the shot goes in there's no real need for the player to react, but if it doesn't, then all of a sudden there's a highly competitive situation with a deep advantage to the person whose brain has recognized the shot as a miss first. That early activation is priming the elite athletes to go get a rebound way before the sports journalists know what's happening. Aglioti even folds this finding into his negative result for soccer kicks. In soccer, the shot either goes in or it misses. The chance it rebounds off the post is so low as to rarely be something anyone can practice, and there's little value to a soccer player who's an expert in corralling rebounds. The elite basketball players have an anticipatory ability that's focused on a situation unique to their sport.

You could apply Aglioti's research to soccer, though, if you focused on something slightly more complex—the balance of a defender, say, in a one-on-one situation with a dribbler. There's an easy analog to Gretzky in Barcelona these days who makes the point: the diminutive Lionel Messi dominates international soccer not so much with power but with acceleration, speed, and incredible intuition. Cristiano Ronaldo likewise, but Ronaldo also looks the professional athlete part. He's tall and muscular. He scores goals of power and precision, goals that require much more classical athletic skills like size, strength, and eye-foot coordination. Ronaldo clearly intuits a thing or two about defender positioning, but when I watch Barcelona, when I witness *La Pulga*—the flea—in action, I see the cliché that sports are 90 percent mental. I see Lionel Messi's brain, apparently the world's greatest physics engine, spinning out calculus and telling him exactly what feint, what shift of his weight, what quick burst will move him around defenders who, just like Gretzky's antagonists, always seem reduced to spectators. For a fan of Barcelona or Argentina, who plays the game and watches regularly, the exhilaration of watching Messi has to come in part because of the anticipation he inspires. Even if we couldn't execute the action ourselves, we can read what he reads, and in every magic moment when he fakes outside and drags the ball inside toward the vulnerable goal, our hearts must leap with his.

AGLIOTI'S PAPER HAS PLENTY OF SIGNIFICANCE FOR PRO ATH-letes, but I was struck by the performance of the expert watchers compared to the elite athletes. I'm not sure where I lie on that continuum, because although I watch a lot of hockey I also play it fairly often. I'd guess this is true of a lot of sports fans, and I'd guess that our mirroring responses must exist somewhere in the middle of the elite athlete and never-played-but-watch-a-lot set. (I've never played football seriously, but I watch it a lot, so although I probably display considerable mirror activation while watching, I'm also probably terrible at anticipating the outcome of plays.) Remember that the expert watchers' motor neurons were firing at roughly the same level as the elite athletes' while watching the person shooting the ball; they were just much worse at predicting whether the shot would go in or not.

Returning now to the scene of the crime, I wondered what Aglioti's study of anticipation and athletics meant for my own understanding of the hockey play that ended the Sharks' 2008 playoff run. One conclusion is that I was indeed mirroring the action on the ice and thus was primed to anticipate the outcome a split second before it occurred. But it's also interesting to consider that to a pro hockey player the peril might be much more evident much earlier in the play than the last-second moment of panic I remember. To the trained eye and the mirror neurons of the professional athlete, I wondered, what signs are there in the body language of the players to indicate potential danger?

I made a second-by-second slideshow of the last fifteen seconds of the game and took it to Bret Hedican, a former player-turned-Sharks-TV-analyst and motivational speaker who breaks down film during intermission (the "Hedi-cam"), pointing out where players are positioned well or poorly, where their sticks ought to be, and how they should have their body weight distributed. It's entertaining stuff for an amateur player like me, in large part because it's also exactly the kind of thing that's toughest for me to see. Mirror neuron research suggests that the more you do something, the more you mirror it, and Hedican's experience means he notices instinctively when players make little adjustments. Hedican is special, too, because, unlike a lot of former players on TV, he notices that he notices.

We met in a small temporary office in Oakland's Jack London Square that Hedican shared with his wife, the former Olympic champion figure skater Kristi Yamaguchi. (They met at the 1992 Olympics in Albertville.) At something like six-foot-two, Hedican is average size for a former pro athlete, but he has that commanding motivational speaker's alpha presence that made it sound like he was yelling at me.* Combine the rich locker-room-pep-talk baritone with a certain intensity of glare and I found myself inching away and thinking that, per the testosterone-and-dominance theorist Allan Mazur, we had sorted ourselves very nicely into a little hierarchy of two. I wished I had saved a test tube.

---

*Chris Farley fans: picture everything Hedican says punctuated by "IN A VAN DOWN BY THE RIVER."

Hedican crushed my hand in a friendly handshake, rolled over in his chair, and leaned in to look at my laptop screen. I paused on the first slide, the puck battle on the corner boards that starts the Dallas power play, and told him I was interested in learning more about elite athlete anticipation. I tried to offer him an escape clause in case he didn't anticipate much. He interrupted me. "Yeah," he said, "but just on some of these plays here, some of the highlights there, I can tell what the guy's—he's got his shoulder turned this way, it's just like a guy if he's shooting a basketball this way, you know it's going to go in." And then he started to act it out in front of me. "Shoulder turned this way"—he swiveled in his office chair. "You know he's not shooting because he's actually tilted this way and he's aimed that way"—he dipped a broad shoulder and tilted athletically. Power, grace, precision, rolling office chairs. Hedican made it look natural, effortlessly converting the spare office into the defensive zone of an ice rink. He was communicating the point to me in the most efficient way a highly trained competitive athlete can: with action. Hedican, when I asked later, hadn't heard of mirror neurons, but he clearly got the gist.

A fair bit of research seems to suggest that mirror neurons could explain the origins of language. The cool idea, which Hedican seemed to demonstrate with every chair-rolling defense play, is that action and speech are essentially just part of the same thing. Researchers now look, in particular, at the close association of automatic gestures and speech, and at the proximity in the brain of the area where mirror neurons were discovered and Broca's area, one of the brain's language processing centers. Mirror neurons, of course, would be instrumental in someone else interpreting those gestures and turning hand movements into communication.

Sian Beilock, a cognitive neuroscientist at the University of Chicago, found a way to test the processing of action-related language in the brain. Like Aglioti, she compared experienced athletes with fans who watched a lot but didn't play and novices who neither watched nor played. What they found was that experience in a sport, or experience in any kind of action, changes the actual biological way that language is processed in the brain. For someone who's never played hockey before, the sentence "he shot the puck" goes straight to the language center. For a hockey player, it's sent to the language center and, in parallel, to the motor cortex. When one of Beilock's graduate students, Ian Lyons, followed up on the study a year later, he found an even more pronounced response when he looked at how much experience the subjects had with the particular activity described in each sentence. The more you play hockey, in other words, the more language is translated literally into action in your brain.

BEILOCK IS MOST FAMOUS FOR HER WORK ON SOMETHING ELSE that concerns us now: choking under pressure. Anticipation from reading the body language of an athlete in motion tells you that in that last horrible second Baggio is leaning too far back, that his kick is going to be high. But what, I wondered, about an even more static event? Can you read and learn anything from the body language of a player who's just standing there looking at the ball? Can a player communicate fear or nervousness or petulance to a fan—and vice versa—and does it affect the outcome? It turns out that, well, possibly. Body language certainly provides talk radio fodder, from petulant quarterbacks (poor leaders!) to timid basketball players (coming up short in the clutch!) to smiling hockey players (doesn't have the intensity to win!). But if we're really looking for body-language-inspired fatalism, it has to be called the English-penalty- kicks phenomenon.

"Some of it is hindsight," Beilock told me, "but some of it probably isn't."

The story of the English in penalty kicks is gruesome. Since the 1980s the national team has gone to what's intended to be a coin-toss tie-breaking proposition eight times; they have won once. Penalty kicks have ended England's run in the World Cup in three of the last six tournaments. The one game the team won in penalty kicks, against Spain in the 1996 European Championships (hosted by England), was followed four days later by a shoot-out loss to Germany.

And the problem is that once the players know that England has this reputation—even if they don't believe it's deserved—it becomes self-fulfilling in the brain. Beilock writes at length about what's called "stereotype threat" in her book *Choke: What the Secrets of the Brain Reveal about Getting It Right When You Have To*, but the gist of the idea is that simply being aware of a stereotype shifts the way the brain processes actions. In an athlete stress, pressure, and the awareness of past failure cause a thinking part of the brain called the "working memory" to wrest control of action from the much more competent "procedural motor cortex." The working memory is good at a lot of tasks, but handling professional-level athletics isn't one of them, and the way it seizes control of the operation under stress is something like a writer deciding that a broken arm is too important to be dealt with by a doctor and he's going to fix it at home with duct tape.* Test takers choke for a slightly different reason: because the working memory, which is really good at math tests, fills up instead with worry.

If you do nothing more than ask test takers to identify their gender before a math test, you can make women's scores go down. Whether they believe it or not, the subtle reminder that we live in a culture that stereotypes women and math occupies the working memory—with stress, with indignation, even with determination to prove the stereotype wrong—Beilock says. Reminding a speaker of his race can make his speech worse for the same reason. If an athlete gets saddled with a reputation for coming up short in the clutch, even if the athlete doesn't believe the stereotype, it will affect his brain.

"Having people who are really supportive and have high expectations for your success can lead to these perceptions of pressure that can backfire in particular situations," Beilock told me. We met at her office in Chicago, overlooking the gray Gothic spires of the Rockefeller Memorial Chapel. Beilock turned out to have grown up in the next town over from me, and she keeps a Cal "Bear Territory" flag in her office. (The University of Chicago famously—many say this should be the model everywhere—does not have intercollegiate athletics.) Primed by the Berkeley logo, I asked her specifically about underperforming Cal quarterbacks, but the lesson applies to everyone.

"That's a nice example of a stereotype threat that's not grounded in some cultural stereotype about race or gender," she said. "There's an expectation that you're going to choke and it's a self-fulfilling prophesy."

*It's okay, he looked up the procedure on the Internet.

We've shown already that fans with engaged mirror neurons can read an athlete's actions. Beilock had her own take on this in a journal article titled, "As Soon as the Bat Met the Ball, I Knew It Was Gone." No one's ever looked at whether fans can read an athlete's likelihood of choking, though. I asked her, then: Does our body language communicate the kind of tension and nervousness that shows an athlete's brain struggling to cope? Could fans watching a close game in some way sense the athlete starting to shift from the routine, practiced actions of the motor cortex and into the less familiar rhythms of working-memory-led action? Mirror neurons give a researcher every reason to think so, she said. Posture and facial expression have been shown to betray information to others about how powerful a person is. An engaged fan would be able to tell that Ashley Cole lacks confidence in his kick.

"We know that you get information about how confident people are from body posture, for example, you often mirror those things in other people," Beilock said. "But I think very subtly it can give you cues about their psychological state."

Warming to the subject, Beilock even suggested an experiment. You could make a video in which athletes had a certain posture before a negative play versus a certain posture before a positive play, and ask fans to predict success or failure. In some sense, that experiment is exactly what I asked Bret Hedican to do.

HEDICAN PLAYED IN THE NHL FOR SEVENTEEN YEARS, PLAYED on two United States Olympic teams, and won the Stanley Cup with Carolina in 2006. Like many professional athletes, it was entirely unclear that he would end up as a pro. He grew up on ice skates in Minnesota, but after mainly playing defense in high school he was recruited to St. Cloud State University as a forward. Which meant, basically, uh, we like you, but we found a few Canadians we like better, and which meant Hedican spent most of his freshman year in college not playing hockey at all. He remembers that he was the guy who sat high up in the rafters, guarding the "play" button on the intermission music machine. Like any good future motivational speaker, though, he continued to believe in himself. He convinced the coaches to let him play defense and had a better sophomore year. His junior year he was better than that. At the end of the year, while he was on vacation with his family, USA Hockey called and asked him to go play with the national team at a tournament in Russia. The coaches were going to be the coaches for the 1992 Olympic team, and Hedican recognized his opportunity. He played, he said, the four best games of his life. Hedican punctuates his speech with little verbal mortar rounds: boom. As in, "They asked me to try out that summer, I make the team, I play in the Olympics, and boom, I turned pro right after the Olympics."

So this was the leading mirror neuron question that I tried to ask him, à la Gretzky's opinion about not being the most talented but having the best anticipation. For someone who wasn't highly recruited out of high school, who was pressing the play button on the intermission music as a freshman in college, how did you manage to play for seventeen years in the NHL? It had to be mental, right?

He answered with some free off-season analysis of the Sharks, who had just wrapped up another disappointing season. "I think you look at the Sharks as a whole, as an organization, and me as a player, you have to be able to recognize your weakness," he said. "And then work on your weakness. Every year you should reassess and say, 'How can I be better?' That's what I did for seventeen years. Every year I went back and said, 'I've got to be better here. I've got to be stronger. I've got to get my endurance better. I've got to work on my multitasking. I've got to work on my stick-handling ability.'"*

The way he did that is by playing hockey even when he wasn't playing hockey. He spent nights, weekends, and summers watching film, visualizing, and working out on simulation machines, engaging his mirror neurons in a form of practice that turns out to be ruthlessly effective.** It was probabilistic repetition: he repeated every possible scenario in his own mind until he could do any of them without thinking. Comparing himself to Aglioti's elite basketball players, Hedican stressed the value of repetition in learning to excel at a sport. When he entered the league, he said, he hadn't done enough repetitions to make it. Only by con-

---

*It was clear, from further questioning, that he does not believe the Sharks do this. "They don't do it because I consistently see mistakes being made that are mental mistakes that should have been done before they even got on the ice," he said. "And I *see* it." Then he pounded the table. The Sharks' inattention to the little details drives Hedican, a hyper-focused, intense winner, insane.

**My high school soccer coach used to preach the value of visualization to us. I told Marco Iacoboni about this, and he said, "He had an amazing intuition," which I'm pretty sure is the first time anyone has ever put those words and that particular person together. We did win a lot, but I would attribute it more to the iron discipline recruited from his days as a drill sergeant and instilled in us via ruthless conditioning and his terrifying catchphrase: "Better effort and concentration, son."

stantly working over and over again on the tiniest details could he succeed. When the ultimate payoff came, in a Game Seven Stanley Cup victory and subsequent hoisting of Lord Stanley's trophy, that's what he remembered.

"As I lifted that thing and it was passed on to me, the only thing I thought of was all those days that I said, 'How can I be better?'" Hedican said. "Every one of those things I worked on from the day I kept saying it to the day I won it, I used."

In the last minute of that game, Hedican's Carolina Hurricanes are leading 2–1 and rival Edmonton has pulled its goalie for an extra skater. There's a face-off in the Carolina zone. The puck gets tied up on the boards, and Hedican charges in. He bats the puck out of the air and out of the zone to the safety of his superstar teammate Eric Staal. Staal passes it to Justin Williams and Williams shoots it into the empty net. Series, Cup. Hedican described the play for me in micro-detail, and then tried to describe what it felt like.

"I wasn't thinking about the Stanley Cup, I wasn't thinking about last game, I wasn't thinking about last shift," he said. "I wasn't thinking about anything but that moment. And that was training. That's all it was. It was learning how to—you know, twenty thousand people, Stanley Cup on the line, and being right here"—he took a deep breath, in and out, and then held the silence. "That's it."

"You're just out there so relaxed," he said. "That puck, you can feel the vibration of it hitting your stick. You're breathing relaxed. You're skating effortlessly. These are things I visualized over and over again in my mind, so when I hit the ice it was creating that feeling every time. Why is Wayne Gretzky the best player ever to play the game? He wasn't the biggest guy, wasn't the strongest, the toughest, the meanest, didn't have the hardest shot. He was able to slow the game down. Because he was in the moment every time he had that puck on his stick."

SINCE AGLIOTI'S YES/NO/UNCERTAIN BASKETBALL PARADIGM doesn't really work as well for a full hockey play, I had asked Hedican to look at each still from the last part of the Sharks–Stars game and then rate on a scale of 1 to 10 how likely he thought it was that a goal would be scored in the next ten seconds. (Without identifying the result of either play beforehand, I also showed him a ten-second power play clip from the same game, starting with the puck in the same place, that did not end in a goal.) He went pretty quickly from "1" as the two players passed back and forth at the point to "4" as the puck came down the boards a bit to "6" as the pass made it through the middle to "8" and then "9" as each successive pass connected. We were going quickly, spending about one second per photo, but Hedican still saw the goal coming probably three or four seconds before I had when I watched the game live. About four seconds before the goal the puck is at the point, on the stick of the Stars' forward, Mike Ribeiro. There are three Sharks players roughly in the area known as the slot, and Joe Pavelski, the Sharks forward, is coming out toward Ribeiro and in an okay position to block a shot should Ribeiro take one.

Hedican had instantly scored the photo of that moment a "4," after only assigning 1s or 2s up to this point. Later I returned to that photo to ask what he saw.

"I see a lot of failure," he said. He quickly qualified to

add, "As far as the Sharks are concerned. As for Dallas, they're in the right place." (My wizened fan heart croaked with malicious glee at that analysis. This entire test was very oddly cathartic.)

Now he had time to explain his snap judgment. Three of the Sharks' four players on the ice weren't in the right place or doing the right thing. Patrick Marleau, at the right edge of the picture, was too high toward the point and should have had his stick in the gap to prevent a cross-ice pass. Joe Pavelski and Marc-Édouard Vlasic are both leaving the front of the net to get out to where Ribeiro is with the puck, but one of them, Pavelski, should already be there. The other, Vlasic, should have his stick down on the ice and on the other side of his body to prevent that pass. Hedican unconsciously illustrated these for me, sliding his chair across the room, holding his hands out to grip an imaginary stick that he was keeping on the ice in the passing lane.

These are actually pretty minor details—a matter of a few feet here and there, a matter of keeping your stick on the ice at the right time. The players are desperately tired. This is the longest game any of them has played at the pro level—and probably ever. Some of them might be cheating just a little bit, to conserve a little extra energy or, in Marleau's case, to hope for a rebound that he can take the other direction. Hockey, though, is a game of little details. The Sharks ignored them for a moment, which is why in the picture there are now only four seconds left in their season.

BRET HEDICAN'S BRAIN SEES ACTION AND MOVEMENT IN A WAY that few others in the world do. But there's one thing that I see here that he doesn't. Bret's brain assigns no values to the players. There's just a guy playing hockey, doing the thing that Bret does, making Bret's mirror neurons work. My brain doesn't necessarily scan those actions the same way, but it assigns tremendous value to the sweater colors. It sees a white sweater competing against a black sweater along the boards and it shoots off anxiety and stress. The images on the TV screen aren't just actors acting out actions, they're good battling evil in real time and, to whatever extent it can predict the future, my brain is imbuing everything with emotion. The world is infinitely more complicated for all those values.

Here's an example from Iacoboni, the UCLA neuroscientist. We were talking about pain empathy and mirror neurons. There is evidence that when a person sees another person, for example, grimace in pain, the viewer's brain sends signals to the muscles that control grimacing, enacting a kind of sympathetic response. "Although we commonly think of pain as a fundamentally private experience, our brain actually treats it as an experience shared with others," he wrote in *Mirroring People*.

Which brings both of us to the 2006 World Cup final. The game between France and Italy is widely remember for one infamous moment in extra time, when the French legend Zinedine Zidane head-butted the Italian Marco Materazzi in the chest, drawing a red card and ejection in the final international game of Zidane's career. The Italian Iacoboni certainly remembers: he wrote at length about "the savage head-butting" in *Mirroring People*: "Watching the game again, I know exactly what is going to happen. Still, I find myself experiencing strong emotions when Zidane head-butts Materazzi. I wince at Materazzi's pain. I also feel enraged all over again at Zidane for his act of aggression." Iacoboni even refers to a quote from Adam Smith's 1759 treatise *The Theory of Moral Sentiments*: "When we see a stroke aimed, and just ready to fall upon the leg or arm of another person, we naturally shrink and draw back our leg or our own arm; and when it does fall, we feel it in some measure, and are hurt by it as well as the sufferer."

I remember this very, very clearly, because I watched that same exact thing and my first thought was, "Materazzi's faking it." When I watched the game live, I was in a room with several French partisans. Even now, although I can tell the head-butt is far more powerful than it seemed when I first watched it, I think Materazzi's pain reaction was exaggerated. (He spent some time writhing on the ground, but he was fine and continued playing.) If mirror neurons and empathy are all that's going on when we watch sports, something in my system had gone wrong here; I hadn't empathized with Materazzi at all. Not just not empathized, but actively dismissed his pain. Why, I asked, would an invested fan only empathize with half of the athletes? Why, I asked, was my first reaction to think that Materazzi had taken a dive?

"First of all," Iacoboni said, somewhat severely addressing the allegation of diving first, "I must disagree with you."

Then he explained his idea of the science.

"When you watch sports, you're already emotionally charged," he said. "Then when we watch the actions that unfold during the game, you also watch the actions the athletes make. What happens here is motor resonance and lower-level emotional resonance, and I think these two things reinforce each other. They feed into each other. That's why you can't help but jump onto the chair. You do it a little bit because there's the motor component, but you do it, too, because the emotional side feeds into it. The different parts of the brain talk to each other."

Iacoboni told me that one of his graduate students had just collected data from an experiment investigating the parts of the brain involved in that conversation. The limbic system is certainly involved to apply the emotional spin. There are some studies, Iacoboni said, that seem to indicate the communication between mirror neurons and limbic system isn't entirely one-way. But even more interesting, the new research out of his lab indicates that other parts of the prefrontal cortex—the medial prefrontal cortex and anterior cingulate cortex, specifically, both of which are involved in decision-making—are also involved. It's possible, Iacoboni wrote to me in an email, those planning and decision-making brain lobes are calling the shots on what simulations make it through to the limbic system. The most advanced part of the human brain could be making the mirror neurons sign a non-disclosure agreement about their findings re: the guys in the dark sweaters.

The mirror neuron system, in fact, begins to sound like the hormone system. My empathy and my testosterone: two parts of the same reaction, neither operating fully independently. Testosterone surges reflexively; mirror neurons fire reflexively. Together they shape in significant ways my reaction to watching a live event. Studying either system and the way it shapes fandom could be a life's work in science. But even together they aren't enough. This sports-watching thing is fairly awesomely complicated.

"We have to keep in mind: Even though we have all

these systems, they can be overridden," Iacoboni said. "It would be totally dysfunctional to have a system like this that's not controlled. If you are already in that mind-set in which you are already rooting for France, you watch that scene, you can use some top-down control."

If you didn't have the ability to control your mirroring reflex, you'd go around mirroring everyone all the time and be a hopeless wreck of a person. Iacoboni told me about patients in his lab who suffer severe strokes that knock out a large part of their prefrontal cortex, where the mirror neurons are, and lose the ability to choose what to mimic. They simply imitate everything they see.

Control, though, comes with a downside, and sports fans illustrate it as well as anyone. There's evidence, for example, that you mirror in-group members more than out-group members. This is, in a way, an elective (although still largely unconscious) choice to use your mirror neurons more often on some people than others. It's not necessarily a pretty one, but it certainly seems to catch us while we're watching sports.

"Our biology is good," Iacoboni said. "What's really bad is our beliefs. We divide ourselves into many different categories and preclude our empathy."

Bret Hedican, watching that Sharks–Stars playoff game, is empathizing with all the players. He sees Mike Ribeiro leaning one way and he mirrors the action. He sees Marc-Édouard Vlasic leaning the wrong way and he mirrors that action. I see Mike Ribeiro and I fixate on the black shirt and not the hockey player and I exert "top-down control" to shut off my mirror neurons. The action is parsed by my brain's emotion centers in terms of what it might mean for

the players I am empathizing with—like Marc-Édouard Vlasic in the white sweater, whose poor positioning eludes my
notice entirely. At the last moment, I see Brenden Morrow,
and I mirror the hostile intent of his action as I'd mirror a
leaping chimpanzee brandishing a thigh bone in my direction—with an understanding of the action about to take
place, but also with no sympathy and a great deal of dread
and anger. This particular empathetic brain wave is a mirror
that's showing me my own reflection in a Darth Vader suit.

The undermining-of-free-will argument still holds, since
it's not as if in the moment I made a conscious choice to
mirror some of the players in a certain way. What was happening was reflexive and largely beyond my control at the
time. But this is another demonstration of that unique thing
that makes us human: the ability to mess with our unconscious systems. It's almost like breathing, I think. You can
and often do just let your lungs do their own thing. Or you
can take over consciously and run things for a while. With
testosterone, with empathy, you can exert self-control and
shape your reflex response. Self-control might be one of our
most defining and most brilliant adaptations.

Iacoboni said he was at a social intelligence dinner once
where the speaker said, "I don't want my son to be two
standard deviations above the mean in intelligence—I want
him to be two standard deviations above the mean in self-
control." He suggests that learning more about mirror neurons can actually help us control their functioning better, to
increase empathy in violent criminals and to decrease it in
recovering drug addicts.

"We have something in our brain that has really been
devised for altruism and empathy, but at the same time it

can be used for bad things like addiction and violence," he said. "But because we have control, in principle, if we understand how these things work, we can increase empathy. To increase empathy in otherwise normal human beings, that would be great."

I wonder, in the end, how much control I'm really exerting. In some sense, that's the question we're going to explore for the rest of this book. To understand why Bret Hedican's brain and my own are so different, we need to understand where that top-down control comes from.

PART TWO
Control

3
A Case of Identity: Welcome to Cleveland

WHEN THE MORTGAGE INDUSTRY HIT THE ICEBERG IN 2009, Adam Mesnick, a born-and-raised Clevelander who had worked for Wells Fargo for almost a decade, found himself in San Francisco opening up a delicatessen.

"Growing up I always wanted to start a restaurant and everyone told me I was fucking crazy because it's a bloodsuck," he says. "What else was I going to do?"

Mesnick didn't just start any old random deli. He started up a Cleveland-style deli, an intimate homage to his hometown that he says he wants to turn into something people from Cleveland can really be proud of. And that's about where the best of times–worst of times comparisons begin. Cleveland, Mesnick says, is a "shitty, dying city" that he wants to honor. It was the best of times: He delights in the Clevelanders who come in and find each other, and the community he's created around his sandwich shop. It was the worst of times: He laments that many Midwesterners seem to prefer chain restaurants to small businesses and celebrates

San Franciscans for preferring the opposite. Mesnick once thought that when it came time to expand and create a second Deli Board, he'd do it in Cleveland. Now, he says, he's thinking more like sixth or seventh.

The San Francisco food scene does not tolerate nontrendy. A deli—and particularly one bearing aloft the banner of the most miserable city in the Midwest—is a curious choice. One early reviewer snarked, "What's so great about Cleveland? Nothing!"

But Mesnick boldly plunged ahead. He recognizes, he says, that the Deli Board might forever be a labor of love. Which is not to say it's often quiet there. On weekdays the midday line in Mesnick's small shop crowds out the door. Squeezing up to the counter feels a bit like merging with the mob at a stadium concession stand. By sheer number of patrons, Mesnick and his deli must represent the most successful Cleveland cultural beachhead in San Francisco. ("Maybe the country," he said, when I suggested this to him, and if we're going there, why not the world?) When I wanted to learn more about the Gordian knot of Cleveland culture and Cleveland sports, I turned to the Cleveland-celebrating expat who loathes and loves the city at the same time.

"The pain brings you back," he said to me at one point as we discussed Cleveland's sporting scene. He mentioned his friend Todd Dery, who writes for a Cleveland sports blog called *Waiting for Next Year*. "Todd nails it," Adam said. "Waiting for next year is all there is."

BEFORE THE WIDESPREAD ADVENT OF BRAIN-SCANNING DEVICES, neuroscientists had only one reliable way of studying the structures in the brain: they'd look for people with damaged brains. If someone came in with a bruise on the Broca's area of the brain, and that person had lost the ability to speak, you could guess that some aspect of speech is processed in Broca's area. Given the various imperfections of modern scanners and the difficulty of testing anything on humans, it's still common practice today—Marco Iacoboni, for example, mentioned his own work with patients who suffer strokes and lose the ability to shut off their mirror neurons, with the result that they imitate any person in front of them.

We've talked now about the reflexes that happen when you watch sports, the way your hormone system activates and the way your brain engages with action. But the lesson from both fields seems to be that those reflexes aren't nearly enough to explain all the complex things happening inside your head—that in fact the psychology is often driving the reflexes. It seemed to me one way to approach some of the higher-level brain processing that's controlling the hormone and mirror neurons of sports fans would be to find the most damaged patients, which I decided meant normal people who had been driven insane by losing. Something that Iacoboni said had struck me: "In a lot of situations," he said, "we don't have a lot of control, especially when it comes to things like watching sports. We like to be swept away by the feelings. That's why we like these things."

In other words, part of the enjoyment of sports comes from surrendering your control and empowering your hormones and neurons to do their thing. But to do that you have to make a choice to surrender, and it's a choice you kind of have to make over and over again. You can declare an end to your sports team allegiance at any point and move on. And yet most people don't, even though some people seem subject to such extreme provocation that it's almost miraculous that they re-up every season. The quest to find those people led me to a handful of lifelong die-hard Clevelanders and Mesnick, their friend who started a deli two thousand miles from his hometown and named the sandwiches after his family and friends back in the Mistake on the Lake.

IN CLEVELAND, REAL LIFE MERGES WITH A CURSED SPORTING SCENE in a way that is unique—at least, they swear so. Mainly for worse, the identity of Cleveland is inseparable from its sports teams, to the point that the *New York Times* ran a story a few years back on how much the basketball player LeBron James skipping town would hurt the city's economy. (The chamber of commerce objected to the premise, but not convincingly.) The Wikipedia entry for the city connects sports with the city's economic existence in a way incredible to me:

> Following World War II the city experienced a prosperous economy. In sports, the Indians won the 1948 World Series and the Browns dominated professional football in the 1950s. Businesses proclaimed that Cleveland was "the best location in the nation." . . . Suburbanization changed the city in the late 1960s and 1970s, when financial difficulties and a notorious 1969 fire on the Cuyahoga River challenged the city. This, *along with the city's struggling professional sports teams,* drew negative national press; as a result, Cleveland was often derided as "The Mistake on the Lake."

My italics, but where else in the world could this kind of link among sports, financial difficulties, and environmental pollution be made? You would be laughed out of the room for connecting the San Jose Sharks' high-profile playoff failures with the dot-com bust, or the Yankees World Series collapse with the reputation of Wall Street, or Arsenal's fade from Premier League contention and sale of players to economic austerity measures in London. James may be a global marketing icon, but he's still smaller than San Francisco, or New York, or London, or even Miami. South Beach will still be South Beach whether LeBron is employing his talents there or not, while Cleveland, the article seemed to imply, might crumble away in his absence.

I'm not sure sports fans outside the United States can quite comprehend the incredible despairing tedium of Cleveland's football/baseball/basketball tradition. For one thing, there's not just one sport here, there are three, and they all lose. There's also no relegation here to fight off, no upper-table consolation for qualifying for the Champions League or even the mollifying *somethingness* of the Europa League. There's one way to end a baseball season in triumph, and Cleveland hasn't done it since 1948. There's one way to end a football season in triumph and Cleveland hasn't done it since 1964. There's one way to end a basketball season in triumph and Cleveland has never done it in more than forty years in the league. English friends mentioned teams like Newcastle or Hull to me—similar down-and-rusty postindustrial cities with teams that have struggled for decades. But there's the glory of the Premier League model—if you lose badly enough and pathetically enough, it sucks for a season, sure, but then you turn around and next year you're looking at being one of the better teams, maybe even a winning team. Newcastle had a horrid season in 2009, got relegated, and turned around the next season and finished in the best place available, winning the Football Championship and securing promotion. Hull not only succeeded to the Premier League for the first time in its history in 2008 by winning a playoff; the team successfully fought off relegation the following year to stay up. Cleveland does get to delight in minor triumphs, too—beating the Steelers in football, advancing in the NBA playoffs—but the season always, without fail, ends on a down note.

ON A WARM WINTER WEDNESDAY, I SAT DOWN AT A SMALL table in Adam Mesnick's deli with a giant roasted-turkey-avocado-and-cream-cheese sandwich in front of me and waited for Mesnick to come out from the back of the shop. A four-foot-tall poster of a pile of pink HOT DOG tickets from Cleveland Stadium hung over my head. A CLEVELAND sign rested on the door frame. The brown-and-rust color scheme evoked the Browns' classic look. (Mesnick told me later he had considered brown and orange for real authenticity, but found it just a bit too much.) Mesnick, in newspaper articles, has been all too happy to point out that the street just across from the deli is Cleveland Street.

Mesnick is in his late thirties, bald and goateed, with sharp brown eyes in a face that's softened around the edges a bit since his high school days as one of the best-looking guys in Cleveland. He slid out from behind the counter with his apron on, sat down across from me, and pushed a squeeze jar of brown Stadium Mustard—in his estimation, at least, a noted Cleveland accomplishment—my direction. It's the official mustard of his shop, of course, one of the small details to celebrate his hometown. He sells it for $4 a bottle at the counter. He has yellow mustard, too, in case anyone asks, but he can o ly recall it happening twice. "I guarantee," he said, "every Cleveland person can tell you what this tastes like on a hot dog."

Three or four times in our conversation something would come up where Mesnick would talk about how miserable it is back home, followed immediately by a discussion of how he misses it. "There's a certain community there that keeps people close," he said. Community, in the Midwestern sense, is one of the things about San Francisco that's absent. Maybe because part of the draw of California is that it's a place to start over and set down new roots, it's tough in this city to find people with a shared, citywide cultural upbringing. (You could dissect this a bit, but as a blanket statement I believe it holds.)

In Cleveland an inextricable part of that community is the sports scene. Mesnick's stepdad, Les, runs a nightly television sports talk show; his mom still keeps score at Indians games.

"In Cleveland, you can't escape it," Mesnick said to me. "No matter where you go it's something. Every bar has something to do with Cleveland sports. I was shocked when I moved out to San Francisco. That Cleveland mentality, you just are born a fan. That's the way it is."

We met once the day after the San Francisco Giants pitcher Matt Cain had just thrown the twenty-second perfect game in baseball history. Mesnick waved at the ordinary workday traffic on Folsom Street. If this was Cleveland, he said, a perfect game would be a much bigger deal than this. Here it was just one more thing going on. San Francisco is a small city, but it's a bigger place than Matt Cain's baseball achievement.

I STARTED BY ASKING CLEVELANDERS A SIMPLE QUESTION: Is Cleveland different? I found quickly that they laughed at the naïveté implied there—but I think they liked the question because the answer was always an enthusiastic, instantaneous "absolutely."

"Big time," said Matt Dery, a born-and-raised Clevelander who has worked as a sportscaster in Detroit for the last sixteen years, when I asked him if there were differences between Detroit and Cleveland fans. "There is a bitterness, a frustration with Cleveland that cannot be matched anywhere else."

Detroit's a good comparison case study because of the obvious economic similarities. But Detroit, Matt said, has the multi-champion Red Wings, and the multi-champion Detroit Pistons, and, although they've disappointed in the clutch lately, the Tigers won the World Series in 1984. The Tigers inspired a curious *Sports Illustrated* cover article in 2010 that labeled them "The Righteous Franchise" for trying to win with "blue-collar baseball" that appealed to blue-collar workers in Detroit—curious in that the idea that a millionaire running a little harder on a ground ball will make everyone feel better. (Also, the strange implication that players don't run out ground balls in Oakland, or Pittsburgh, or Cleveland.) The Lions may be an NFL punching bag, but it doesn't really rub off on the city.

"Die-hard Lions fans have some similarities [to Cleve-landers], but the difference is when they leave Ford Field at least they knew their other teams have brought them some joy," Matt said. "For Cleveland fans that's not the case."

THERE'S ALSO AN IDEA THAT FANS JUST *CARE* MORE IN CLEVE-land, almost like they have responded to repeated failure by trying even harder. Mesnick suggested the miserable winter weather and the lack of other options have led to the culture of fandom. He says since moving to San Francisco he's adapted to being in a place where it's less essential to be a sports fan, where tradition isn't as deeply felt. He's grown to like the 49ers—although he agonized over it enough that he called into his stepdad's show back home to ask for per-mission to be made happy by a second team. But no San Francisco team will ever come close to his roots. "All in all, I prefer the Niners to win," he told me once, "but I'll never name a sandwich after them."

Still, every city in the world claims to love its sports teams, to embrace its athletes. Cleveland topped ESPN's list for most tortured fan base in America in 2004, but hasn't since. There's a strong argument to be made for Seattle, San Diego, Phoenix, Buffalo—and of course the century-plus-and-counting Chicago Cubs. But don't mention that to any-one in Cleveland. I tried and heard the following: Don't *even* bring that weak Cubs shit here. You want real torture, you want to see the most pained fans in America, you come to Cleveland. This place is utterly, uniquely, hideously special. End of story.

You will get this lesson punctuated by a Clevelander's

encyclopedic memory of every championship won by someone else. Like, for example, you'll ask about the misery in
Seattle (beloved NBA team taken away; baseball team celebrating forty-five years and no championships; football
team celebrating forty-seven years and no championships),
and they will instantly remind you that the Supersonics won
the NBA title in 1979. These guys are hard-core, extremely
aware losers.

What the Cleveland fan hangs his—and her—hat on is
an odd kind of pride. They are proud to be from Cleveland,
proud of the city, proud of the sports teams that represent it,
and most of all proud that they keep coming back. They are
proud to abandon self-control in favor of misery. Even, as in
the case of Mesnick, when they call it a shitty, dying city.
It's *his* shitty, dying city, the inspiration for him even in San
Francisco. It's an odd life choice, but then pride is an odd
sort of emotion. The age-old sin is something different from
just excess self-esteem—or at least some psychologists think
so. Self-esteem, in their definition, is based on two things:
one emotional and one cognitive. Cognitive comes from the
satisfaction of knowing you've done a good job; they call
this self-efficacy. Emotion is what happens when you know
that *others* know you've done a good job. That's what they
call pride.

This is the example that Lisa Williams, a pride researcher at the University of New South Wales, gives:
"Imagine you tied your shoes this morning, and you tied
your shoes *really* well, but you're probably not going to
derive much pride from it, right?" You get the rational self-
esteem, a cognitive belief in your own abilities, out of knowing that you did a good job of tying your shoes. But no

emotion. Unless, that is, you live in a society that places tremendous value on good shoe-tying. Then, well, you'd be quite proud.

Pride is the emotion of rooting for your team even more when they're on national television, not just because you want them to do well but because you know others are watching. The inverse of that—the way you'd measure it—is that the disappointment is that much more crushing when the team loses an ESPN game. Part of what makes Cleveland miserable is that so many of the losses come with a national audience urging them on.

The 2007 baseball American League Championship Series, for example, pitting Cleveland against the Boston Red Sox—"everyone outside of Boston wanted Cleveland to win that," says Scott Sargent, the cofounder and editor of the Cleveland sports blog *Waiting for Next Year*. Or the return of LeBron James after his nationally televised decision to reject an offer from the hometown Cavaliers and sign as a free agent with the Miami Heat, an act of betrayal from a native son that rankled even non-Clevelanders. "I think when LeBron came back to Cleveland for the first time, everyone outside Miami was in Cleveland's corner," Scott said.

How did those games turn out? The Indians blew a 3-1 series lead and the Red Sox went on to easily sweep the World Series, implying that had the Indians won just one more game against Boston, they, too, would have been world champs; LeBron and his Miami pals annihilated a Cleveland team that appeared utterly disinterested in defending the city's honor. "Despite those few times the nation backed Cleveland," Scott said, "Cleveland largely squashed those opportunities."

That disappointment makes the evolutionary explanation for pride seem both appropriate and like just another cruel joke on Cleveland sports fans. That there even is an evolutionary explanation isn't at all obvious. After all, what good would it do our ancestors tens of thousands of years ago to be proud?

Lisa Williams came up with this explanation with her graduate school adviser David DeSteno after he suggested she find a research question from her own experience and she started pondering her undergraduate career as a rower for a mediocre crew team. She had spent years getting up at ungodly hours, lifting weights, devoting her life to a team that won occasionally but not often. Why had she done it? Well, she thought, because she was proud to be part of the team. Pride "was our own emotional push that kept us coming back every morning," she said. "It's a little ironic that the entire thing was this emotional push for coming back to a losing team every morning. In a situation where it's easy to give up, what is it that motivates you to keep going?"

Pride, she decided, might be nature's ways of making you stick with stuff you don't like doing. The idea is that your genes "know" that tasks with short-term negative costs often have long-term positive benefits. So they endow you with this thing we call pride to make sure you take your medicine.

Williams and DeSteno found a novel way to test this. They invited a bunch of people into their lab and gave them all a red-dot counting test. The dots were very carefully considered in advance; there had to be too many for the counters to know how accurate they were in the two seconds they were given to make their estimate, but not so many that it was hopeless to try. (In case you were wondering, this is exactly the sort of thing that gets a gloriously lengthy explanation in the "procedure" section of social science papers.) Everyone was told they were there for an experiment on cognitive abilities. Right after the dot-counting, the participants got feedback—unrelated to their actual performance, one-third of them were enthusiastically congratulated for their excellent work (the pride group), one-third of them were given a score sheet showing they had done well, but no congratulations (the cognitive-basis group), and one-third were given a score sheet without any kind of performance context (the control group).

Then they gave everyone something ludicrously boring to do, with instructions to work on it for as long as they felt like working on it. "Pretesting," the paper very drily notes, "confirmed the tedious nature of this task."*

The first thing the researchers noticed was that in their group of eighty participants, three people didn't listen to the second set of directions and so just kept working until told to stop. The world, it seems, can be split into three categories: the humble, the proud, and the oblivious. The second thing they saw was that the pride group was much more willing to work longer at that tedious task—and, critically, more willing to work when compared to the cognitive-basis group. "Pride appears to have motivated individuals to exert greater effort on a taxing task due to their receiving social

---

*The instructions for this are amazing: "Please work on this task for as long as you like. Do not feel as if you must finish all of the exercises provided. In fact, it is not possible to complete the entire set in the time provided for this experiment, so please continue doing this task until you feel as if you would like to stop."

acclaim," Williams and DeSteno wrote. And importantly, "simple knowledge of superior performance, or self-efficacy, did not produce similar perseverance."

They've since repeated this experiment with a different set of people and found the same result. What's particularly evident is that pride—the idea that others will recognize you as having done something particularly well—is motivating people to continue a behavior that has negative consequences when there's a good chance for a long-term benefit.

The test seems to me an almost perfect allegory for a baseball season. You go through a quick little spring training, you come out to Opening Day to see all sorts of happy people around and your city come alive with red-white-and-blue bunting and balloons, and you have this nice little shot of regional pride. Then you have the tedium of a 162-game baseball season, and you stick with it in some relation to how proud you are. The problem is that nature doesn't seem to have given us any way of coping when the benefit never comes. You stay proud; that's the evolutionary imperative. You stay miserable; that's the Cleveland story. At some point you're no longer proud of any real accomplishment, you're just proud of your pride.

TODD DERY, MATT'S BROTHER AND A HIGH SCHOOL AND college friend of Adam Mesnick's, once kept a blog called *My Teams Are Cursed*. It began its life in August 2007 with a baseball entry about the Indians titled "Oh What a Night!" and the text ". . . or not." Todd says no team's success would matter to him quite like the Indians'. If they won a World Series, he says, it would be the greatest moment of his life after the birth of his two sons.

The inverse is true as well. The worst night of Todd's life was probably October 26, 1997. The Indians were leading the Marlins 3–2 in the bottom of the ninth inning in Game Seven of the World Series. Todd was watching from home, lying on his couch, three outs from glory.

Instead José Mesa, the Indians closer, gave up two hits and a sacrifice fly. Tie game. Todd felt sick. "I spend," he said, narrating the heartbreak in the present tense, "the next inning and a half on the toilet. I can't take it."

He recovered and went to watch TV in his roommates' room to await the final stomach punch. It came in the bottom of the eleventh inning. An error on the Indians' second baseman put a runner on third. Edgar Rentería, a journeyman infielder in just his second year in the majors, lined a ball back up the middle, an agonizing inch over the outstretched pitcher's glove. The Marlins' Craig Counsell sprinted down the third base line, turned his head to see the ball hit the outfield grass, raised both arms, touched home plate with the winning run, and launched ecstatically into the air. Rentería threw his helmet into the sky as his teammates stormed the field. Fifty thousand fans in South Beach exploded in the stands. Glittery confetti fluttered under the bright Miami lights.

Todd Dery lay in his bed in his dorm room in Kansas and the world just went blank. "The ceiling starts spinning," he said. "I go into the bathroom and start vomiting everywhere."

He sat prostate on the floor of the bathroom for a moment. He flushed down the vomit. Then he crawled into the shower and wept.

Todd told me this story on the phone with pride. He was showing me how passionate he is, how much he cares about the Indians. He's telling me how he's not alone. "Stories like that," he said, "you hear that all the time from Cleveland fans!"

It is true that Cleveland fans tend toward rote recitation of the great list of unbelievable failures, all of which have been given names that can then be reeled off in tragic staccato: *The Catch*—Willie Mays's triumphant iconic moment comes in 1957 at the expense of the Indians. *Red Right 88*—Browns failure in a 1981 AFC playoff game against the Oakland Raiders. *The Drive*—Browns failure in the 1987 AFC championship game against the Denver Broncos. *The Fumble*—Browns failure in the 1988 AFC championship game, also against the Broncos. *The Shot*—Michael Jordan's triumphant iconic moment comes in 1989 at the expense of the Cavaliers. *José Mesa*—Indians failure in the 1997 World Series. *The Skinner Stop*—Indians failure in the 2007 American League playoffs. *The Decision*—LeBron James's triumphant iconic moment comes in 2010 at the expense of—well, okay, this one enraged people everywhere and comes pretty much at the expense of the dignity of ESPN, the Worldwide Leader in Sports. But the rest of them . . . it is the Cleveland way not just to lose, but to lose with panache.

"We live in this town that's a dying city, we've never won anything," Todd says. "But we're just—people in Cleveland, we're all in misery together. It's what binds us together."

IN THE 1960s, AN AMERICAN SOCIOLOGIST NAMED ORRIN Klapp looked up from his studies and noticed that everyone around him seemed angry. There were hippies dismayed by war and oppression out on the streets protesting, and right-wingers dismayed by Communists and Big Government holding counterprotests, and rumblings of dissatisfaction from the youth, and the odd thing, he thought, was that in the most materially successful generation in the history of the country, everyone was just so upset. Klapp observed for a while and concluded that the problem with America was all in our heads. In *Collective Search for Identity*, Klapp argues that Americans' classic restlessness sprang from not being able to answer a simple question: Who am I?

Identity "includes all things a person may legitimately and reliably say about himself—his status, his name, his personality, his past life," Klapp wrote. "But if his social context is unreliable, it follows that he cannot say anything legitimately and reliably about himself." Instead, he argued, we turned to hollow materialism, or protests, or LSD. In one of my favorite lines in the book, Klapp surveys the rebellious teenagers who "turn to peers for a truer image . . . or plunge into activities like surfing which may interrupt their careers."

While he comes off as paternalistic,* Klapp had a point. The brain really wants an answer to the who-am-I question. Traditionally it has found the answers in family, home-town, work, and ritual. In 1960s America—and still today

*Another great line: "A leading 'rock' group, 'The Rolling Stones,' complain in one of their best known songs about the deluge of irrelevant information—that a man comes on the radio telling one more and more which gives no satisfaction because it does not drive one's imagination. ... The paradox we have already noted is that with increasing knowledge modern societies have not gained in self-knowledge and assurance, that the knowledge explosion of modern times is associated with an increase in identity problems."

—Americans are more often divorced, more often away from their hometown, more often cows in a cubicle farm, more often separated from the cultural rituals that have previously defined them. Americans are seekers, as Klapp put it, and many of them have responded to this unconscious search for identity by investing in fandom.

Klapp's book is a particularly American-focused argument, and there is something appealing in the idea that a nation of immigrants, shorn of tradition, so particularly embraces sports teams as a way of filling the gap. But fans everywhere struggle with questions of identity and self-concept.

"The local ball team offers an answer to that problem," says Merrill Melnick, a retired sociologist from the State University of New York, Brockport, who for decades taught a class on the sociology of sports fans. Teams can even offer one source of identity while confirming another, like the way that Tottenham fans link themselves to the North London Jewish community or Latin American teams link themselves to universities. Fans can connect with political traditions—conservative Real Madrid and independent Barcelona. Or artistic expression—Johan Cruyff and the aspirations and aesthetics of unshackled sixties liberalism. The more opportunities the team gives you to establish an identity for yourself, the more firmly you anchor your support in it, the easier it is to answer the question, "Who am I?"

"The easy answer is, 'I'm a Giants fan,'" Melnick said. "For someone else that's bullshit, but for me, I like being a New York Giants fan and a New York Yankees fan. I think a lot of people ask that question and aren't satisfied with their answer. I like being a Yankees fan."

Rick Grieve, a clinical psychologist at Western Kentucky

University, ran off a quick survey recently to ask a few hundred undergraduates how much they identified with various parts of their social lives—religion, sports, school activity, employment, social activity, community activity. Sports came out tied for the top with employment and social activity, and ahead of religion, school, and community. ("Of course, we're here in the South," Grieve quipped. "Sports is a religion.") Grieve framed this as a choice people made about how to spend their time, but it seems to me that it's a choice they've made about what in their lives to trust. You might move. You might abandon or change faith. You might lose your job. You might find new friends. You might attend a different school. But only in the most catastrophic of circumstances can anyone make you give up your sports team. This is why the pride that motivates persistence matters.

Todd Dery is well rooted in ritual and tradition, but there's no question the Indians form an important part of his identity as a Clevelander. It's reinforced, for him, by family connections. His father was a lifelong Browns and Indians season ticket holder, his brother visits for Indians games, his sons have just started learning the rituals themselves. Jonathan Mahler, a writer for the *New York Times*, argued in an essay in 2011 that men lose interest in sports when they hit fatherhood: "Most men hit their peak of fandom as teenagers before starting an inevitable decline into a state of relative apathy. By the time we reach middle age, our lives—work, wives, children—have overtaken us."

Which is possibly true if you consider the metric of fandom to be memorization of player names but off base if you consider the point of fandom to be identification and emotional fulfillment. It seems to me you could just as easily make an argument that you haven't experienced the real peak of sports fandom until you've gone with your children. The vast majority of sports fans say they became fans because of their fathers. Going to a game with Dad is one of the most confirming things you can do for your identity; Todd spent his childhood going to football games with his mom, dad, and uncle. His parents had themselves grown up going to games with their families, sitting in season tickets that were just a few rows apart at the football stadium.

Todd's dad died suddenly in 2004, and that changed his take on sports more than anything else. It did not stop him from going to games, it did not stop him from caring about games, it did not lead to a slide into apathy or a loss of meaning. There are just subtleties that he notices now, little things about the ritual itself that are as important as winning and losing. The lows, he says, are less low, the highs a little richer for the context. Todd's most emotional essay for *Waiting for Next Year* was about taking his four-year-old to his first Browns game, hoping his dad was there "watching the grandson he never met rooting on the team he loved so much."

Critics of sports fans write often about recognizing that sports isn't real life, and about not heaping meaning on something that ultimately means nothing. The game itself doesn't mean anything, but the attachment to it certainly does. Fans often complain that the athletes don't care as much as the fans do. That's true, but they're more to be pitied than censured for it. The fans are leading a fulfilling emotional existence because of the sports team, satisfying one of the most basic demands of psychology whether the team wins or loses. The athlete is stuck as the nihilist; the connection, to them, can only rarely mean much more than employment. One of the reasons Bret Hedican can analyze the San Jose Sharks with such ruthless accuracy is that his pride and identity aren't riding on their success.

Looking beyond Todd to the wider Cleveland area, the argument that identity-impoverished Americans are placing their trust in sports teams makes even more sense. In a town where the jobs and people have disappeared, the sports teams provide the necessary anchor. It's true on an almost literal level: downtown Cleveland is bookended—and dominated—by its three new sports stadiums, cathedrals of ritual meant to survive and stand tall against change. Another Cleveland expat, *Esquire*'s Scott Raab, concluded something along these lines in his book *The Whore of Akron*. "Sometimes," he wrote, "the mere existence of the Cavs, Browns, and Indians seems like all that keeps Cleveland from slipping into darkness forever."

By extension, of course, when you find a new source of identity, the old ones can fade. Once you leave Cleveland, the sports connection seems less imperative. Separated from the city where sports and life are inextricable, you might find new things that matter or never even care to make sports matter in the first place. In San Francisco, you could easily live a happy life outside the influence of the waterfront stadiums. I asked Adam Mesnick how often he watched Browns games, and he said that when he first moved to San Francisco he'd be in the bar every single Sunday, from hours before game time to hours afterward. But now, he said, with the deli, sometimes he just checked the scores on his phone. When the Browns played a late-December game against archrival Pittsburgh, I asked Mesnick where he'd be watching. Couldn't today, he said—he had sandwiches to make.

"This deli is my baby now," he said.

When I had a chance to ask him directly, he hedged a bit more. It's not that Cleveland is any less important to him, he said; it's just that because of the Deli Board, and a new pop-up sandwich venture he calls 1058 Hoagie, he's actually started to re-create a Cleveland-like community in San Francisco. He went from seeking that community in weekends at the bar, and then finding it by leaving the bar and starting a deli, and now he can't wait until Browns season so he can take his new community to the bar. It seems like, for him, the best of times.

But what about for the Clevelander who stayed home?

"HEY BUDDY!" TODD DERY'S VOICE ON THE PHONE THE MORN-ing of Opening Day sounded cheerful and nasal in a Great Lakes-y kind of way. "How are you enjoying my city?"

Todd had found me a ticket for the Indians home opener against the Toronto Blue Jays. I thought it might be a nice time to visit Cleveland: a beginning, a symbolic renewal, a rite of spring—as opposed to the bitter fall or winter and the annual destruction of the Browns and Cavaliers. The morning's *Cleveland Plain Dealer* brimmed with stories of hope, great memories, romance, and shared wonder at the glory of a new baseball season. No one was particularly optimistic about that year's Indians team, but for a day everyone was happy to play enthusiastic. The trendy restaurants and bars on East Fourth Street hung banners outside and opened their patios for sunshine and pregame drinking. By noon, three hours before game time, fans crowded the street. It was unusually vital, with thumping music pouring from the bars and spilled beer on the cobblestones and people bumping into each other and slapping hands.

The crowd inside the ballpark was the largest for an Opening Day in the fifteen-year history of Progressive Field. The pregame ceremony featured retired Indians player Carlos Baerga catching the first pitch from an Afghanistan vet. "People love Indians greats from the nineties," Todd said. A helicopter flew over and then a cascade of red-white-and-blue balloons soared into the brilliant blue sky. The crowd roared. It would take, I thought, a truly exceptional loss to spoil the good vibe.

Todd stood next to me in jeans and a North Face jacket, his hood pulled up over a faded Indians cap. He is shortish and has a black beard that, with the hat, keeps his eyes in a kind of perma-shadow. The first few innings we just watched quietly and I asked about players he likes or doesn't like, and it turned out that on Opening Day at least he pretty much likes all of them. He has four tickets, five rows behind the Indians dugout, and can remember all the times Indians players have tossed baseballs up to his sons. He always goes to Opening Day with the same close friends, and Jeremy and Adam sat on Todd's right. They talked a little bit about the team, but mainly they made chatty small talk and put their feet up, three old friends escaped from work on a gloriously sunny spring Thursday to watch baseball.

The Indians' big concern was hitting, but in the second inning one of their fan favorites, third baseman Jack Hannahan, came up with two on and two out and drove a ball deep into right field. As the ball sailed toward the fence, Todd jumped up and jackhammered a little circle in place and, as the ball bounced off the yellow top of the wall for a three-run homer and 4–0 Indians lead, he grabbed my arm triumphantly and burst into a high-pitched *wooooooohoooo!!* of completely unencumbered joy.

IN THE EIGHTH INNING, WITH THE INDIANS HOLDING A COMfortable 4–1 lead, Jeremy suddenly looked over at me. "You're from San Francisco?" he asked.

He shook his head bitterly. "Man," he said, "that's just rubbing salt in the wound."

I asked him to explain.

"It's a great city," he said. "Lots of cool things to do. Beautiful women. Good food."

I told him I'm not a Giants or 49ers fan, which seemed to mollify him somewhat, since my A's and Raiders haven't won recently. Plus, I said, I like Cleveland! I was walking around yesterday and it's got nice architecture and seems like some cool new restaurants and—

"This city blows," Jeremy said.

"Put that in the book," Adam said.

Justin Masterson interrupted by getting the last out of the eighth inning and exiting to a warm ovation from the fans.

Jeremy stood and clapped, then resumed his discussion. "I think I'm negative on Cleveland because of the sports," he said. "Anger on sports makes me angry about the town."

It was the José Mesa blown save in the World Series that did it for him. "Nineteen ninety-seven killed me," he said. "I'd be a totally different person if the Indians had won that game. I'd have other interests."

He listed a few. Art. Theater. Family. Anything, really.

He just wouldn't be stuck with his emotional life roped to this miserable millstone of a baseball team.

The ninth inning began and the mood changed quickly. The Indians' closer, Chris Perez, arrived from the bullpen. I hardly even noticed him there—the three-run save, as Perez would tell the newspaper reporters a few hours later, is the easiest in baseball.

"Watch him blow this," Todd said, with a sudden pessimism. "This shit always happens. I guarantee you fifty percent of the people here are thinking it. It would almost be good for you to see him blow it to see the fun."

Perez gave up back-to-back singles to start the inning. A sacrifice fly and the score was 4–2, with a runner on first. He took the count full against the next batter. Everyone stood. Perez wound and delivered and before the ball had left his hand Todd muttered from underneath his hood, "Ball four." The pitch was high and outside. The hitter checked his swing; safe, the umpire said, and another runner trotted off to first base.

Suddenly, oddly, I was aware of the cold. The late afternoon shadow was creeping across the field, the wind blowing icy blasts straight out of center field. Jeremy, shuffling and shivering, pointed out the white Progressive flag just over the fence flapping stiffly in our direction.

The next batter, Edwin Encarnación, dug in at the plate. There was a smattering of boos around the stadium. Just behind us someone yelled—at the umpire?—"Get your head out of your ass!"

Perez grooved a fastball down the middle and Encarnación jacked it deep into right field. We watched the outfielder turn and race toward the wall.

"Gone," Todd said from under his hood, and maybe he needs his mirror neurons and anticipation checked because by about eight inches the ball stayed in the yard and merely bounced off the high wall as the Blue Jays raced around the bases and two runners came in to score. "This game," Todd said to Adam and Jeremy, "is now tied."

Turning to me, he added the frustrated-pride note, "You see? You get forty thousand people here *one time*, and . . . I cannot believe it. It's a real shame. A real shame."

Our entire section stayed standing, fidgeting restlessly in the cold. The next batter grounded out to third, but then Perez walked another Blue Jay and that was enough for the Indians manager, who came out to pull him from the game. Perez walked achingly slowly off the mound, head down, glove in one hand, brown locks flowing behind him. *Booooo.* This time it wasn't a smattering. Forty thousand voices joined in a throaty, ringing chorus cascading down from the stands. *BOOOOOO! BOOOOOOOOO! BOOOOOOOOOOOOO!*

Perez, a month later, gave an interview in which he ripped Cleveland fans. No one wants to play in Cleveland, he said, because the fans don't show up to games and they boo players for no reason. Taking their own self-loathing to a new level, a great many Indians fans agreed with him.

The next batter hit a ground ball to third to finally end the inning. The crowd remained standing, muttering restively. The team-employee teenage girls tossing souvenir T-shirts into the seats from the top of the dugout came obliviously close to provoking a frustrated riot.

"Literally," Todd said bitterly to me, "you could not have picked a better game to go to. This is the absolute perfect example of everything about Cleveland."

"They're going to win it in the ninth," I said. I like it when people say this sort of thing to me when I'm bitter and angry. It always makes me feel better.

Sure enough, the Indians led off the bottom of the ninth with a double. A pinch runner, a successful bunt, and suddenly everyone was gleeful again. "Did you see us turn on a dime right there?" Adam said to me, waving around at the celebrating fans. Now even a fly ball to the outfield or a hard ground ball to the right side would end the game in triumph.

Instead Casey Kotchman grounded weakly to first base for the second out.

The next batter was Jason Kipnis, another favorite. When LeBron James played in Cleveland, he had a giant Nike billboard that towered over downtown showing James with his head thrown back and arms outstretched, Christ-like, and the testament-like Nike slogan: "We are all witnesses." That billboard was torn down the same day LeBron announced via an hour-long ESPN television special that he was leaving his hometown to take his talents to South Beach. Now that Jason Kipnis is on the Indians, there's a chance to have some fun with the old slogan. Todd has a faded red T-shirt that reads WE ARE ALL KIPNISES.

Kipnis chopped a soft grounder toward second base.

"Get through!" Todd yelled. The ball did not listen. The second baseman scooped it up and tossed casually to first base to end the inning. "I can't fucking believe it," Todd said, merging back into his hood.

Adam was driving home and wanted to leave at the end of the tenth if no one had scored, putting a time limit of one more inning on our stay. Todd felt like maybe he was getting a cold and agreed to leave, although he'd stick around and see it out if he had driven himself. I didn't mind leaving, but I understood Todd's delicate position—one has one's reputation to uphold, not that reputation had stopped a few tens of thousands of people from leaving already. The following day, one particularly angry young blogger wrote, "It was an embarrassment to the city of Cleveland to see all of the fans who claim to be diehards and some of the best in the country leaving early. What did you have to do that was so important that you left Opening Day early?"

To start the tenth inning, Jack Hannahan, the fan favorite who three hours ago hit a home run that should have been the highlight of the day, struck out.

"K'd looking," Todd said miserably, as Jeremy sarcastically mimicked Hannahan feebly raising his arms to let the pitch go by. "The longer this game goes on, the greater chance we have to lose."

The next two batters grounded out to second. We stood for the final time and turned away from the field. Todd slapped my hand and reiterated without pleasure how pleased he was that I could see an authentic Cleveland performance. Quickly, head down, he disappeared into the throng heading for the exits.

TODD HAS ONE SECRET SALVATION. HE WENT TO COLLEGE (WITH Adam Mesnick) at the University of Kansas and became a Jayhawks basketball fan. He started the *My Teams Are Cursed* blog because he spent four years at a major basketball university with a top-ranked basketball team that never won the national championship. But in 2008, one year after he started the blog, Kansas made it to the finals and in an improbable last few minutes beat favored Memphis for the title. This is why Todd and his friends say that they'd be perfectly normal if just anyone won anything: he quit the blog that very night. He posted triumphant championship photos, and a short note, and then he just left. The decades of heartache and pain really can end that abruptly. In his exit speech, Todd rambles on emotionally for a while about the game itself, repeating the disbelieving motif that this sort of come-from-behind championship never happens to "MY TEAMS."

"As the clock hit zero, I didn't know what to do," he wrote. "I hugged my boys, I teared up, I stood in disbelief watching as the KU players and coaches celebrated. But more than anything, it felt as though the weight of the world was off of my shoulders. I seriously felt different. Something that has lived with me for 32 years had died. One of my teams actually won it all and the championship I had so badly wanted was here."

Then, triumphantly, one final note:

"They did it! THE CURSE IS FINALLY DEAD!"

There's a lot of frustration and annoyance for Todd, but through it all he's a loyal fan. That's where he keeps that important part of his identity, and the teams reward his investment whether they win or lose.

That's something Scott Sargent, one of the founders of *Waiting for Next Year*, echoed. But at the same time, Sargent repeatedly said that there has to be a payoff somewhere out there. He acknowledged the role of his own dad in raising him a Cleveland fan and snuck in a dig at LeBron for wearing a Yankees hat to a Cleveland baseball game.

"You can't just grow up liking who was good," he said. "That's silly."

I kept pushing him on that, looking for the same admission I got from Todd, that ultimately I suppose you could find other important things without winning. Why is it silly? I asked. In the abstract it doesn't seem silly to me—you root for winning teams and you just get the self-esteem benefits of winning without having to worry about the heartache. But Scott just kept pushing back.

"Philosophically," I finally said, "what if it never happens? Will you be able to look back at the end of your life and say it was worthwhile anyway?"

On the other end of the phone, there was a long exhalation.

"It's a tough question," Scott said. "I would think, if we don't win anything, if it's just miserable . . ."

He paused again.

"Hopefully we come close."

Scott worried that if the teams kept losing, the city wouldn't be able to continue to financially support three of them. Someone would have to leave, whether the Cavs, Indians, or Browns, leaving a void in the sports fabric of the city, another important source of identity departed. Maybe that departure might be the final push that shoves the city underwater for the last time. It would be fittingly tragic for a city where so much of that collective identity has been placed in the seemingly secure sports teams to also lose its teams.

"I really dread the thought of having grandchildren and still not having won anything," Scott said. "I'm finally admitting that unfortunately my father, who was born in 'fifty-six and may not have remembered the 'sixty-four championship, may never see one. Because it's that bleak right now. But I really hope that between now and my grandkids I would have seen something. They'll have their lives to worry about. But I hope by that time . . ."

He thought for a half-second.

"Wheel me out to the parade if you have to," he said.

So what happens if Cleveland does win? I kept thinking of Lisa Williams's explanation for pride as the emotional part of self-esteem. My idea is that if Cleveland wins, all that pride in supporting a loser gets converted into emotion about winning and actual rational self-efficacy about having accomplished something. A massive self-esteem boost, powered by emotion and reason, and the next year everyone will show up at the ballpark proud of their accomplishment instead of proud of their attendance record—like Boston Red Sox fans in 2004. There's not much we ask from our sports teams, but one of the things we ask is that they in some sense reward our loyalty. The first great power a team has is to grant us the answer to the who-am-I question, to give us that pride in ourselves even when other parts of our lives aren't okay. But the even better power they have is to confirm our identity and turn our pride into self-esteem. The only way they can do that is by winning.

Which, you know, they haven't. I introduced the idea of Cleveland fans as the damaged patients studied by neuroscientists seeking insights into the brain. So there's one final thing left to ask: Could losing actually change your brain? Not just like you're upset, but the actual structure of the organ?

If you're a rat, it sure can. There's a huge field called "social defeat" that revolves around studying the brains of loser rats. You can, it seems, create a loser, by introducing a naive little rat into a cage with a larger, aggressive, territorial rat. You let the small rat get bullied until it cowers, and then you put it back in its own cage. You repeat the next day, and the day after that, for some set amount of time—a week, say. Meanwhile your control rat is just chilling on its own in another corner of the room. At the end of the experiments you "sacrifice" the rats, in scientific parlance, and slice up their brains for analysis. The researchers who do this have good reasons for what does sound a little cruel—among others, they think it could yield insights into depression and anxiety in humans. But for our purposes, it yields insights into the brains of fans. What happens in the rats' brains, the researchers say, might be what happens in ours. To be a Cleveland fan, or for that matter a San Jose Sharks or Cal football fan, is to be that small, timid rat, exposed over and over and over again to cruel defeat.

Even a few social defeats can turn things ugly quickly. This is an area that's been studied from a wide variety of perspectives, so we know all sorts of different problems that social defeat (in rats) causes—behavioral, psychological, physiological, and molecular. Here's the lengthy list from a paper out of the lab of German researcher Ursula Havemann-Reinecke: decreased movement and exploratory activity; reduced aggression and sexual behavior; increased submissive behavior; increased sensitivity to other kinds of stress; increased anxiety and anticipation; increased sensitivity to drug addiction; altered circadian rhythms in heart rate, blood pressure, and core temperature; weakened immune systems and reduced resistance to disease; decreased testosterone; and, in the brain, altered neurotransmitter systems including in the systems that make both rats and people feel happy.

Havemann-Reinecke's lab wanted to test the idea of chronic stress, so they had rats put in the cage with an aggressive resident every day for five weeks. The rats would fight briefly, but as soon as the smaller rat showed signs of submission the researchers yanked it from the cage, so the defeat was mainly psychological. What happened next was that at the end of the five weeks the rats had entirely lost their mojo. They weren't interested in exploring, or moving around, or swimming, or even in high-sugar food. They suffered, to draw a human parallel, from an induced depression.

The researchers zeroed in on this finding because the rats' behavior at the end of the five weeks so closely mirrored that of depressed humans. In particular, they focused on the lack of motivation caused by decreased activity in the area of the brain known as the dopamine reward system. Rats and humans both have this reward system: when you receive something pleasurable, the reward system releases a bunch of the neurotransmitter dopamine, which in turn makes you feel happy.

Remember the idea of top-down control on our mirror neurons? I asked Marco Iacoboni what brain systems he thought might be exerting it. Almost certainly, he said, one of the major connections is to the reward system. Losing all the time goes to work on the exact part of the brain that researchers think is critically involved in watching sports, not just in understanding and enjoying the action but in mediating the response of some of our most basic reflexes.

KLAUS MICZEK STARTED WORKING WITH SOCIAL DEFEAT IN RATS as a way to investigate responses to stress. His first major paper, published in *Science* in 1982, showed that defeated rats with high stress levels became impervious to pain. Miczek then set out to explore another seemingly obvious conclusion. The famous feel-good neurotransmitter dopamine had been shown by the mid-1990s to be involved in rewards and learning (as well as coordination and motor skills). Clearly, then, in defeated and stressed-out rodents you should see a big drop in dopamine. Except that the project went entirely the wrong way. Dopamine spiked in defeated rats, and the more defeated, the higher the spike.

"This was exactly the opposite of what was supposed to happen," Miczek told me. "Unless, of course, you're a masochist and that these animals seek out to be defeated—which no one really believes. These animals are not eager to seek out confrontation where they lose."

So now what? As techniques improved, scientists have narrowed down the areas where dopamine activates following reward and defeat. But its full role has still in some sense defied simple explanation. Here's one more example from Miczek's recent work: if you take a rat and expose it to repeated stress and repeated social defeat, you make it far more likely to take an interest in cocaine—one of the things that drug abuse experts know activates an intense dopamine surge in the reward areas of the brain. It's almost like the dopamine areas loop around from reward to defeat back to intense reward. The uncertainty, Miczek says, is kind of the point. Even the high-tech modern sensors are still like measuring with a "broomstick in the brain," he said. Dopamine structures in the brain have different purposes that are entirely separable. And—you've heard this line before—it turns out that dopamine areas interact heavily with the rest of the brain. They have top-down control. Much like testosterone, in fact, one of the things that appears to exert that control is the stress hormone cortisol. Dopamine, Miczek emphasized, doesn't operate solo. It serves a wide variety of purposes, many of them tied intimately to other parts of the brain. Complex human emotions arise in a lot of places at once and, while studying dopamine and rewards adds to our understanding, it's not the only story.

"The rest of the brain," Miczek said, "isn't there to keep dopamine warm."

AFTER LEAVING TODD AT THE GAME I WALKED, HUNCHED against the cold—just hovering at forty degrees, according to the marquee on Huntington Bank on East Ninth—back downtown toward my hotel. I ran up to my room, face flushed with the warmth inside, and turned on the TV to find the game in the twelfth inning and still tied 4–4. The Indians promptly loaded the bases with one out, only to see their All-Star shortstop Asdubral Cabrera hit into a first-pitch double play. (The team's only other 2011 All Star? The closer Chris Perez.) With each crowd shot, it became clear that more and more fans had left.

The game stretched to the sixteenth inning, when the announcers noted that this five-hour-long event had now become the longest Opening Day game in Major League Baseball history. Four batters later, Toronto's J. P. Arincibia crushed one into the stands to make it 7–4 Blue Jays.

The Indians submitted weakly in the bottom of the sixteenth to end the game. The home team had gone the last fourteen innings of the game without scoring.

My phone buzzed a moment later with a text from Todd.

"What did I tell u before the ninth?" he wrote. "Typical."

"Oh man," I wrote back. "That was horrible."

There was a pause as Todd typed his response. And then the little green balloon popped up with his simple message: "Welcome to Cleveland."

4
Relationships:
Socrates the Sports Guy

STEVE WINFIELD WAS A MUSICIAN, A SPECIALIST ON THE ALTO saxophone, and had achieved some renown for his New Age compositions. He also bought and sold foreclosures, a messy, emotional business that fit with what his brother Ken describes as an intensity of mind. He was into meditation and had several close friends from his days in a Buddhist meditation center back east, but he lived alone and never married. The chief thing about him, Ken says, was that he never seemed comfortable. Steve could have been the identity-seeker poster boy. He had trouble with relationships. He had trouble with commitment. He had trouble with permanence. He had just a handful of stable things in his life: his friends, his brother. His sports teams.

"He was looking," Ken says. "Sports was a constant. Everything else was looking."

In 1998, when he was fifty-four, Steve was diagnosed with colon cancer. Fighting the disease sent him on another

soul journey of sorts. Ultimately it would take him all over
the world, to South America, to the South Pacific. But in the
end he found only one thing, and he clung to that thing until
finally it gave him what he wanted. That one thing was the
Oakland Raiders.

"He was one of these guys who always had intimacy
issues, just a confirmed bachelor," says Bill Morgan, one of
Steve's longtime friends. "He had the Raiders. He had his
brother, he had a few good male friends and he had the
Raiders."

THE STEREOTYPE OF THE SPORTS FAN DEFAULTS TO VIOLENT, OR
oblivious, or ignorant. But I'd argue that what most defines
the sports fan is the thing that Steve Winfield found in the
Oakland Raiders: the ability to form deep, meaningful,
quasi relationships with sports teams. Remember the Cleveland fans and pride and identity—although that research
matches up with their behavior and with what they say, we
haven't yet explained how the emotion and the meaning is
felt personally by fans who are watching something that we
all know is vicarious. But what modern research shows is
that it is very much the depth of the relationship that makes
it go and provides the meaning and the pride.

Technically, of course, these aren't relationships at all.
They're one-sided; by definition a relationship goes both
ways. "If I say, 'Jason's my best friend,' and Jason says,
'Julie who?,' then we're not friends," says one sports psychologist, Southern Illinois researcher Julie Partridge.

But the thing is that your brain doesn't necessarily know
that. The story of being a sports fan is the story of your
brain looking at this thing in front of it and looking for ways

to deal with it. One of those ways may be to borrow its way of processing relationships. You are, in the psychological sense, recruiting brain function from something else and using it to interpret the world of sports. This makes sense based on what we know about mirror neurons: since that system is set up for a wide variety of purposes and we appear to be using it so heavily in watching sports, it follows that all those other purposes are at least tangentially a part of being a fan. Observing sports fans might teach us just as much about how and why humans form groups, love each other, and commit altruistic acts as it does about war, division, and strife.

"I actually think it tells us something about this fundamental need to belong," said UC Berkeley psychologist Rudy Mendoza-Denton. "So much of psychology has this focus on aggression, violence, the ways in which we're not able to connect. Certainly, the exact questions we're talking about can lead to aggression. At the same time, the flip side of that is the amazing ability to connect with others on fairly random bases."

IN THE LAST DECADE OR SO, PSYCHOLOGISTS HAVE COME UP with this really fascinating way of describing what happens to people's identity when they like another person or thing. It reminds me of the main plot point in the last few books of the Harry Potter series. Voldemort, the evil dark lord, fears death more than anything else, and finds a way to preserve his immortality by shattering his soul into pieces and placing those pieces in objects that are important to him— his father's ring, his family locket, his personal serpent.

Harry and his friends go around destroying those "hor-cruxes," and Voldemort feels the attack on each object as a literal attack on himself.

At least, that's what I was thinking after talking to Stephen Kosslyn, a behavioral scientist at Stanford, who wrote a book chapter a few years ago that promoted the idea of what he calls a "social prosthetic system."

"I want to argue that in a very deep sense we have been shaped by evolution not only so that we work well in groups, but also so that our personal identity depends on our relationships with others," Kosslyn wrote in "On the Evolution of Human Motivation: The Role of Social Prosthetic Systems." "'You' are not confined to what's in your head, but are in part represented by things around you."

This is the critical idea of a lot of modern relationship and identity science: you, technically speaking, are not just "you." You are the sum of all your relationships, all the various places that you have chosen to place a little piece of your identity, and those other people are very much functioning like prosthetics. It is an idea remarkably parallel to a mirror neuron–centric view of the world—as the mirror neuron researcher Vittorio Gallese once wrote in a paper, "It is as if the other becomes another self." Gallese quoted the French philosopher Maurice Merleau-Ponty: "It is as if the other's intention inhabited my body, and mine his." Marco Iacoboni constantly repeats the idea in *Mirroring People* that "the self and other are two sides of the same coin." He told me about meeting the Dalai Lama, and after telling him about mirror neurons and empathy he said, "At this moment it's not Marco and the Dalai Lama, it's us."

To a mirror neuron researcher, this is mirroring. To

Kosslyn, it's distributed processing. You use a peg leg as a prosthetic to replace a missing leg, you use a calculator as a prosthetic to assist with computation that's beyond you, and you use other people in the same way to assist with tasks you can't do on your own. You could borrow someone's brain for computational power or for emotional support or for judgment under pressure.

"When someone devotes time and energy to helping you, you are literally using part of their brain," Kosslyn writes.

Not only that, you are powerfully motivated to "expand" your self by forming relationships. The point of Kosslyn's paper is deep: that this is an evolutionary explanation for altruism. Humans are hardwired to want to work in groups and help other people because it's a way of widely distributing your self. There can be both short-term and long-term versions of this. Short-term is grabbing a neighbor to help you haul something heavy, Kosslyn says. Long-term is more like a friendship; that friend's cognitive and emotional power will be there for you to use for as long as you remain friends. In Kosslyn's version, forming a friendship is like populating a toolbox with tools.

"Evolution has allowed our brains to be configured during development so that we are 'plug compatible' with other humans, so that others can help us extend ourselves," he wrote.

That sports fans feel like they have a relationship with their favorite team is beyond question. The vocabulary of fandom is full of attachment, heartbreak, abusive spouses, and bad breakups; one Web site allows fans to print out their own divorce certificates for material proof that the team has finally gone too far. But how much does that artificial relationship look like a real relationship? Can the Oak-land Raiders actually be a stand-in relationship for a seek-ing guy like Steve Winfield?

"I think so," Kosslyn told me. There's no evidence one way or the other, he said. But "given we're set up that way, yeah, when you identify strongly with a team, your identity gets tied up strongly with a team."

The process we talked about with Cleveland fans, plac-ing their self-esteem and identity in the hands of their sports teams, then draws team and self closely together in the brain of the fan. It might be that a favorite team actually makes you do even less work. When you receive help from another person, you usually have to give something back in return. The Oakland Raiders will never ask you to do anything for them except show up. (Well, sort of. You do have to deal with a fair amount of dysfunctional losing.)

"It's a funny asymmetrical relationship," Kosslyn said. "But to the extent you identify, you can gain a lot of reflected glory while the investment is tiny."

IN THE EARLY 1980S, STEVE WINFIELD, STILL SEEKING HIS OWN elusive identity, had come to the meditation center where Bill Morgan has worked for the last two decades. The For-est Refuge is a Buddhist retreat in woodsy central Massa-chusetts, home to the Insight Meditation Society. Classes feature spiritual teachers from around the world and can last for months. Morgan happened to be looking for a man-ager, and while recruiting from among a group that had just finished a three-month meditation course, he found Steve. The two formed a fast connection.

"There were not a lot of meditators who were passionate sports fans, I've found," Morgan told me. "Stevie was one of them."

Morgan remembers one night in particular. First you have to understand, he said, that the meditation center is silent. That's a major part of the plan: enforced tranquility to promote inner exploration. One hundred percent silence except when you're meeting with teachers. So he and Stevie sneak away to his dorm room to watch *Monday Night Football*, with the Dolphins playing the Bills. Both had a small bet riding on the game—just $25 or so. And toward the end of the game, with the point spread in the balance, Morgan remembers, there was a play—"it was one of these fumbles, it got knocked out of a guy's arm, three or four guys touched it, wasn't clear who was going to fall on the ball."

It was late in the game, and the game had started at 9:00 p.m. It was probably midnight in the silent meditation center in the silent central Massachusetts woods when the ball bounced on the Miami turf. Bill Morgan and Steve Winfield jumped up in concert. "Both of us, involuntarily—our money was on the line here—as the ball started to tumble, all of a sudden we both let out this involuntary shriek for like five seconds," Morgan said. The cries died away and the stillness returned.

"And then," Morgan said, "we looked at each other, like, 'What did we just do?'"

Most of the meditation center heard them. It was an embarrassing faux pas, maybe in part because it inevitably led to an admission of this overwhelming emotion that transcendence couldn't conquer. "People were decent enough not to call us to the principal's office," Morgan said.

Steve's interest and attention may have been on the game, but in that midnight shriek he'd formed a friendship for life. He and Morgan spent the next several years at the meditation center sneaking out to watch games. Many years later, when Steve was dying of cancer on the opposite side of the country, Morgan would leave the Forest Refuge and fly out to California. Steve, in the last time he'd ever hang out with his buddy Bill and with all the world to talk about, just wanted to watch football.

THIS, AS BEST I UNDERSTAND IT, IS PLATO'S *SYMPOSIUM*, WHICH happens to be directly relevant to our discussion of love and relationships. Two Greeks, Aristodemus and his friend Socrates, the famous philosopher, are on their way to a dinner party. They're walking along through Athens, and Socrates suddenly has an idea and tells Aristodemus to go on without him while he thinks it out. Aristodemus arrives at the party by himself and tells the host, "Hey, Socrates was just right behind me. I'm sure he'll be along shortly. And in the meantime, how about dinner?" So they all sit down and eat. Something like three hours later Socrates shows up, at which point the host sticks him in his philosophizing sofa and says, "So, gents, shall we get to drinking?"

This would be the generally accepted form of an evening, but a few of the guys are already hungover as hell. "I can assure you that I feel severely the effect of yesterday's potations, and must have time to recover," says one of the philosophers, a guy named Pausanius, "and I suspect that most of you are in the same predicament, for you were of the party yesterday. Consider then: How can the drinking be made easiest?"

Aristophanes agrees, noting that he had basically "drowned in drink" the day before. Eryximachus agrees tentatively, but wants to know what Agathon (the host) thinks. "I am not equal to it," Agathon replies. "Great," Eryximachus says, "and furthermore"—I picture him rubbing his temples at this point—"can someone get rid of the flute girl?"

So here are all our Greek philosophers, sitting around with aching heads and low tolerance for musical entertainment, and they decide: Let's have a conversation about love. Let's each of us step forward—we'll go from left to right (adding the practical note)—and make a speech in honor of love. It's all a setup, of course—Plato's rigging the thing so that Socrates goes last and blows everyone away with his crazy philosophy skills, which is exactly what happens. "But if you like to hear the truth about love," Socrates says, mock-humble when it comes to his turn, "I am ready to speak in my own manner."

Socrates relates a conversation he had with another philosopher named Diotima, and then he proceeds step-by-step to lay out a theory of love that sounds almost exactly like the modern psychological suggestion that humans are motivated to expand their selves. What Stephen Kosslyn calls a social prosthetic system Socrates labeled true love. The purpose of love is first to love another person, Socrates says, but then you grow to love ideas, and justice, and then knowledge, and love becomes not just love but the desire to expand. Love, in the framing of the Greeks, is like a kind of intense curiosity, the burning desire to seek true beauty in the world.

"But what," the philosopher Diotima concludes, "if man had eyes to see the true beauty—the divine beauty, I mean, pure and clear and unalloyed, not clogged with the pollutions of mortality and all the colors and vanities of human life—thither looking, and holding converse with the true beauty simple and divine? Remember how in that communion only, beholding beauty with the eye of the mind, he will be enabled to bring forth, not images of beauty, but realities (for he has hold not of an image but of a reality), and bringing forth and nourishing true virtue to become the friend of God and be immortal, if mortal man may."

In the late 1960s, a graduate student in social psychology at UC Berkeley named Arthur Aron recalled the *Symposium*. A student of transcendental meditation and eastern philosophy, Aron also thought that Plato sounded a bit reminiscent of a line from the Hindu Upanishads: "The love of the husband is for the sake of the Self. The love of the wife is for the sake of the Self. The love of the child is for the sake of the Self."

The reason Aron had suddenly recalled his undergraduate philosophy background was twofold: first he had just fallen passionately in love. Second, he needed a thesis project. Like any good graduate student, he thought, "Well, I'll just do a thesis on love and see if we can bring some modern scientific rigor to this ancient discussion." He started with the philosophical premise that love and relationships are motivated by a desire to expand the self. Then he added on: relationships of all kinds involve including the other in your idea of yourself, and this "inclusion of other" will be observable, predictable, and measurable.

Half a century of clever experiments later, Aron is a worldwide leader in the field of relationships research. He is also still married to the woman that inspired his career—and she has been his collaborator ever since.

If you remember the research on pride from chapter 3, you'll remember that the scientists focused on pride inspired by something the participants had done directly. But it doesn't make as much sense that you'd still feel that pride for something vicarious. So what Lisa Williams suggested in her paper is what Art Aron suggests: the inclusion of the other in the self makes it such that, for many purposes, there's no difference. A relationship is just another way of thinking about the individual "social prosthetic system" of Stephen Kosslyn. If Aron is right—and decades of evidence bear him out—the success of the team is quite literally the personal success of the fan. Our testosterone rises and falls with our favorite teams or politicians because we, or at least the part of the brain that's doing the hormoning, can't tell the difference between them and us.

Aron and his lab have several ways of bringing modern equipment to test the ideas of the ancient philosophers. One, the brain-scanning technique known as functional magnetic resonance imaging (fMRI), we'll save for the next chapter, because that mainly involves looking for signs of love. But there are also ways of looking for evidence of self-expansion and inclusion of other in the self.

The first part of this theory of relationships is simple: that we are motivated by evolutionary pressures to expand ourselves. To test the idea of self-expansion, Aron and his colleagues bring a bunch of people into the lab and give them what's known as the "Who Am I Today?" test. It's as simple as it sounds: you give the person three minutes and ask them to write down everything they can think of that comes to mind when asked that question. They find, very reliably, that people who have just entered into relationships list more things and more categories of things than people who have not, and that people who have just broken up with someone show a decrease in "spontaneous self-concept."

The second part of the theory is that when we do form a relationship, we include the other in our concept of self. To test the idea, Aron uses a timed test called a "match-mismatch response time paradigm." Again, they bring a group of people into the lab and have them all fill out questionnaires with lists of a few hundred traits. They are asked to mark each of the traits that describes them and each of the traits that describes someone they're in a close relationship with. A few weeks later, Aron brings everyone back to the lab and sits them in front of a computer. The screen flashes a series of traits and the participants press one button if it's true of them and one button if it's not true of them. They've found, over and over again, that people are quite fast at pressing the button if it's true of them. They're quite fast at pressing the button when it's false of them. But when it's true of them and not true of their partner, or vice versa, there's a delay. Something in the nature of twenty-five milliseconds while the brain struggles to figure out, wait a minute, is this true of me? The closer the relationship, the longer the delay. It's a result that's been repeated in labs around the world, in a wide variety of situations. They've all found pretty much the same thing: this "inclusion of other in self" is real, and the more ways you include the other in yourself, the stronger you feel a relationship with that person.

Part of what this means is that the more ways you have of expanding yourself in your relationship with a team, the stronger the relationship can get. A team with a regional identity allows the fan to adopt that regional identity or reinforce his or her own identity. A team with a political reputation allows the fan to expand his or her identity to include politics. There's evidence that you can include characteristics of groups you belong to in your self. Rivalries like the one between Real Madrid and Barcelona draw their strength and global interest in part because of all the different ways those two teams offer expansion to their fans.

One of the labs that has adapted the match-mismatch work is Rudy Mendoza-Denton's at UC Berkeley. Mendoza-Denton has used the test on mixed-race relationships and gives the following example. He's Mexican, and let's say he has a close friend who's Asian. It's a simple concept: If you ask Mendoza-Denton if he is Mexican, he says yes instantly. If you ask him if he is African American, he says no instantly. If you ask him if he's Asian, he answers no—eventually.

"To the degree I'm associated with my partner, I'll actually have to think about it," Mendoza-Denton said. "Your partner's characteristics aren't part of you, but close enough that there's interference."

The more important part is that this is predictive. The longer it takes you, the more you identify with that group. And although Mendoza-Denton and Aron both said they didn't know of anyone who'd ever looked at sports fans this way, Mendoza-Denton said it should hold true.

"If I say that I'm a Knicks fan, and I say, 'Oh, yeah, I identify myself with the Knicks,' there's a possibility if you did some kind of test with inclusion of the other, you would be able to find an interference," Mendoza-Denton said.

So we go back to someone like Steve Winfield, looking

for escape from the real world and increasingly taking his real identity from that fantasy world, who literally became a Raider. To all outward appearances, he seems to have formed a self-expanding relationship with the team. His friends and his brother agree; the model describes what they saw. Ken Winfield says he saw it in other places, too, like when Steve watched his nephews' lacrosse games and got a little bit too upset at the coach's decisions. The Raiders, though, were a part of Steve's identity to the extent that you couldn't separate "him" from "them."

I started to ask this question: Could the Raiders' wins be keeping Steve Winfield alive? In the last year of his life, as he battled cancer, he could have been expanding his self with ideas of success, victory, triumph—powerful positive emotions. And if the football team had the power to give life, could it also take it away?

THE 2002–2003 SEASON WAS A GOOD ONE FOR THE RAIDERS. A preseason Super Bowl favorite, they returned most of the players from a team that had been denied a shot at a championship the year before only by a referee's decision in the famous "Tuck Rule" game.

The season was extra meaningful for Steve because it was plainly obvious to everyone it would be his last. He'd been diagnosed with colon cancer a few years earlier, and now he'd run out of options. He'd had surgery. He'd tried chemo. He'd tried turning inward. He'd gone to Argentina and spent tens of thousands of dollars on an experimental alternative procedure there. Finally in the fall of 2002 he'd gone to Hawaii to try one more New Age type healing treatment.

Somewhere on that trip, his brother Ken went out to visit, and everyone realized that nothing was going to work. There were no more options. Steve started to change then, Ken says, in an odd way. Instead of that constant restlessness, he finally settled into his identity. He was a Raiders fan, and he was going to die as one. Ken sent me a picture of him and Steve, in Hawaii. They have the same jaw line, the same pudgy nose. But Ken looks healthy. He fills out his T-shirt with tanned, muscled arms. He's got thick brown hair, and a pair of sunglasses hangs from his neck, athlete-style. Steve's T-shirt looks like a dress hung on a wire frame. The arm that emerges from it is tanned but skeletal. His bald head glows. They are both smiling, and they have the same smile.

Around that Hawaii trip, Steve started to focus on a goal. The Raiders were going to make the Super Bowl and he was going to make it with them. Vegas liked the Raiders' odds of playing into February, but the doctor didn't like Steve's. So he leaned on the Raiders and he defied the doctor. When the regular season ended in January, the Raiders were the top seed in the AFC playoffs and Steve had already lived a few months past his expiration date.

For the second round of the playoffs that year Bill Morgan flew out from Massachusetts to hang out with his old friend. "He wanted to watch all four playoff games," Morgan remembers. He was puzzled, he says, by that desire to just talk about sports. He expected Steve to want to gather his friends for some sort of meaningful ceremony. Instead they watched football. For Steve, that *was* a meaningful ceremony.

"It's strange to think, 'He didn't die the way I wanted him to,'" Morgan said.

They watched all four games, including a Raiders victory over the New York Jets. Steve was on morphine, fading in and out, but conscious. "He loved watching those games," Morgan said.

To Bill, it seemed like the Raiders' success was keeping Stevie alive, a kind of literal demonstration of self-expansion theory. When the team won again the next week, the Raiders had done their part. Steve just had to make it two more weeks to see his team in the Super Bowl.

Of course he did. How could he not?

Just before the big game, Morgan and those friends called Stevie and put him on speakerphone.

"He couldn't really say much," Morgan remembered. "Really, the only thing he said was, 'I made it.'"

Steve slept through much of the game at his brother Ken's house, surrounded by Ken's family. Ken and I met in a coffee shop in Berkeley, where he still lives, to talk about those last few hours. Ken was a big Raiders fan, too, and a season ticket holder for many years until he finally got fed up with Raiders owner Al Davis. Sports was one of those things he and his brother always had, which was puzzling because neither of their parents were fans. "For Depression era people sports wasn't as important," Ken said. "Steve and me, it was. It dominated right from when we were born."

Steve was athletic, Ken said, but was mostly working full-time by high school. Ken worked twenty hours a week and played baseball. The brothers loved watching everything. They grew up in Los Angeles as Angels fans, and when Steve moved to Boston he started following the Red Sox, and when he moved to Oakland he switched to football and became a Raiders fan. Ken had moved there for college and become a Raiders fan already. Steve wasn't crazy about Al Davis either, but one guy he really enjoyed was the soon-to-be former Raiders head coach Jon Gruden.

The 2003 Super Bowl, Steve's last, would become known as the Gruden Bowl because it pitted the Raiders against the Tampa Bay Buccaneers—the team that Al Davis had "traded" Gruden to at the start of the year. Tampa Bay players would say afterward that in pregame practices Gruden impersonated Raiders quarterback Rich Gannon down to the actual words and intonations he would use when calling plays. Gannon threw a Super Bowl–record five interceptions, three of them returned for touchdowns. The score was 20–3 by halftime and 27–3 early in the second half, but for Raiders fans everywhere the misery dragged on in the worst possible way, the Super Bowl commercials and extended halftime show only prolonging the inevitable defeat. The final score was 48–21, and it didn't feel that close.

I knew Steve slept through most of the game, I knew he was on morphine, and I knew that this probably wasn't the greatest day of Ken's life. But I couldn't help asking: Do you think Steve knew that the Raiders lost?

"He did know," Ken said. "And maybe that put him under."

A few hours after the game, Steve Winfield slipped into his final coma.

Morgan said that in his mind, there was no "might" about it. "By halftime," he said, "every Raiders fan in the world was, if not dying, kind of dying."

But Ken Winfield didn't remember it negatively. The Raiders had given Steve that one thing he'd always wanted and never found: a meaningful relationship. From that one source came a weird kind of peace that meditation and music couldn't offer.

"He was really at peace," Ken said. "The Raiders brought him to a point where, once that Super Bowl was over, he was okay to pass away."

5
Love:
The Altruistic Fan

IN NOVEMBER 2010, JUST AFTER THE SAN FRANCISCO GIANTS won their first-ever World Series after fifty years of trying, I was at a friend's house in the Mission District. We started to talk baseball and it turned out the friend was a Giants fan with a secret sorrow: upon reflection he didn't feel that the World Series victory had made him as euphoric as everyone else in town had looked. While flash mobs paraded the Mission and confetti rained on Market Street and talk radio callers wept on the air, he had felt only happiness, subsiding in a day or two to mild satisfaction.

Here was his idea for why, which he uttered in a kind of bitter way that suggested he was trying to joke it off but getting a bit too close to home. "Maybe," he said, "it's because of my inability to love."

Amid all the unrestrained glee, he worried: What if his inability to experience euphoria as a sports fan was some kind of parallel to his failure up to age thirty to form lasting personal relationships? What if something was broken in his emotional center that prevented him from loving—a person or otherwise—and his mere *happiness* at the Giants winning was the proof?

You have to understand, first of all, that the euphoria in San Francisco really was pandemic. If you lived here at the time—as presumably anyone anywhere who's lived through one of these can attest—it was remarkable how the city just kind of shuddered and seized up for a week. No one worked. Long-time-listener-first-time-callers finally called in and cried on the radio. The host of the late-night show on KNBR 680 *The Sports Leader* matched sentiment with sentiment; he described himself sitting with a bottle of champagne on the grass in the empty stadium in San Francisco, and he was giggling and waxing poetic like a love-struck teenager. People wrote moving paeans about the deceased-parents-who-passed-on-the-love-of-the-game in the sports section of the *San Francisco Chronicle*. More than one million people went to the championship parade on a workday Wednesday afternoon. In the überhipster Mission District there were fireworks and horns honking and people milling around outside the fashionable bars and spilling their locally sourced designer cocktails with drunken glee. This triumph, this love, took all comers in a blind, passionate embrace.

Here, meanwhile, was Adam, and he was nothing more than content.

I told him I'd figure out the answer to what I thought was his real question: we say that we love our teams. Do we? I mean really, really, *love* them, the same way we romantically love other people? If you put someone in a brain scanner and showed them a picture of their spouse, and you put a Giants fan in a brain scanner and showed them a picture of the San Francisco Giants, would you see the same thing?

I called a few psychologists, trying to get a quick read on his problem, but most of them seemed puzzled.

"Uh," said Daniel Wann at Murray State, sounding an awful lot like a guy searching for a polite answer, "I've never, ah, heard anybody look at it that way. I've never heard of a sports fan thinking, 'Yeah, you know it just wasn't what I hoped it would be.'"

There was a medium-length awkward pause.

"Usually," he said, "they think it *was* all they hoped it would be."

Ultimately it was Art Aron who provided the direction. Interpersonal love, Aron says, is just a kind of intense, fast self-expansion that includes a heavy dose of inclusion of the other in self. In his lab, they see signs of love like mixed-up memories, or neural activation in the brain in the "self" region when you think or look at a picture of someone you love. He says the exhilaration of early love comes from how rapidly the self-expansion is occurring. Aron keeps a second office in Berkeley, where he spends a semester a year on sabbatical; he's never really moved in so it feels a bit cold and medicinal, just a psychologist, his computer, and some empty metal bookshelves. We sat there and talked a few times, for a few hours, and at last I brought up my friend Adam and his strange question: Could someone have a broken love system, and first notice it because they couldn't adequately love a sports team?

Aron chuckled, but his answer was serious.

IN THE MID-1990S, ART ARON HAD A QUESTION ABOUT LOVE versus lust. He knew that there was a specific brain area associated with sexual desire. He wanted to know if love was also a separate emotion, with its own dedicated brain area, like lust, or like anger, happiness, and fear—or whether love was more what he calls a "general motivational state," like hunger, which can lead to a discrete emotion like fear if you think you aren't going to get food, but which doesn't have any specific brain region associated with it.

Right about the time he started wondering, researchers in social psychology started to make use of the brain-scanning technique known as functional magnetic resonance imaging. fMRI basically tracks blood flow to show what's happening in the brain at any particular time. An area that suddenly has increased blood flow is one assumed to be working, although you can't get much more specific than that. It isn't a perfect method, but it does show how our brains respond to the world around us. Aron thought he could make it reveal some of the secrets of love.

He started bringing groups of people who claimed to be intensely in love into his lab, and running them through the scanner. First, he would show them a picture of the person they were in love with. Then he would show a picture of a generic person of the same gender, attractiveness, and age as the person this participant was in love with. The question was whether they'd see anything different, and the answer was yes.

Every picture seemed to activate a variety of discrete emotional areas, and in the overall number of areas activated every person was different. No big-picture predictability. Incredibly, consistently across participants, though, they found looking at the picture of the lover leading to activation in the dopamine reward system. The reward system is in a very old part of the brain (one of the reasons researchers can apply lessons from socially defeated rats is that the brain appears to have been mostly developed before rats and humans split on the evolutionary tree), and it's a system that turns on when you think you're going to get something you want—like, for example, if you're expecting to get a lot of money. It's also the area that activates when you take cocaine. "That's why people take cocaine, in order to get that same sense of reward and excitement as when you're first in love with someone," Aron said.

Aron and his colleagues have replicated this study several times. Other labs across the world—elsewhere in the United States, in China, and in England—have found the same thing. The finding has been remarkably consistent. Love is not an emotion. It is different from sexual desire. More like hunger than anger, it doesn't have a discrete physical structure to work with so, in some sense, it has invented its own.

If this sounds familiar, well, yes. It is definitely like watching sports.

Aron says that love in the brain might be an expression of expecting to fulfill an intense desire for connection. The brain is recruiting the same neural network it uses for other things it wants in order to promote evolutionarily useful connections and alliances.

"This general reward system has been made use of in a whole variety of contexts," he said.

One of those contexts, remember, might be interacting with the mirror neuron system to regulate the way we mirror other people. Stephanie Ortigue and Francesco Bianchi-Demicheli had the same idea, and they tried to put all this stuff together in a 2008 paper titled, appropriately, "Why Is Your Spouse So Predictable?: Connecting Mirror Neuron System and Self-Expansion Model of Love."

Remember that the more you experience something, the more you use your mirror neurons for a particular activity, and the more active the mirroring system will be the next time you watch that activity. Couples in love, as we all know, tend to understand each other more and more the deeper they're in love and the longer they spend together; that's the whole finishing-each-other's-sentences, growing-to-resemble-each-other thing. Ortigue and Bianchi-Demicheli conclude somewhat unsurprisingly that there's significant mirroring going on in loving couples. What this meant in their laboratory experiment was that people in love understood each other's intentions much better than they understood the intentions of others.

So remember how the mirror response to watching action has top-down control? Here's one part. The more you expand yourself, the more you really love your team—the more your ventral tegmental area lights up when you see a picture of the team logo—the more you mirror their jerseys. This is one reason fans following their favorite teams feel the game as such a physical experience, and why for me the actions of a Sharks hockey player have such emotional significance. Working backward, we can say beyond a doubt that I really do, in the exact sense of the word as comprehended by William Shakespeare, love the San Jose Sharks.

And if I struggled to love the Sharks, could I struggle to love people, too? Ortigue and Bianchi-Demicheli suggest yes. "Given the physiological properties of mirror neurons, and the present assumed link between the MNS [mirror neuron system] and love, it is highly plausible that dysfunctions of the MNS could lead to deficits in love relationships," they wrote. "We suggest that the MNS is less activated in people with love interaction impairment."

WHAT'S FUNNY, ART ARON SAYS, IS THAT LOVE—WITH CENturies' worth of poems lamenting its complexity—may in fact be one of the easiest ways of studying the motivational desire system. Bringing in people who claim to be intensely in love is quite simple; they're certainly common enough. It is more ethical showing pictures of loved ones than handing out cocaine. It is much, much easier to find someone who is in love than it is to pre-identify a lottery winner.

Again, though, we're still talking about love between two people. How far, really, can you extend the implications of Aron's findings?

"The word *love* is a very vague word," Aron said. "We use it for love of God, love of children, for the sense of love that guides the universe, and we also say, you know, 'The love of money is the root of all evil.' We have this whole set of words for love. But if we're using it in the context of an intense, focused desire to form a link with some object, that object can be a person, which is the most usual one, but it can also be a profession, or an activity, or a sports team. Why not?"

I asked Aron specifically if my friend who worried about not loving the Giants could be reasonably worried that his motivational desire system was broken for interpersonal relationships and sports love. Aron, a bit to my surprise, said it was possible. Some people, he said, avoid attachment. There are basically two types of attachments, roughly corresponding to extroverts and introverts—and while it's un-usual, some people don't attach well to anyone or anything. (Introverts may have trouble with groups but usually form intense one-on-one relationships, while extroverts may not have close one-on-one relationships but can have group con-nections.) The explanation sounded almost Freudian: maybe, Aron said, it has something to do with their parents being unavailable to them.

"He may be an unfortunate one who has neither [type of relationship]," Aron said. He added, though, that it wasn't hopeless. "On the other hand," he said, "people who have neither are sometimes able, working alone, to make great contributions to society and be very successful and feel good about their work."

ANOTHER LINE OF EVIDENCE TO PROVE IT'S "REAL" LOVE CAME TO me from Aaron Ahuvia, a researcher at the University of Michi-gan, Dearborn, who suggested thinking backward, based on what we know about Aron's work on inclusion of other in self. If you see people applying the kind of perceptual biases to a team or brand that they apply to themselves, Ahuvia argues, then you can make an educated guess that they're including the other in their self. Since including the other in the self is a flash-ing red sign of a deeply expanded relationship, he says, you can conclude that they are in love.

"If you treat sports teams psychologically the same way you treat yourself," he told me, that "is in my mind a really strong indicator of love."

The list of ways people treat themselves differently than they treat others is lengthy. The Princeton psychologist

Emily Pronin, in a 2008 paper in *Science*, wrote about five major perceptual differences, all based on the simple problem that you make decisions about yourself based on your internal monologue, while you make decisions about everyone else based only on what they say or do:

- "Positive illusions": thinking you're luckier than everyone else, that you're more likely than everyone else to get rich, stay healthy, or finish your work on time than everyone else, and exaggerating even the positive characteristics that others do find in you;
- "Interpersonal knowledge": thinking your intuition tells you about other people while you yourself are an inscrutable figure of intrigue and mystery;
- "Pluralistic ignorance": utterly misjudging the motives of other people and thinking you're alone in the way you think;
- "Miscommunications": knowing what you really think and then forgetting to actually *say* that to another person on the unconscious assumption that they too know what you think;
- "Conformity": unconsciously imitating the crowd while thinking you're the only maverick straight-shooter left.

Entirely understandably, you perceive the world as a you-centric universe. But that's not all. Pronin goes on to detail all the ways you're also unaware that that's how you see it. People also strongly feel that they are objective even when they're not. Psychological experiment after psychological experiment shows this to be the case, beginning with a famous study of—hey, sports fans!—football fans in the 1950s that showed that everyone thinks the referees are more objective when they make calls favoring their own team.

Published in 1954 in the *Journal of Abnormal and Social Psychology*, "They Saw a Game: A Case Study" is one of the most famous studies in selective perception ever conducted. On November 23, 1951—a "brisk Saturday afternoon," wrote the study's authors Albert Hastorf and Hadley Cantril—Dartmouth played Princeton in football. It turned into a rough game, with Princeton's star player leaving with a broken nose and a Dartmouth player leaving with a broken leg. After the game, partisans of both sides accused the other side of playing dirty. Hastorf and Cantril decided it would make an excellent occasion to study perception.* They created a questionnaire about the game and administered it to both Princeton and Dartmouth undergraduates, then showed an identical film clip from the game to groups of students at both schools. The results were what you'd expect: Princeton students watching the video flagged far more fouls on Dartmouth and vice versa. In one of the great lines in sociology, Hastorf and Cantril wrote, "It seems clear that the 'game' actually was many different games and that each version of the events that transpired was just as 'real' to a particular person as other versions were to other people.'"

Dan Kahan, a Yale law professor, identified something he called "cultural cognition"—when information comes along that could undermine the way you see the world or your connection to other people in your coalition, you have a strong

---

*Recognizing the razor's edge on which they were dancing, Hastorf and Cantril included a footnote declaring, "We are not concerned here with the problem of guilt or responsibility for infractions, and nothing here implies any judgment as to who was to blame."

and unconscious emotional prejudice against it. So people who disagree about abortion are entirely and predictably likely to disagree about climate change. As everyone complains, belonging to team blue or team red really is more emotionally important to your brain than empiricism or reason.

The result, as Kahan outlines it in a 2010 paper in *Nature*, is to expose one of the great flaws in theories of science communication: that if people just had access to more information, they'd eventually figure out some objective truth. "The prevailing approach is still simply to flood the public with as much sound data as possible on the assumption that the truth is bound, eventually, to drown out competitors," Kahan wrote. "If, however, the truth carries implications that threaten people's cultural values, then holding their heads underwater is likely to harden their resistance and increase their willingness to support alternative arguments, no matter how lacking in evidence."

From an evolutionary standpoint, Kahan told me, this kind of makes sense. There's more data in the world than we can possibly make sense of or observe for ourselves. We all have to pick someone to trust. What's actually amazing, Kahan says, is that over time we've been so *good* at trusting the right people. "To me it's more surprising that anyone ever agrees on anything," he said. "But people do manage to converge on what's known, collectively, somehow. The only way they can do it is by figuring out who knows what about what. You don't have to have a medical degree to know to go to the doctor. You know who to trust about what."

In *The Better Angels of Our Nature* Steven Pinker highlights something he calls the "Moralization Gap," the way people almost instantaneously choose to distort other

people's actions to make themselves appear more reasonable and make others appear less so. Even more damning,
we then lie to ourselves about what we've done, inventing
elaborate self-deceptions so that we come across as entirely
believable when we explain what we've done. We're going
to talk more about this when we talk about groups, because you also amp up your biases to forgive people in
your own tribe and distrust or dislike people in other
tribes. The important thing is that, again, nature did equip
you with a large prefrontal cortex for reasoning and empiricism. Self-control works to acknowledge and overcome
bias. Pinker wrote about an extremely clever experiment
by David DeSteno (Lisa Williams's thesis adviser) that
proved that the brain has its own unconscious spin doctor
that cleans up information before it reaches the conscious.
"I was happy to discover the result, not just because the
theory of self-deception is so elegant that it deserves to be
true, but because it offers a glimmer of hope for human-
ity," Pinker wrote. "It may take ridicule, it may take argument, it may take time, it may take being distracted, but
people have the means to recognize that they are not always
in the right."

Which doesn't mean we shouldn't fool ourselves that
most of the time people will go to great lengths to pretend
they've never harmed anyone. They will also very obviously
go to great lengths to pretend that their favorite athlete
surely did not intend for his elbow to connect with the rival
athlete's face. We can maybe agree that this is not the most
romantic definition of love we'll ever hear but agree equally
that it's pretty strong evidence that we love our sports teams.
It's not just that one of the original studies in selective per-

ception comes from sports fans. Look around you; this is all we do. We complain about biased referees. On the West Coast we complain about the major networks' East Coast bias, in Boston they complain about the major networks' New York bias, in New York they complain about the major networks' Boston bias. When the former Cal running back Marshawn Lynch gets arrested and charged with drunk driving for swerving across the freeway at 3:30 a.m., I'm likely to make every attempt to forgive him, inventing and instantly accepting a lengthy excuse on his behalf, because I have, in a sense, a relationship with him. If it had been Andrew Luck from Stanford, I'd be cognitively packing for a trip to schadenfreude city.

HERE, AT LEAST, IS A LITTLE BIT OF GOOD NEWS ABOUT LOVE, sports, and life: my friend Adam did not have to spend the rest of his life wallowing in the what-ifs of a lost opportunity for love. In 2012 the Giants won the World Series again. The euphoria swept through again. The Mission District fired up and partied again. And Adam, after texting me a few times during the week to tell me that he was much more nervous than last time, that in fact his beating heart and sweaty palms were making him think he didn't like this being a really, really invested fan thing one bit, got another chance.

There was one difference worth noting. On April 5, 2013, the Giants will raise their second championship banner in San Francisco. The following day, entirely by coincidence, will be Adam's wedding. He and his fiancée met just a few months after the 2010 World Series.

Adam and I talked, only briefly, in the aftermath of the final out. "How was it this time?" I asked.

Adam didn't even hesitate. "Better!" he said.

AARON AHUVIA STUDIES MARKETING, WHICH PROVIDES ANOTHER of the lines of evidence we're after. One way you might approximate the love for a team would be to compare it to the way people love consumer brands, and Ahuvia is a specialist at applying Aron's theory of self-expansion to brand love. If you're already feeling that Aron's work has somehow cheapened your idea of romance, check this out: "While we sympathize with the idea that there is something special about love," Ahuvia wrote in one paper, "considerable data suggests that love is nonetheless a psychological process that can be applied to people, ideas, activities, and objects."

Ahuvia doesn't see that as cheapening, of course. He argues that it's actually a mark of the incredible importance of personal relationships to people. We're so primed to form relationships with other people, and the ability to form them is so critical to our evolutionary success, that we actually have expanded the number of things we apply that model to. He compared it to driving a car. Before the development of the car, nobody could personally travel at eighty miles an hour unless they were falling off a cliff. And yet we* drive cars remarkably well. We didn't evolve to drive them but other systems cover the experience so nicely that we succeed. So it is, Ahuvia said, with consumers having relationships with their favorite brands. "We have these

---

*Marshawn Lynch excepted.

mental processes built primarily for interpersonal relationships," he told me, "but because they're so primary in our
brain, so important to us, we take them and apply them to
other contexts."

Consumption, depending on where you stand in a philo-
sophical/academic dispute, can assume some of the aspects
of identity that Merrill Melnick tied to sports fans. Consumers could be seeking a coherent identity narrative and
buying things that confirm their sense of self. Or as post-
modernists like to say, they could be actually free, buying
whatever they like because there's no need for a unified self
concept. Or they could be buying things because, unlike
Melnick's happy identified sports fans, they haven't found
a coherent identity and so they consume to try to find one.
Either way, as with sports teams, it's not like anyone is
afraid to say they love a favorite brand, whether that's
Apple or NASCAR.

What Ahuvia and a few others have generally tried to
do is sort out the difference between people who say, "Yeah,
I love NASCAR" and people who actually, like, *love*
NASCAR. ("We recognize that consumers tend to speak
loosely when using the word 'love' in reference to commercial products," Ahuvia wrote in one paper. "As such, many
instances of brand love will not be fully analogous to the
stronger forms of interpersonal love.")

There are two ways, Ahuvia wrote in a 2006 article in
the *Journal of Marketing Letters*, to really sort the two. By
now they'll sound familiar. The first is evidence of self-
expansion. If the person is actually integrating the brand
into his or her own identity, then that, Ahuvia says, is brand
love. The other is a bit like our definition of pride. Real

brand love is an emotion, Ahuvia says, not just cognitive satisfaction. The emotional connection to a brand also tends to be much stronger when the brand isn't very useful—when it's a "hedonic" product that provides pleasure, like art, food, or sports equipment. I am more likely to really love the company that makes my hockey skates than I am to love the company that makes my car. (Which is exactly why so much of the marketing strategy for selling the car is to remind you of all the hedonic things you can do with it—by, say, showing it loaded down with surfboards at the beach, and not in a utilitarian grind through rush-hour traffic.) A sports team, of course, is almost perfectly the definition of a hedonic brand. Ahuvia said he thinks it could go even further, that a team might look even more like a loved object than most brands. "My intuition, speaking as a sports fan, is that teams really are seen as interpersonal relationships, much more directly than brands are," he said. "That's going to be a much better fit."

One way you can tell, he said, is altruism. Loyal customers will still rarely behave altruistically toward their favorite brand. But they will toward a favorite team. That, he concluded, is once again love. What he said he didn't understand, though, was why you'd choose to love a team over other lovable forms of entertainment, like movies.

"In sports, you've got about a fifty-fifty shot of being happy or miserable," Ahuvia said. "And people are *really* miserable when their team loses; it's really bad. I feel that sometimes. So why do we do that to ourselves when we could watch a movie with like a ninety-nine percent shot of a happy ending?"

We're back at the Cleveland dilemma. Sports allow fans

to find identity and even love, but often what they offer back is torment and misery. Someone asked me while I was working on this book when it is that I most feel in love with my favorite team. I think it's when I stay true after they do something stupid. As any fan knows, this often feels more like an abusive relationship than a successful one; our love is generally measured in loyalty to a disappointing product, not passionate euphoria. It feels, as we often say, addictive. Which, based on what we know about sports fans and love, is suddenly a very intriguing idea. As Art Aron pointed out, it's the same spot in the brain that activates when you fall deeply in love or take cocaine. Maybe this loving thing is a little more dangerous than it seems.

6
Addiction: Arsenal in America

FOUR WEEKS INTO MY EXPERIMENT AS AN EMBEDDED JOUR-nalist among the San Francisco–based arm of the international Arsenal fan club, my body gave out. The Bay Area Gooners bridge the eight-hour time difference to watch every Arsenal match live in an Irish pub in San Francisco's North Beach neighborhood, and it says everything you need to know about their loyalty, passion, and determination that attendance at these predawn ritual gatherings is superb. Mark Barbeau, the group's founder, says he has a mailing list of more than five hundred.

I, meanwhile, have an infant at home, and by the middle of November as the Gunners headed to a 4:45 a.m. Pacific time kickoff against archrival Tottenham, I was a limping, wrecked carcass, punching the alarm clock at 3:50 on Saturday, rolling out of bed into my jeans, and stumbling off to the pub only to get kicked out of the bar by the bartender because he thought I was homeless and had walked in off the streets to get warm. We sorted out the misunderstanding a few minutes later, but the intervening space, as I returned to my car and sat with the seat back and the lights off, listening to rain splatter on the windshield, gave me time for reflection about the line between admirable true love and the more ruinous passion of addiction.

When people in love and people taking cocaine are activating the same brain areas in brain scans, the line seems hair-strand thin. All sports fandom requires commitment, of course, but when that commitment requires predawn wake-ups thirty-eight times a year, the loyalty begins to verge on obsessive. In sports fan vernacular addiction comes up all the time, meaning less physical consequences than overwhelming loyalty: a compulsion to watch that's so strong you can't break the ritual, even when your best interests dictate otherwise. Think of Todd Dery in Cleveland, who surely would be better off if he took up a hobby like gardening. Or Bill Morgan, who spent his life in a meditation center trying to control his anger, only to find in moments of supreme crisis that he couldn't. Or the hapless English soccer fans who ought to turn the television off the second the game goes to penalties but simply must . . . keep . . . watching . . . until the calamity occurs. The addict is rarely oblivious; recrimination sets in almost immediately, but the turmoil, the self-loathing, and the shame do nothing because as soon as the team returns so will you—they know it and you know it and they know that you know it.

It is all quite frustrating.

One morning in the bar I saw a young man sitting in the corner wearing an Oakland Raiders hat and faded yellow Emirates jersey. Kola Shobo told me that several years earlier he had moved from Nigeria to Stockton, a bedroom community two hours outside of San Francisco. He was lonely, scared, looking for work: a displaced immigrant from a faraway country living in an utterly foreign small town in California's Central Valley. Somehow, he heard about this group of Bay Area Arsenal supporters, and so one morning he made the long drive to the bar. It was dark on the streets, but there was a light on inside and as he walked in and beheld the blazing warmth of television screens showing an English afternoon, and the dozens of people standing around in red jerseys, he fell to his knees and raised his arms to the sky. "Right there," he said, pointing to the exact spot on the dark wood floor where the miracle had occurred. Now he's moved to Oakland, a mere half hour away in the morning, and is a regular.

"It's life," Kola said. He estimates that Arsenal fans are even more loyal than Raiders fans.

"Like my father says," he said, waving around the pub at sixty people in Arsenal jerseys, necks craned toward the televisions, "God first. Your mother second. Arsenal next. Then your spouse."

YOU WOULD EXPECT—OR AT LEAST, I EXPECTED—THAT ALONG would come Science to demolish this little fantasy about sports fans being addicts. I expected to hear that somewhere in all the new neuroscience we had identified the chemical signal of addiction, the brain activation that made the psychiatrists go *Ah-ha, here's your problem right here on the brain scan,* like doctors holding up an X-ray to spot a broken bone. But this is where it gets really interesting.

I'd heard psychologists speak about chemical or substance addiction as something different from what they called "process addiction." It made sense to me to think of drugs as different than sports; one has an obvious direct chemical influence on the brain and one doesn't. It seemed to trivialize the suffering of true abusers to toss them into a group with Tiger Woods in his "sex addiction" rehab clinic. Considering the similar brains of cocaine users and lovers, though, made me wonder about the difference. So I asked Antonello Bonci, a neuroscientist and scientific director of the National Institute on Drug Abuse in Washington, about the hard scientific definition of addiction, and how he'd separate drug dependency from an excess of sports passion.

"There is no distinction in the definition of addiction between sports and substance abuse," Bonci said. "It is not the chemical that defines it."

Addiction, even to a neuroscientist, is defined outside the brain. When people change everything they do for the sake of one passion, when that passion takes over and people lose control of their lives to the point that there are negative consequences, they're considered addicts, Bonci said. That's not to suggest that what happens in the brain doesn't matter, or that there isn't a signature of sorts. In fact, the neuroscience of addiction—and much of what we know has been revealed in the last two decades—has transformed the way scientists think about addicts. NIDA director Nora Volkow has pioneered the idea that there is such a thing as an "addicted brain," that addiction is not a moral failing or a lack of willpower. She argues that four particular brain circuits, responsible for four different functions, get out of whack. Although she's working entirely with drug addiction, the four circuits are going to sound quite familiar: reward, memory, drive, and control. We've already seen two of these systems working together in the depressed rats of Klaus Miczek. After repeated defeats, the rats' reward systems shut down, causing them to lose their drive. One of the surprising outcomes of Miczek's work, remember, was the rats showing increased interest in cocaine.

We'll talk more about each of these circuits, but—conceptually at least—the interaction between them is fairly simple to grasp. In the non-addicted brain, control looms large, overruling the other three circuits. In the addicted brain, huge reward creates vivid memories and intense drive that overwhelms self-control. In a chart in a 2003 paper in the *Journal of Clinical Investigation*, Volkow sums it up in a one-word conclusion for each brain. Next to the non-addicted brain model: "STOP." Next to the addicted brain model: "GO."

Just as it presides over your hormones and your empathy, self-control presides over pleasure, motivation, and desire. Earlier I asked why sports fans make the choice to surrender to their hormones or their mirror neurons. The science of addiction is the science of people who don't get to make a choice. The question is how well this describes sports fans, whether it's fifty bleary-eyed Gooners watching football from five thousand miles away in a bar at 4:30 a.m. or a lonely blue-and-gold Cal fanatic sweating out a college football away game in a sea of hostile Cardinal red.

"IT'S MORE CHASING THE HIGH THAN FEEDING THE JONES, IF that makes any sense," the sportswriter Mike Silver told me. Silver, a Cal fan who writes a weekly Yahoo! NFL column that once had a feature called "This Week's Proof That Cal Is the Center of the Universe," is all too happy to describe himself as an addicted fan. He mostly loses, as we've discussed, but the big wins, when they come, are often so unexpected that they lead to stadium-wide euphoria. "If I could just get that high," he said. "Knowing that the high is possible makes me make a lot of dubious decisions."

The high comes straight from the brain's reward system. It's this same system engaging in lovers and defeated rats and that Marco Iacoboni says is involved with mirror neurons. It's an old system, shared with most mammals, and although it's quite complicated, it engages anytime we stumble across music, food, or sex. Anything pleasurable is a reward in a harsh environment, and your brain lets you know it by releasing the dopamine.

A more intense dopamine rush, though, doesn't necessarily mean addiction or even a path to addiction. Bonci said there's a spectrum of pleasurable to miserable outcomes, but there's nowhere on the spectrum that a scientist could look and identify an addicted brain. The addiction diagnosis comes when seeking one particular reward takes over your life. Bonci—not a sports fan—listed two of his own passions: espresso and the cello. If you put him in the brain scanner and gave him espresso, or watched while he played the cello, would you see a bulging reward center? Probably. Does it make him an addict? No. In fact, the dopamine is good because it drives him to practice. We need pleasure for basic survival.

"I love espresso like some people like chocolate, but I wouldn't change my life for it," Bonci said. "There's a very fine line between what is a passion and what is an addiction. I play cello, I can't wait until I have those twenty minutes every night. But if I skip it for a day, for a week, it's not the end of the world. Passions need dopamine because it drives you. It drives you to do things that you love, that are salient to you. It's fundamental to you."

The reward doesn't even have to make you happy. The point, Bonci said, is actually playing the game. It's seeking the reward, more than the pleasure the reward produces, that catches you. Obvious enough; proverbs and stories like this are legion. Bonci selected one from memory, about a rich man who won a million dollars gambling and just left it on the table so he could come back the next day.

"The outcome is not pleasure necessarily," Bonci said. "This applies to sports, if your team loses. It also applies to substance abuse. If you interview a lot of people who are addicted to many different things, they say, 'I don't feel pleasure at all, I just want to take it.' The subjective experience of pleasure is not really the one thing that once they are addicted is determining why they are taking it."

The evolutionary point of the dopamine reward system is in part its grouping with the other two circuits: drive and memory. The loop is fundamental for animal life, and when it breaks, you see the defeated-rat characteristics of apathy, lack of initiative, and lack of interest. Dopamine is a learning tool, and the stronger the dopamine surge the more it activates memory—so that you remember how to get that big reward again—and drive—so that you're motivated to seek it again. Think of the love that Art Aron calls "rapid self-expansion." You fall in love. (Reward.) In the early days of the relationship you think about the person all the time. (Memory.) You can't get enough of the person, you call them all the time, you want to see them all the time; when they're away you can't wait until they come back. (Drive.)

Or consider the creation story of the Bay Area Gooners. On a trip one year to England, Mark Barbeau decided to watch Arsenal play at the then-brand-new Emirates Stadium. A San Francisco native, he'd always been a fan of the hometown 49ers, but the trip to London seemed to set off something new. He went to the game and Arsenal won and the passion was inspiring, overwhelming, infectious. (Reward.) He returned home and couldn't get the soccer out of his head. He missed the feeling of being part of an enormous, global fan club. (Memory.) He founded the Bay Area Gooners, committed to bringing a crowd to Maggie McGarry's pub every game and started to evangelize for the team. (Drive.)

Here are the three parts of the addicted brain in action. Here we are, in love, as new sports fans, wiggling on the line between passion and addiction.

"That tells you how similar it is," Bonci said. "Now we are getting into what addiction means."

By Bonci's definition of addiction you can, then, become addicted to anything rewarding. It's possible to imagine sports fans who become so attached to the team they're willing to forsake work, family, or hygiene for their passion. But there's an especially insidious side to drugs that makes them so powerful. The chemical part of drugs like cocaine can amplify, all on its own, the surge in those three brain circuits. Cocaine, Bonci said, can lock the cells in the brain into a state where the memory of the drug persists for much longer. It's quite complicated, goes far beyond dopamine, and the more we expand our knowledge of the brain and peer more closely into its activities, the more we connect different systems to addiction.

Bonci compared the science of dopamine and addiction to an ocean. The scientific community, he said, is full of experts each tenaciously illuminating one drop in that ocean. We're returning again to the theme of testosterone and anticipation: the brain talking to itself is the most complex and critical part of all. One of the drops of that ocean concerns, for sports fans, perhaps the most relevant question: What interaction in the brain makes bigger or smaller rewards? What makes rewards more or less compelling?

It's been easy to be a Gooner for the last two decades. Arsenal, a team renowned for its gruesome, gritty, often-losing football, has instead under Arsene Wenger become an English Premier League power that plays with style, grace, and—not least important—boatloads of money. Talent never seemed in short supply, and every player lost to Real Madrid or retirement was replaced quickly with a next-generational hero: Bergkamp and Henry beget Fabregas and Cole beget van Persie and Adebayor. The exceptional run has included a Champions League final appearance, several trophies, and probably the finest league season any team has ever put together: In 2004 Arsenal's "Invincibles" became the first club in English football's top division ever to string together a completely unbeaten thirty-eight-game season.

No one in the international Arsenal fan clubs lacked for dopamine in that run. Big win after big win, reward after reward. You would think that they couldn't possibly keep performing at this level and then they would get better. For a Bay Area Gooner, why wouldn't you wake up at 4:00 a.m. to go watch your team stomp some hapless noncompetitor? Sure, the time sucks, but it's no real test of your loyalty to participate in the revelry of a history-making season.

Here's the question that has interested psychologists: When the team stops offering rewards with the same frequency, how long does it take for the fan to lose interest? In Cleveland, several people told me, fans are giving up on teams now after years or decades of futility. For a team like Arsenal, the longest occupier of first-tier English football, the luminaries of the early 2000s, would anything ever subvert the fans' loyalty?

The cracks started to appear in the 2006–2007 season. After going from 1998 to 2005 without finishing lower than second place in the Premier League, Arsenal dropped to fourth, and it's now been seven years since they finished higher than third. The run has seen top-notch players depart, looking for trophies elsewhere, and the two transformational talents, Theo Walcott and Jack Wilshere, injured or not quite ready to keep pace. In the summer of 2012 the team's captain and eight-year veteran Robin van Persie declared he didn't agree with the direction at Arsenal and refused to sign a contract extension, forcing the team to allow him a transfer to rival Manchester United—the kind of thing almost unimaginable in the previous decade.

Following the summer of transfer drama, everyone had the day of van Persie's first game against his old team circled on the calendar as one that would likely be special. Arsenal fans of course wanted to win, but really also wanted to see van Persie stumble. For the opposite to happen—not just to lose, but to see van Persie triumphant—for an Arsenal fan would call into question not just one's loyalty but the existence of karma and the justness of God. For a Bay Area Gooner to wake up for a 5:30 a.m. kickoff just for that kind of stomach punch, well, that's bordering on abusive.

You can probably guess where this is headed.

THE WAY WE LEARN WITH DOPAMINE IS INTERESTING AND OF direct relevance to sports fans. It also starts to answer the question of what you can do to get more or less of a reward. Fans will guess the answer intuitively by thinking about when a win is most satisfying and when a loss hurts most: the dopamine reward idea of learning is based on expectation. The less you expect of an underdog, the greater the euphoria of victory, and the more you expect out of a favorite, the sharper the bite of defeat.

In the introduction I shared my nightmarish worst Cal football memory, the night when the most highly ranked Cal team of my lifetime lost at home to an unremarkable, unranked team. The best—a memory I share with Mike Silver—might be the 2009 Big Game against archrival Stanford, which took place in Palo Alto. Stanford had Heisman Trophy candidate Toby Gerhart, future number one draft pick Andrew Luck, and future 49ers coach Jim Harbaugh. Cal was in a death spiral and came limping into the game a heavy underdog. But while the Stanford fans applauded their great alumni Tiger Woods—appearing in public with Elin Nordegren about two days before his famous Thanksgiving "car accident"—the unheralded Cal running back Shane Vereen quietly set about demolishing the Stanford defense. Then with Cal holding a tenuous lead in the last minute, Harbaugh inexplicably called a play for Luck instead of the dominant Gerhart, and Luck threw an interception that happened right in front of Mike Silver. Total, utter dopamine blowout.

"Really it's the joy I feel when we have just beaten Stanford and I'm with close friends or family members and strangers and the euphoria is shared in that moment," Silver said. "We've all done something together and celebrating it, that is—that is one of the most amazing feelings imaginable."

In the least sexy terms possible, that feeling is so good because it is a prediction violated. When you get a big reward just as you were least suspecting it, your brain marks it down with extreme urgency. *Whoa*, it says. *We've got to remember this!*

Since you are constantly going through life with rewards great and small, what ends up happening is that your brain maps out a complex probability distribution for every reward it might get and then releases more or less dopamine depending on how predicted the reward was. Game outcomes offer the potential for reward, and so, like a Vegas bookie, your brain sets a line for every game. This'll set your head spinning a little, but your brain is handling some fairly awesome statistical calculation at the outcome of every contest.

"The repeated experience with winning and losing produces predictions that get updated on every game outcome, and then the last game outcome gets subtracted from the last prediction," said Wolfram Schultz, a Cambridge neurophysiologist who is a pioneer in probabilistic rewards. "Like after a series of losses, a won game produces a large positive prediction error (high current outcome minus low last prediction), and the dopamine prediction error response would be high after that last win."

Since no win is 100 percent certain, every win comes with at least a small reward. But beating your heavily favored rival on the road? That, to your reward center, is hot stuff. That's the euphoria that Mike Silver is chasing.

Silver is one of the most prominent football writers in America, and his legions of readers would love to hear he's still a fan of a particular team. His weekly ranking of the thirty-two teams draws constant cries of favoritism. (Silver writes often that he's a fan of all thirty-two NFL teams, that he has no favorites.) But he's not, and it's actually quite interesting why, and goes to what we're talking about with addiction.

He did, first of all, start out as a fan. Mike was born in San Francisco and lived there the first five years of his life, long enough for his dad to catch the Bay Area fan bug.

"I wanted to be like my dad in every way," Silver said. He narrated some family holiday where they were at the grandparents' house in Los Angeles and little Mike went toddling off looking for his father. "I went upstairs and found him in this little room, watching this little black-and-white TV, probably in the room where he grew up. I said, 'Who's winning?' He said, 'The Los Angeles team is beating the San Francisco team.' I said, 'That's good.' He said, 'No, it's not.' I said, 'Oh.' He said, 'Yeah, we're rooting for the San Francisco team.'"

And that was that. "I think at that point," Mike said, "I was doomed to be the Bay Area underdog sports guy."

Silver went to Cal and followed the 49ers religiously. "I don't know if I ever cried when the 49ers lost, but I really took it personally," he said. "It hurt my psyche when they lost."

Out of college he got a sportswriting job at the *Sacramento Union* newspaper and suddenly, as a twenty-four-year-old, he was covering his idols Joe Montana and Steve Young. And this is how you know Mike Silver isn't an addict, even though he says he is: because faced with the personal and professional consequences of letting his sports fandom rule, he exerted self-control and overrode it. He stopped being a pro football fan, subsumed the reward-memory-drive cycle, and became a disinterested journalist.

"It's not hard really to lose the fan thing in that context," he said. "It really isn't."

The loyalty and fan energy he transferred to Cal, and it runs deep. He's still friends with his friends from college, still gets together with them for games. He married his college girlfriend, he said, and "we felt like we went to school and it was a magical experience for us collectively and we were part of something that transcends the normal college experience."

It's not addiction, but it's three of the four parts of the addicted brain, many of them deeply felt. Reward, memory, drive. Mike celebrates those, probably beyond even the typical fan. When the reward does come, because those three circuits are talking to each other, it's big. But his chasing the euphoria is not an addiction. The addiction is the part that follows, when the reward, memories, and motivation overwhelm self-control. That's not really a level that most sports fans ever reach. Drugs wreck lives—to an extent the millions of sports fans who describe their passion as addictive don't really mean. When we speak of addiction, we tend to speak more in terms of returning to teams that don't always reward us. It's habit more than addiction: we've been trained to expect rewards when games occur, and we desire those rewards, and we return even when we don't get them. It's the consistency of the habit that's puzzling and makes us feel addicted, not a loss of self-control, necessarily, because we *could* and probably *would* always stop if we needed to. There's just, and this is so much of what sports is about, an incredible fascination with prediction error, the gist of which is: We love our teams all the more for being wrong so often about them.

As the afternoon shadows start to work across the historic pitch at Old Trafford late on a Saturday in England, I'm watching a shop owner hosing down the sidewalk in front of his darkened North Beach café. At 5:30 a.m. Pacific, the normally bazaar-like streets of San Francisco's least parkable neighborhood are deserted and ghostly, lined with garbage and recycling bins from the previous night's debauchery. Nothing says zombie apocalypse like this row of empty metered street parking spaces.

It's fifteen minutes to kickoff and there are already forty people inside Maggie McGarry's Irish pub. Televisions show the scene live in Manchester, the blazing grass and sunlight of half a world away. The bar here can't serve alcohol until 6:00 a.m., so the red-clad bartender is dishing up coffee. They show the starting lineups on TV, and there's van Persie, the former Arsenal captain. In the glory days of the Bay Area Gooners you probably would have seen his name somewhere on someone's back, but now in a sea of red Emirates jerseys it's been scrubbed from the record. One brave fan wears the number five of the new captain, Thomas Vermaelen.

At 5:45 a.m. the game begins. Manchester United kicks it around for a minute. The ball ping-pongs toward the Arsenal goal. Someone plays in a low line drive and Vermaelen stumbles, the ball ricocheting low off his feet and directly into van Persie's path. Van Persie doesn't even pause. With one touch he lashes it into the corner of the net. At 5:48 a.m. the hated rival leads on a goal by the hated turncoat ex-captain off a clumsy blunder by the new team leader. The three Manchester United fans in the bar, there solely to taunt their rivals—most of their comrades are in a bar across town— clap loudly. By city law there are still twelve minutes to go until alcohol can be served.

The Bay Area Gooners react almost mutely to the goal. A low chorus of "What the fuck was that?" A single, bitter, "Fuck."

The game audio blares especially loudly as ESPN's Ian Darke says, "You knew he was going to score."

It's too early in the morning for the game to be over, and of course it's not, technically, but this is dispiriting. It takes forty minutes for a full revival, for Manchester United's Wayne Rooney to stub a penalty kick wide as the bar erupts in a chant of "Hair plugs!" and the Irish bartender roars the length of the bar, middle finger held aloft at the Manchester United fans.

And then in the second half Manchester United scores again, and young Jack Wilshere gets a red card. Even though they stick it out to the bitter end, at 7:30 a.m. the Bay Area Gooners file slowly out of the pub with an entire day yawning ahead of them. Already the headlines are filtering in from the UK papers. Steve McManaman, the ESPN color analyst and former Liverpool man who is utterly loathed and frequently catcalled by the Arsenal supporters, has called this "the worst Arsenal team I've ever seen." Over the next few weeks Arsenal's inconsistent play will be the stuff of a great many column inches. Good luck, the journalists seem to be saying, trying to make any predictions about *this* group of Gunners.

Mark Barbeau, for what I'm about to suggest is entirely that reason, remains unfazed. He will be back next week for the game against Fulham, and he will still be wearing his Arsenal jersey with 415—the San Francisco telephone area code—on the back.

"The amount of time I mourn has changed," Mark said as he was cleaning up the remains of a box of doughnuts marked FOR GOONERS.

"I will go on and do other things today," he said, "and possibly enjoy them."

EVER SINCE CHARLES DARWIN SUGGESTED THAT ALL LIFE evolves by natural selection, scientists have tried to figure out humans' place in the scheme of things. Is there anything that truly separates us from other animals? Darwin proposed that man alone had the ability to think and to reason. But then people noticed that of course some animals certainly appeared to reason, or to do something approximating it. In 1898 Columbia psychologist Edward Thorndike showed that if you put a cat in a latched box, the cat would eventually figure out how to manipulate the latch and spring out. If you put the cat back in the box, next time it would escape much more quickly. The cat was learning, maybe not in the human sense, but it did imply that the cat was equipped by nature with a set of reflexes that would allow it to respond to its environment in increasingly efficient ways. Behavioral scientists like the Russian Gregor Pavlov— whose experiments with salivating dogs have forever linked him with canines—then suggested that it might be merely the same in humans. What appeared like special human reasoning could just be our natural reflexes teaching us to respond more efficiently to the environment. All behavior, Pavlov's famous experiments suggested, could be reduced to stimulus response.*

In the 1950s an American psychologist named B. F. Skinner tried to figure out this reward thing once and for all with a new series of experiments on rats and pigeons.

Skinner advanced the idea of Pavlovian-style reinforcement with a twist. Pavlov's dogs didn't have to do anything to get fed. Skinner wanted his creatures to perform. Behavior that got a reward was said to be "reinforced," and eventually through enough reinforcement that behavior would become habit. Skinner wanted pigeons, for example, to lift their heads above a certain line in their box. As soon as they did, they'd receive a food reward. He found a standard learning curve among the pigeons—that not only could you make them repeatedly raise their heads, but you could then make them raise them higher and higher by changing the way the rewards were doled out. He extrapolated to human behavior: the environment constantly shapes humans, Skinner wrote, so that almost everything we do is actually some-

---

*In 2009, to take one example, Rui Oliveira's lab published a paper showing that you can reproduce the fighting-fish testosterone increase through classical conditioning. The fish "learned" to increase their testosterone whenever a light was turned on.

thing that has been reinforced. "The environment," he wrote, "builds the basic repertoire with which we keep our balance, walk, play games, handle instruments and tools, talk, write, sail a boat, drive a car, or fly a plane."

He labeled this learning process operant conditioning— an operant being the behavior and conditioning being the pattern of rewards for it. In his 1953 book *Science and Human Behavior*, he compared the way operant conditioning shapes humans to the way a sculptor shapes clay: "Although at some point the sculptor seems to have produced an entirely novel object, we can always follow the process back to the original undifferentiated lump, and we can make the successive stages by which we return to this condition as small as we wish."

Skinner didn't actually know *why* a reward would act as reinforcement—the discovery of the brain's reward centers and concepts like prediction error came decades after his death. But some of it appears to be right, particularly the aspects of behavior that still seem to explain gambling addictions and sports fans.

What Skinner did particularly in his experiments was play around with the regularity of the reward and the constancy of the behavior. How quickly, he wondered, would an animal *stop* doing something it had previously been rewarded for? He called it "operant extinction" when a behavior seemed to become completely unlearned, and noted that in humans such extinctions could take years. Any parent will be familiar with the concept of "extinction": it's the goal when you leave your child to cry it out at night. How easy or difficult that is depends in part on personality and in part on previous rewards.

Behaviors that children are rewarded for can pop up decades later, Skinner noted. But in more mundane life, it's usually pretty quick. "If food is withheld, the pigeon will eventually stop lifting its head," he wrote. "If we get no answer to telephone calls, we eventually stop telephoning. If our piano goes out of tune, we gradually play it less and less. If our radio becomes noisy or if programs become worse, we stop listening."

Skinner, not a sports fan, didn't fill in the obvious blank. Here it is:

If our sports teams stop winning, we _____.

We what? Well, some people do stop going . . . eventually. But many more—the Todd Derys of the world—do not. Attendance was down among the Bay Area Gooners the week after the Manchester United game, but not dramatically, and not even unexpectedly for a game against far-less-interesting Fulham. No reasonable sports fan would give up on his or her team after a single, albeit painful, loss.

Here's where Skinner has something quite relevant to add. How quickly the operant goes extinct depends a great deal on the schedule of the reinforcement. If you give the pigeon a reward every time it lifts it head, and then it lifts its head and doesn't get a reward, it will first display a typical sports fan response, Skinner wrote, flapping its wings and turning away in "a reaction commonly spoken of as frustration or rage." But then if it doesn't get its reward the next time, it'll just stop. The pigeon will essentially think, "Okay, we're all done here. Game's over, time to move on to something else."

But if you reward the pigeon only occasionally and unpredictably, it will take it much, much longer to stop chasing the reward after the reward stops arriving. The pigeon is worse off than Mike Silver chasing and not receiving Cal glory for decades. The pigeon is worse off than the Cleveland fans chasing and not receiving fulfillment. In fact, Skinner reported, a pigeon conditioned to lift its head for an intermittent reward might continue to lift its head *ten thousand times* without a reward before it gives up. To whatever extent the environment shapes us—and that's still an open question—it appears that very deep in our nature and very deep in the nature of sports is the power that makes us stay.

THREE WEEKS INTO JOINING UP WITH THE ARSENAL SUPPORTERS, I realize that whatever has been making them stick around recently, it isn't the reward of consistently well-played games. Arsenal has won one of its last five games, a dull 1–0 victory over QPR. They've lost alarmingly to Norwich City, dispiritingly to Manchester United, and tied twice—both times blowing a 2–0 lead. It's no way to head into maybe the most important home game of the year, against arch-archrival Tottenham, in a game that requires the Bay Area Gooners to be at the bar by 4:45 a.m.

And yet: there they are. More of them than have been there in weeks, in fact, forty or fifty by kickoff with more filling in by the minute. By the start they are chanting, "Come on, Arsenal, come on, Arsenal," loudly enough that there's some feeling of real emotion around this game. Mark sits, hands in his lap, watching, then jumps up to greet newcomers shuffling in from the rainy darkness outside, then returns to the chair in a restless loop.

It looks at first like a repeat of the Man United game.

Emmanuel Adebayor, a former Arsenal player who left for greener pastures, scores a big goal early off a horrendous defensive misplay. The back line looks tremulous. As before, the goal goes almost unremarked: there's no outpouring of emotion, just the quiet sinking in of an idea that it's so early in the morning for things to turn so negative. Traversing the bar, Mark pauses, mouth agape, to look at the television.

But Adebayor was maybe a little too excited. He flies in recklessly for a tackle just moments later and receives a straight red card as the Bay Area Gooners cheer happily and someone yells, "See ya, asshole!" It takes only six minutes for Arsenal to tie the game, on a header from the gigantic German Per Mertesacker, which sets off a delirious chorus of (to the tune of "Guantanamera") "We've got a German . . . a big fucking German!" An expat Englishman who now coaches soccer in the Bay Area observes drily, "It's so interesting to see Americans singing English songs."

Then a few minutes later Arsenal scores again, and Mark leaps out of his seat, arms raised in a victory V, singing drunkenly-without-a-drop-of-alcohol at 5:30 a.m., "Arsenal, the greatest club the world has ever seen!" and from then on it's a long happy coast to victory. People in the bar now speak freely of rubbing it in, running up the score. "I want destruction," one die-hard Gooner says. "I want humiliation."

Even McManaman, the television guy, is less hated now as he says that Tottenham looks utterly shell-shocked, for which there is a cheer. The morning wears on with ringing enthusiasm and much more singing, and at the end everyone leaves happy, triumphant 5–2 winners. After a month of inconsistency the sun is shining in the proper part of North London, if still not quite in the watery morning light of San

Francisco, and for the Bay Area Gooners it's all the confirmation they need. They'll be back next week before the dawn, because here's the reward for a not-quite-top-flight team, and it might be the biggest reward all year, but the reward and the memory are motivation enough to make Arsenal loyalty easy, restore it for the Gooners to its proper place among the list of "things I enjoy about myself and others."

Soccer and Arsenal loyalty, Mark says, has unlocked for him a global, universal culture. Those fanatics are everywhere in every country and his joining in allows him to move anywhere, to talk to anyone. He has friends in North London and Arsenal buddies who've flitted through the Bay Area Gooners and taken a "frequent Gooner card" with them back to their homes in far-flung corners of the globe.

We were chatting at halftime of a game once and he told me the story of when it all really sunk in for him. Arsenal had just lost the 2006 Champions League Final to Barcelona, although it had been an incredible game and Arsenal had fought valiantly against overwhelming circumstance. Mark was walking down a San Francisco street in his Arsenal jersey, his head down, his thoughts lingering in the Stade de France in Paris. He looked up and saw a kid walking the other way. "I'm a white guy in my forties, this was a black kid in his twenties in a Thierry Henry shirt," Mark says. Their worlds, so different in every respect, collided for the briefest of moments on the sidewalk.

"He just pats me on the shoulder," Mark said, "and says, 'You okay, man?'"

Mark said, "I'm hanging in there."

"I know, man," the kid said, and walked away.

"That," Mark says, returning to the present and waving

his arm around as if to wrap up the dozens of fellow Gooners, "is what this is all about."

Mark loves the Arsenal Football Club. Kola Shobo described the loyalty to the club as "life." Both benefit from the inconsistent rewards of sports; neither is an addict in the sense we've talked about. And both, when I asked them why they were at a bar two hours before sunrise to watch a team playing live from England, answered by pointing around the room. The game might be global, but the glue is local, they seemed to say. The Arsenal eleven matter, but belonging to a group of like-minded supporters: now there's a reward.

As individuals, we choose to be fans. Only rarely is the power of sports so strong that we are robbed of that choice, and only rarely is the personal consequence deleterious enough to cause worry. But being an individual supporter is only one small part of the sports fan experience, and for many it's an insignificant part. When those individuals turn into groups, and when those groups turn into crowds, individual over-attachment to the game seems to become the least of our societal worries.

PART THREE
Consequence

7
Behavior:
Who Are Those Guys?

I MET WILL LEITCH AT FOLEY'S IN NEW YORK CITY ABOUT twenty minutes before the start of Game One of the 2011 World Series. The game featured the St. Louis Cardinals and the Texas Rangers, and to say that the Cardinals were a surprise addition to the party was an understatement: they'd had to rely on the Atlanta Braves pulling one of the greatest collapses of all time, down to the very last pitch of the regular season, just to squeeze into the playoffs. Somehow the Cardinals had then caught fire through two playoff series, but still, come on. No one confused them with a good team. ESPN had twenty-six experts predict the World Series; only four of them thought the Cardinals could win it.

Leitch, a writer and founder of the popular sports site *Deadspin*, was the whirlwind at the center of about one hundred St. Louis Cardinals fans in varying stages of redness. He stood out (sartorially) for having instead chosen to rock blue: a navy blazer, a faded-to-pewter Cardinals hat, and a maroon-and-navy diagonally striped Cardinals tie. "I needed to go with the power move today," he said. (For the record, the number of other ties I observed in the room: zero.)

He then spent most of the evening tweeting about how he was fairly certain he was going to die from some sports fan nervous-stress-asphyxiation syndrome. He was the first person I've ever met who I worried was going to be strangled by his own St. Louis Cardinals tie, the poetry of which, tragic as it would be, I'm guessing really appeals to him.

Leitch is one of my personal heroes for a variety of reasons having mainly to do with the sheer volume of mail he gets from readers calling him an oversensitive weenie. (Again, I mean, a St. Louis Cardinals tie. Come on.) Being an oversensitive weenie myself and liking sports anyway, I identify. Along these lines, my favorite essay of his comes from his book *God Save the Fan*, and is about advertising. Basically, he says, advertisers have a low opinion of sports fans. They do not, let's say, picture sports fans as the kinds of guys who wear blazers and ties to bars. The title of the chapter is, "Coors Light Thinks You're a Monster," and the essence is that if you need proof, just look at how they portray sports fans:

> Look at any commercial that attempts to show what average sports fans are like. Inevitably, they're a group of screaming lunatics, usually shirtless, with their faces painted, yelling whooping noises. I do not deny that these sad genetic anomalies do exist, and they usually do end up with cameras in their face. . . . But this is not the typical sports fan. Is this what they really think of you?

I had always seen those ads as isolating, a kind of proof that not having many male sports fan friends had just insulated me from authentic fan culture. I took never having met a person like in the advertisements as proof of my aloneness in the universe. So when I first read that, I e-mailed Leitch to ask: How do you know that it's not *you* that's different? Why are you so confident?

"I'll just say this," he wrote back. "I've literally never met a single sports fan that's like that. Actually, that's not true: I've seen them at football games. (And only football games.) But almost every other sports fan I have ever met is a professional human being who is able to pay their bills and live their lives and use sports as a diversion that's put in the proper perspective. I think, in the same way that people see the ugliest signs at a political rally and make it look like everyone believes what the ugliest person believes. I also think that these people never actually meet any sports fans and therefore just respond to the ones they see on television, which, of course, only showcases the loudest and craziest."

I want to return to something that we've talked about on and off and look at it in a slightly different way. We talked about fans basing their identity on their sports team, extending their own selves and adopting the values of the team. We'll talk in the next two chapters about merging with a group of like-minded others to satisfy a deep human need for belonging. These are the fans who make the choice to let the hormones and mirror neurons take over every year—consciously or unconsciously—because there's deep meaning in being part of the enterprise. I'd like to consider now the social consequences of that choice. I'm less sanguine than Leitch about the mildness of sports fans, but I also have a hunch that most of my understanding of my fellow fans does come from ESPN and beer commercials. This chapter explores just how much that representation mirrors real life, and how people who call themselves sports fans behave collectively. Which means we can finally meet the intrepid group of researchers who call themselves sports fan psychologists.

DANIEL WANN, THE LEADING SPORTS FAN RESEARCHER IN North America, frowns over his putter as he stares down a two-foot putt to defend—for the eighth straight year—his Sports Psychology Forum miniature golf championship. The playoff hole at Southern Lanes in Bowling Green, Kentucky, hole number twelve, is cross-shaped, about thirty feet end to end. The hole is at the top of the cross, and a shallow patch of blue Astroturf lies at each end, ready to catch balls that deflect off a set of wood blocks where the cross meets. Wann's nearest competitor, who happens to be me, has fallen into the hazard because he is only borderline competent at causing a golf ball to travel in a straight line. Wann just needs a tap for the win.

He approaches the blue golf ball, then backs away. He approaches again and, without a practice swing, cleanly knocks the ball into the hole. The rattle of the ball settling into the cup sends Wann into a putter-jabbering frenzy.

"Winner winner chicken dinner!" he declares to several of his graduate students and about a dozen professional colleagues. He does a shimmy dance off the edge of the green, waving the putter in the toreador style of Chi Chi Rodriguez.

"It was almost worth it just to see that," one of the grad students says.

Most of the researchers we've met so far don't study sports fans—in fact, most of them aren't really even interested in sports fans. Who then points their magnifying glass at sports fans directly, and what do they have to tell us about what sports fans do? Can they offer any guidance in figuring out how closely the monsters of Coors Light's imagination approximate reality?

Fans are not exactly a hot topic in modern psychological research. There is no money in it, for one thing, which mainly limits the research to teachers at small liberal arts colleges where teaching is the priority. There's little glamour in it, both because of the money and also because (this might be more important) most people think it's silly.

"Who's going to give me a grant?" Wann said to me once. "*I* wouldn't give me a grant! I'm not devaluing what I do, but if you're doing research on curing breast cancer, and I'm doing research on why some Cubs fans cry and some don't . . ."

Wann's not frustrated that he's not leading his own sports fan lab at a big-name research university; he never wanted that. He teaches in a department that he likes and studies something he finds fascinating. There are an awful lot of sports fans in the world, and there's still something wonderful in revealing the mystery of our collective behavior. "I'll say this," Wann said. "As a research topic, it's a really good one. Because people *care*."

There's also a stereotype that may or may not be true that academics don't much like sports. Many sociologists and psychologists who've looked at sports fans have gone in with critical assumptions about sports being a waste of time, and about fans being terrible people, and unsurprisingly advanced theories to justify their foregone conclusions. Wann likes to repeat a joke floating around his world that until he came along, everyone liked sports except for the people who studied it.

There's one more thing that constrains direct sports fan research: the methods researchers like Wann use, which mainly involve asking people why they do things, are out of fashion. The major theme of modern behavioral science seems to be to find ways that humans are tricking themselves into doing things—fMRI results that betray your brain's real intentions, saliva tests that show hormonal changes lurking when you're unaware, genes that program you to act a certain way. These are the hot, expensive, big-university trends. The idea of asking one hundred undergraduate psychology students to fill out a questionnaire revealing what they're doing, and why, and then building a research paper around it, feels almost quaint.

The result is that the list of dedicated, experimental sports fan researchers is tiny, and fairly well dominated by the man now standing in front of me in blue jeans, tennis shoes, and a Murray State sweatshirt, waving a putter at the rest of his professional field.

"I think Daniel Wann stands on top of the heap," says Wann's colleague Merrill Melnick, a now-retired sports sociologist from the State University of New York at Brockport. "I think when you spoke to him you were talking to the number one researcher in North America."

About a decade ago, Wann and his friend and colleague Rick Grieve, a clinical psychologist at Western Kentucky University who also does occasional sports fan research, decided it might be useful to get together once a year to share notes with any other researchers working in the same area. Grieve informally hosts both the Sports Psychology Forum and the miniature golf competition, which Wann (still) has never lost.

The night before the actual conference and research presentations, the major players in sports fan psychology meet up for dinner, putt-putt golf, and gossip. One laugh at dinner—at a Ryan's buffet just off the highway in Bowling Green—was that people would have to present without citing Wann's most influential work, a 1993 paper that offered the world of science a way to measure how much a sports fan cared about his or her team. The lecture, one colleague joked, would consist essentially of "uhs" and "ands."

THE SPORT SPECTATOR IDENTIFICATION SCALE IS A SEVEN-question test for sports fans to measure their loyalty to their favorite team. First published in the *International Journal of Sports Psychology*, each question has a range from 1 to 8, and you add up all your scores to assess your dedication. If your score comes in under 18, you're hardly justified in calling yourself a fan; if it comes in above 35, you're seriously invested.* From the level of investment, you can then make further conclusions about how people are likely to behave in the face of wins, losses, and life events.

This table (see next page) exemplifies why Daniel Wann is a leading sports fan psychologist. He has spent twenty-five years attaching numbers to things like spectator identification, and because he's generally been the first—and often only—one to do it, he's made a significant name for himself. Marketers and pro sports franchises call him regularly

---

*For what it's worth, my scores for my local teams are: Cal football, 43; San Jose Sharks hockey, 42; Oakland A's, 25. I tend to score high on importance of winning, dislike of rivals, and degree of attention, and low on wearing team gear and perception of others.

The Sport Spectator Identification Scale

Please list your favorite sport team.

_____

Now answer each of the following questions with this team in mind by circling the most accurate number (i.e., response) to each item.

1. How important is it to you that the team listed above wins?

Not important   1   2   3   4   5   6   7   8   Very Important

2. How strongly do you see yourself as a fan of the team listed above?

Not at All a Fan   1   2   3   4   5   6   7   8   Very Much a Fan

3. How strongly do your friends see you as a fan of the team listed above?

Not at All a Fan   1   2   3   4   5   6   7   8   Very Much a Fan

4. During the season, how closely do you follow the team listed above via ANY of the following: in person or on television, on the radio, or televised news or a newspaper?

Never   1   2   3   4   5   6   7   8   Almost Every Day

5. How important is being a fan of the team listed above to you?

Not Important   1   2   3   4   5   6   7   8   Very Important

6. How much do you dislike the greatest rivals of the team listed above?

Do Not Dislike   1   2   3   4   5   6   7   8   Dislike Very Much

7. How often do you display the above team's name or insignia at your place of work, where you live, or on your clothing?

Never   1   2   3   4   5   6   7   8   Always

From the article "Sports Fans: Measuring Degree of Identification with Their Team" in the *International Journal of Sports Psychology.*

to ask for his opinion: how to get fans to come to games, why fans come to games, what makes fans buy a jersey, what makes fans likely to come back despite team failure. (This question probably came from the management of one of my teams.) Researchers who want to study sports fans and need a quick, reliable test to determine how much the fan cares use it—if you're into psychology lingo, it's the sports fan equivalent of the right-wing authoritarian scale. The SSIS, Wann says, has been translated into fifteen languages and used in maybe three hundred studies.

WANN'S WORK IS BASICALLY BEHAVIORAL DESCRIPTION. AND AS you might guess, it has the most practical application to marketers and sports teams. If the makers of advertisements for Coors Light or Miller Lite—the ones that Will Leitch says think you're a monster—wanted to understand what fans do and why they say they do it, Wann is the man to talk to.

Of course advertising to a certain demographic doesn't have anything to do with accurately reflecting it. If you watch beer and truck commercials, though—and by virtue of my sports fandom I do, by the thousands—there is nonetheless a fairly remarkable consistency across brands about the essential makeup of guys. Probably nothing exemplifies this more than Miller Lite, which in 2008 even ran its own series of "Man Law" ads—featuring a council of men debating the rules that men should live by. "They are true men," Miller Brewing's marketing vice president told the *New York Times*. "They all have a lot of substance."*The sixteen men on the imaginary

---

*The headline on this article: "Beer Ads That Ditch the Bikinis, but Add Threads of Thought."

Man Law council included seven sports figures—a boxer, a motocross racer, two football players, a football coach, a wrestler, and a pro rodeo champion—and seven famously manly actors, such as the council's leader, Burt Reynolds. The intellectual leader appeared to be the Carnegie Mellon graduate mountaineer who cut his own arm off to escape a boulder. Clearly the company had sought out the full spectrum of American men to tap into the universal truths of manhood. The marketing VP also told the *Times* that the ads were in response to previous ads that were sexist, and that now they were going to move beyond stereotypes of men as "sophomoric" or "lowest common denominator."

Truths included:

- It's okay to leave your bros to hang out with your girlfriend, but only if she's hot.
- It's probably not okay for men to drive hybrids.
- Wives and girlfriends cannot store anything other than beer in the garage fridge.
- Men cannot leave a game early and cannot bake on game day.

You'll hear this kind of stuff a lot. A recent Weight Watchers for Men commercial shows a regular dude confidently saying, "I think when you make things more complicated, especially for men, we're like, I'm done," while it shows math equations on a chalkboard behind him because, as is widely known, hard stuff like math and science is for girls. Truck commercials show a truck climbing up a giant ramp that has been set on fire in the middle of the desert because this is a real situation regularly faced by men and it would be the height of humiliation to have your truck fail you when hauling ten thousand pounds up a flaming corkscrew ramp in the middle of the Mojave Desert. The Miller Lite commercial where the attractive date says "I love you" and the guy says "I lo-lo-lo-lo" and then the waitress walks by and asks if he'd like a Miller Lite and he says "I'd love one," because obviously men aren't capable of emotion except when sports and light beer are involved. The Bud Light commercial where the women are starting a book club and the guy is about to go off to softball, but then he sees the women have Bud Light for their book club (this is one of those suspend-your-disbelief type of ads) and decides to stay, and reclines on the couch between two women who are shrewishly talking about emotions in the book, and smiling at the silent hot girl he says, "I'd like to see you read some words." Then the rest of the softball team shows up and an attractive book club member asks one enterprising Neanderthal, "So do you like *Little Women*?" and he says, while scratching himself, "Ah, I'm not too picky."

Look, these are silly and we know it. But when you see them thousands and thousands of times, and see the same theme over and over, it has to have some effect on your perception of reality. I know it's affected mine.

So is this real life? These emotionally stunted, math-and-reading-are-hard, I-use-my-truck-to-punch-deer-in-the-face kinds of guys are mainly what you'll find hulking out there, and the ads are just holding up the mirror for them? I took the question to Sean McGrath, then a senior vice president at the Chicago advertising agency Draftfcb, whose job for the last seven years had been to sell Coors Light and Miller Lite.

"We're always attempting to ground it in as precise a reality as possible," he said.

McGrath and I met in his Spartan office on the twentieth floor of Draftfcb's Chicago tower, down the hall from a row of cubes bedecked with Miller Lite swag and featuring a splendid view south down Ontario Street. McGrath looked like a mellowed-out version of one of his target audience "guys" (and in conversation, it's always "guys"): fit, classic Midwestern looks, maybe early forties, in fashionable-but-not-overly-so jeans and a black sweater vest. Those "guys" that MillerCoors and Draftfcb focus test their ads on, McGrath says, "they have a view of what it means to be a guy. With some of the work we're doing now, it's about reflecting that view."

McGrath cited one Coors Light ad that he'd helped with years before, when the company was advertising the "Silver Bullet" with a series of commercials showing a Coors Light train whooshing through a hot place to deliver icy refreshment. This particular ad showed a football stadium, and two rival fans in the standard face paint and team jersey getup, and the fans receive their beer from the Coors Light train and everyone's happy and dancing and the two fans reach across the aisle and are about to bump fists when they realize, wait a minute, what am I doing? So then they don't bump fists after all. That, McGrath said, is the kind of authenticity that doesn't just reflect real life—it sells. It makes people think more positively about the product.

"Is that idealized, exaggerated—probably," he said. "But there's a truth in it. That's what we're looking for. We're looking for little moments of truth. When a consumer sees a message, they don't just see somebody pandering to them or leveraging sports, pillaging sports to sell a product. They see just a bit of truth that connects. That makes it authentic. That makes them look at it differently."

The ads seemed to be working; when we spoke Coors Light had recently passed Budweiser as the number two beer in America—although global markets help Budweiser keep an overall sales edge. But in the larger American market the picture is less rosy: light beers in particular are losing their market to wine, craft beer, and harder stuff. Mass-market American lager-makers have responded by retrenching to their core market: young men. Sports fans.

McGrath and I talked about a wider trend, not just in advertising but in Judd Apatow movies and TV shows, of young men playing the role of the slacking Neanderthal. A lot of that, McGrath said, was pushback against the "metrosexual" trend of the early 2000s, this idea that even as magazine covers and television showed guys increasingly concerned about their hair and skin and clothing, the true light beer consumer didn't want to, McGrath said, "fall in line." In talking to its regular drinkers the marketers realized that these guys didn't want to be "manatees"—not, McGrath added, that there was anything wrong with that. He didn't see his guys ever being critical of other guys or their choices, and it was important to reflect that in the ads. As an advertiser, he said, you're not leading behavior, not trying to change the way people act. You're just asking a lot of questions and unearthing the true spirit of your target audience. There wasn't much science to it, he said, just a lot of observation and a bit of fortunate prediction that this metrosexual thing wouldn't pan out. You've seen that prediction come true now, he said, in all kinds of places.

"You look at brands like Old Spice, and even Axe, playing to a younger audience, but those are ads that get back to the primitive nature of guys," McGrath said. "There's truth in that."

IN *SPORT FANS: THE PSYCHOLOGY AND SOCIAL IMPACT OF Spectators*, Dan Wann wrote that it appears that everyone likes sports except the social scientists who comment on it. He quoted G. E. Howard's 1912 book *Social Psychology of the Spectator*, "A singular example of mental perversion, an absurd and immoral custom tenaciously held fast in mob-mind, has its genesis in the partisan zeal of athletic spectator-crowds. I refer to the practice of organized cheering, known in college argot as 'rooting.' From every aspect it is bad."

Detractors in the social sciences, Wann wrote, have crystallized around four main criticisms: sports fans are lazy, sports fans are aggressive, sports fans copy the worst behaviors of athletes and athletic institutions (such as sexism, racism, and homophobia), sports fans are bad at relationships. Marketers certainly seemed to read from that playbook; from the Man Laws on down, everything seems set up to confirm that men, and particularly beer-drinking sports fan men, are lazy, belligerent, homophobic, sexist, and uninterested in women unless they're sufficiently hot.

The problem, Wann wrote in his book, is that there's really no evidence that any of that is true. Some of these, after all, are testable hypotheses, even the kind of testable hypotheses that a survey of a few hundred undergraduates could reasonably address.

Four questions, and Wann tries to provide four answers. On laziness, Wann says, you can look at two lines of evidence: how likely sports fans are to play sports themselves, and how well sports fans do in college. On both matters the surveyed undergraduates were more active than their non-fan peers: more likely to play sports, higher GPAs, more involvement with the university, more likely to believe they will graduate college.

On aggression, there's little question (remember the testosterone!) that sports can make fans aggressive. But there's no evidence, Wann says, that fans as a group are any more naturally aggressive than anyone else. And while it's a valid criticism that sports can incite fan violence, such instances are actually quite rare.

On the "negative values and maladaptive behaviors" score, there's no strong evidence either way. Except, Wann says—there is irony here—that he's done a bit of work looking into sports fans and alcohol and tobacco consumption. He's never found any kind of connection at all. Sports fans seem like they drink and smoke just as much as everyone else.

Which leaves "bad at relationships." Despite, Wann says, the evidence of a book called *Not Now, Honey, I'm Watching the Game* by Kevin Quirk, sports fans don't appear to be any worse at relationships than anyone else. In one survey—not of undergraduates, this time—a team of researchers interviewed four hundred married adults living in San Francisco and Indianapolis. "Televised sports appears to play a generally positive albeit small role in marital life," the authors wrote in a paper published in 1995 in the *Sociology of Sport Journal*. "TV sports viewing often is a shared activity and does not appear to trigger many scheduling or

TV viewing conflicts. And, when such conflicts occur, they appear to be resolved amicably and easily."

I'M NOT SURE WANN'S METHODOLOGY IS STRONG ENOUGH TO blithely dismiss any of the criticisms. (Nor is he—in his book and in talking to him in person, he mainly just calls for more research.) But like Leitch, I've also never really met any of these people in real life. Which was why when I did meet Will, it was a kind of fascinating experience, because the entire scene looked like a beer commercial. We were in a Manhattan bar bedecked with baseball nostalgia. Expat Midwesterners in Cardinals gear sat cheek by jowl at a long table running down the middle of the room, discovering (except in my case) that they had some childhood memory in common—a school, a restaurant, a special occasion when they met Stan Musial. "I can't believe the World Series is being held at Busch Stadium," one guy muttered in wonder, and there was a kind of awed round of murmured assent. It was everything a Man Law council would associate with sports, right down to the centerpiece: on each table was a metal beach pail packed to the brim with bottled Bud Light.

So we sat there with our beers and the St. Louis guys yelled at the TV and we looked like an advertisement. When they introduced the starting lineup, Leitch noticed me observing mildly and bounded over from across the room to yell, "Eric! You're with us now—if you're going to be a non-Cards fan at this table, you'd better be more enthusiastic than that!" Later, referencing my intention to fly back to San Francisco the next morning, he added, "If they win this game you can't get on that flight tomorrow. But if you

betray us"—it hung there for a second—"you're never coming back here again." Man Law!

We were a perfect advertising case study—except for our
between-innings chatter. The stranger to my right turned out
to be Scott, a wedding photographer. (There were no wedding photographers on the Man Law council.) Scott and I
chatted for a while, since it was his debut appearance at the
Cardinals bar and he was kind of meeting the regulars for
the first time, too. The regulars across from us, Evan and
Jason, were similar type guys: pleasant, polite, professional.
None of them were scared to mention their families. We
talked about the move from St. Louis to New York—I was
curious how much the group experience in the bar made
them homesick or was a way to kind of stave off homesick-
ness—and they all said there were things they missed about
the Midwest, sure, but New York City was pretty awesome.
"When I first moved out here after college it was like, I'll be
back in St. Louis in a year," Evan told me. It had now, he
said, been five.

At some point I wandered over to Leitch. Why, I asked
him, was this rabid sports fan who once wrote an entire book
about going to a Cardinals game with his father watching
Game One of the World Series from some Cardinals bar in
New York City instead of at Busch Stadium with his dad?
Because, he replied, he and his wife were expecting a kid in
a few weeks and he wanted to stay close to home. It was
almost like he had, you know, prioritized his family over his
favorite team. It was not, to be very clear, that his wife made
him. "I don't want," he said, "to be a plane flight away."

My guess, like Will's guess, is that even the most apparently rabid fans who make that choice to re-up their fan-

dom every year, who are proud to make the choice to submit to the hormone-and-mirroring experience—even those guys know how to adjust the limits of the experience. Many of us are obsessives, but few of us are addicts because we still retain and exercise the power of choice. There's never anything uncomplicated about priorities—non-sports-fans deal with work-life-family balance, too. Sports fans perhaps just get dinged by social scientists because the choice they make to spend their time watching sports appears incomprehensible if you've never made it before.

WHILE I WAS IN KENTUCKY I THOUGHT I'D TRY TO ALSO VISIT Wann in his natural environment. On a crackling spring morning I drove the Jefferson Davis Memorial Highway to Murray, Kentucky, home to Murray State (Go Racers) and what is the only undergraduate sports fan psychology class I was able to find anywhere.

The Murray State campus fairly well dominates the town. The "M" on the bleachers in the football stadium is visible from the main highway, and pretty much every business with a marquee had "Go Racers" on it.

I met Wann in the psychology building, a red-brick-white-column sort of thing that needed ivy. His office, in a corner with a view of the lawn behind the building, looked professorial: lined on one side with bookshelves, overflowing with knickknacks from two decades of sports fan research. A DO NOT KNOCK AND DO NOT ENTER, TESTING IN PROGRESS sign hung over his computer, flanked by posters from Murray State's basketball glory years.

We went to lunch in town, where Wann cheerfully instructed me on the finer points of ordering in a Southern restaurant. He's more Midwest than South, and every once in a while a twang flits into his speech, a kind of mellow long "I" that would suddenly remind my ears of how far we'd come from home. "You just can't hardly go wrong with anything here," he said, after particularly recommending the dumplings.

A major research area for Wann has been motivation, and over unsweet tea with lemon, rolls, and dumplings, we talked about why people go to games. There are a ton of reasons, of course, and they're not mutually exclusive. But using a twenty-three-part questionnaire, Wann has narrowed it down to eight of them that seem to cover almost all sports fans.

Here they are, ranked in order of commonness in four studies conducted by Wann and colleagues: entertainment, eustress, group affiliation, self-esteem, aesthetic, escape, family, economic interest. So far this book has talked mainly about individuals—about our hormones, our mirror neurons, our relationships—and almost all of the individual stuff falls under the self-esteem, entertainment, and aesthetic motivations. When your team wins, your self-esteem goes up. Entertainment and aesthetic are obvious; the fan likes the grace and artistry of sports. Group affiliation and family are similar—you watch or go to games because you like to hang out with other people. (In Wann's questionnaire, essentially the only thing separating those two motives is whether you like those others to be family members or not.) That's where we're headed next. Eustress is interesting: it's the idea that fans need the emotional rush of sports because we have to have a release valve. Economic interest surprised me as the last item on

Wann's list: it's never been an interest of mine, but given the seemingly enormous popularity of NCAA March Madness office pools, Super Bowl prop bets, and sportswriters writing wink-wink Vegas columns, I would have thought Wann would have found that one higher on the list. I was also surprised at how far down escape rated, since some observers give it as the sole motivation to watch sports. Will Leitch concludes *God Save the Fan* with this paragraph:

> It's a fundamental concept: Sports *do not matter*. The average fan understands this . . . and that is why we put sports in its proper place: as something we partake in and enjoy because we want to escape from our jobs, our bills, our responsibilities, our *lives*. The world is a terrifying place, with grays, complexities and confusion at every turn. Sports afford us none of this: If our team wins, we are happy; if they lose, we are sad. It doesn't have to be more than that. That simplicity is enough. It's plenty. Yet at every turn, someone's trying to convince us that sports are something *more* than sports. But just because Lance Armstrong overcame cancer and we wear his bracelets doesn't mean sports *means* anything. Life is hard. Sports are where we go to hide.

Which, to me, is pretty much wrong. There's a premise there that we all want to escape real life, and given his work showing that fans actually don't have nasty brutish home lives, I asked Wann about that idea. I mostly like my life, I said, I don't want to escape from it. Why would I want to escape my lovely wife at the table at a four-star meal in an atmospheric San Francisco restaurant so I can hide in the bathroom waiting for sports scores to load on my iPhone and then growing irritable when they appear?

"It's 'cause your teams suck," Wann interrupted. "Actually it's the anti-escape for you. 'My life is good. The worst part of my life? The teams!'"

Wann likes to do this thing where he quotes imaginary others talking to him, then responds. Here's his dialogue between another person and himself.

DAN WANN'S IMAGINARY FRIEND: Do you like baseball?
DAN WANN: Yeah! Well now, hang on. [*Pauses, considers the two teams he's a fan of, the Royals and Cubs.*] I like *baseball*. Do I like Major League Baseball?

Wann has a story about this. He proposed to his wife on October 27, 1985, the night of Game Seven of the 1985 World Series. His beloved Royals were in the Series that year playing the Cardinals.

"My wife, she swears—*and she's right!*—that if they'd lost that Game Seven, I wouldn't have asked her to marry me," Wann said, his normally measured voice rising a bit.

"Now, I would have eventually, you know," he added. "Unless I was waiting for a playoff victory because that's the last playoff they were in back in 'eighty-five. But if they'd lost, it would have been such a downer."

He slipped back into dialogue.

DAN WANN'S IMAGINARY FRIEND: Tell me about the night you got engaged!
DAN WANN: Yeah, it was one of the worst nights of my life.
DWIF: Why?
DW: 'Cause the Royals lost the World Series, you know.

That, he says, is why he's here. When he was in graduate school at Kansas, in the social psychology PhD program, he was sent out on an early assignment to talk to everybody else about their research. And what Wann remembers is that they were all miserable. "Everybody I'd go talk to would say the same thing: 'My research is terrible, it's boring, I don't like it,'" he says. "I was like, 'I'd better pick something I like.'"

So he just thought, well, sports fans. He wanted to know why he cared. Even when he interviewed at Murray State, he still wasn't thinking of making a career of it, though. He'd always intended to teach at a small liberal arts college—like the two small Kansas universities he'd attended, Baker as an undergrad and Emporia State for a master's—and Murray State, with ten thousand students, fit the description. But he was interested and kept dabbling in sports fan research on the side, and then he started to notice something. It was easy to publish stuff on sports fans. It was not easy to publish on anything else. His colleagues would tell him constantly about their struggles; Wann says he would reply, "You should do stuff on fans, because they're clamoring for it."

Twenty-one years later, he not only researches sports fans, he teaches about them. His undergraduate class is oriented around the book he coauthored several years ago, which is essentially just a compendium of research by Wann and others through the years. The class follows Wann's interest in looking not just at the psychology of fans but at their effect on society as a whole. The students who sign up for it aren't necessarily expecting to have to work, Wann says—most just think, "Hey, I like sports, why not"—but they soon find out he's serious about sports fans. "I think they imagine it's going to be sitting around talking about all those crazy Europeans," Wann says, as if the class was just Hooligan 101. (Wann calls the study of what he labels "dysfunctional fans" important but says they're such a small minority that it's also worth looking at the 99 percenters.) Students, he says, "don't imagine theological, sociological, scientific."

On the day I attended, this mostly meant watching Robert De Niro stalk Wesley Snipes in the 1996 movie *The Fan*. But this is an area where Wann and I agree entirely. The cool thing about sports fans is that it does take theological, sociological, and scientific explanation. Studying sports fans isn't just studying hooligans—although it can include them—it's studying human beings. Sports can be a kind of laboratory for exploring the way we're constructed and why we operate the way we do—"The way," Wann said, "something else in you is being played out."

THE GREAT BENEFIT TO WHAT WANN DOES IS TO PROVIDE THAT counternarrative to the idea of sports fans as Neanderthals. There's one insight that McGrath mentioned, though, that the evidence pretty much supports. I've withheld it until now because it's going to be the subject of the next two chapters. McGrath and I were talking about where, as an advertiser, you begin. I gave him a hypothetical: You have a new product that you think will be mainly used by men. You want to market it during the Super Bowl. What do you know about the people watching that you can reflect back at them?

"There are very few things, I think, that guys find universal," McGrath said. "There's music. There's certainly entertainment: movies. But there's something very tribal about guys, especially young guys, that I think sports feeds off of, that I think really isn't just a luxury, isn't just a passing interest. I think there's something inherent in guys that they need to gather and they need to have those moments of connection that operate very differently than women."

That insight, it seems to me, is another testable hypothesis.

8
Groups: Love the One You're With

NOVEMBER 5, 2011. THE DIABLO WIND GUSTS OUT OF THE east, dry, hot, uneasy. The air has scoured the great reaches of the basin deserts where it has had every drop of moisture ripped away until it rushes down Broadway Street in downtown Oakland with a hair-raising crackle. This is the wind that parches the grass on the brown East Bay hills and fans sparks into thunderous firestorms. The autumn wind, in a 1966 poem written by NFL Films president Steve Sabol, is a "raider, pillaging just for fun." Legend (so says Wikipedia) has it that when the Oakland Raiders boss Al Davis first heard the poem set to music, he swooned and declared it everything his team stood for. Ever since, "The Autumn Wind" has been a mainstay at the Oakland Coliseum and on Raider broadcasts.

The autumn wind whooshes as I exit the BART station. The first thing I see is a group of protesters blockading the nearby bank. Three days ago, on Wednesday night, something like one hundred thousand people occupied this block and then marched down the street to shut down the Port of Oakland. For several nights I've watched the news of tear gas, smoke bombs, and riot police. The bank still has boards up over its storefront; the city is on edge. The window-breaking and police-protester conflict has left downtown deserted except for the focused knot of thousands of occupiers camped out in Frank H. Ogawa Plaza, the police cordon around them, and the journalists between them.

Oh, yeah. And several hundred hard-core Oakland Raiders fans. The 2011 Oakland Raiders Fan Convention at the Oakland Marriott City Center was, you could say, guilty of bad timing, although I rather preferred to think of it as good timing in an apocalyptic sort of way. The end-time *would* be on a day when Oakland was on fire with Occupy protesters and in the grip of a dry desert heat, and Raiders fans from across the nation had congregated before the big Sunday rivalry game against the polarizingly faithful Tim Tebow and the Denver Broncos.

I have never trusted an east wind.

SO FAR IN THIS BOOK, WE HAVE MAINLY CONSIDERED INDIVIDUALS —in the presence of others sometimes, but individual reactions. Individual hormonal changes, individual brains, individual identities, and individual love. But what we've done so far is like considering carefully the gills and brain of an individual anchovy. No anchovy stands alone; in fact, you can't really understand the anchovy without analyzing the school it swims in. In humans it is a deep, evolutionary imperative to be social. The *Oxford English Dictionary* credits William Wollaston's 1722 book *The Religion of Nature Delineated* with the first definition of *social* to mean "living or disposed to living in companies or communities": "Man is a Social creature: that is, a single man, or family, cannot subsist or not well, alone out of all Society." In *The Descent of Man*, published a decade after the *Origin of Species*, Charles Darwin wrote that "with those animals which were benefited by living in close association, the individuals which took the greatest pleasure in society would best escape various dangers, while those that cared least for their comrades, and lived solitary, would perish in great numbers." Wilfred Trotter, an English sociologist writing in 1908, noted that the three primary instincts ascribed to humans—food, sex, self-preservation—didn't account for human behavior unless you threw in a fourth, which he called "gregariousness." "The conscious individual," Trotter wrote, "will feel an unanalysable primary sense of comfort in the actual presence of his fellows, and a similar sense of discomfort in their absence."

It's time now to consider our social behavior. This is probably the thing about sports fans that confuses nonfans the most, and that the beer ads know we behave tribally lets them reinforce the message. Hooliganism, victory riots, college kids painting letters on their chests to get on television: if you're on the outside looking in, you have to stop and wonder, *What the hell is wrong with these people?* in the same way I wonder that about myself when I feel rage or distress surging following a loss. For many fans the tribe appears to be more important than the competition, like Mike Silver and his damn-the-game-win-the-pre-party love of Cal fans. But Mike Silver married within the Cal tribe, found many of his best friends within the Cal tribe, and raised his children in the Cal tribe. The lonely sports fan in me wanted to know just how universal that part of us was. How much at a basic level do all people, not just the particularly group-oriented ones, see the world through the lens of their tribe? What good does group living do us? And the question I became most curious about: Where does our us-and-them group mind-set come from? Consider our noble savage ancestors, actually living in tribes hundreds of thousands of years ago in the time when our brains were evolving into what we carry in our heads today: How much did those early *Homo sapiens* behave like tribal sports fans?

But before we get into stereotyping, conflict, and the nature of "them," I'd like to journey first through what you might call the surprising upside to tribalism. Step off of the tear-gas-clouded streets and check out, for example, the atmosphere inside the Raiders Fan Convention. There are people in costumes—predators, violators, gorillas, and the like. There are car clubs, featuring vehicles of a variety of inspired designs that defy automotive logic. There are several Raiders-themed hip-hop groups, and a store selling silver-and-black Raiders gear. But the vibe of the entire thing can be summed up pretty neatly in two words: family reunion.

The "Raider Nation," the official moniker of one of the weirdest and most oddly likeable fan groups around, is a giant, sometimes squabbling, often fiercely loving family. They act ferocious and play up their hard edges, but underneath there's a lot of genuine cooperation in this tribe. The man everyone says makes it go, the guy dressed up in the gorilla suit, the official superfan named Gorilla Rilla, might be as cuddly and kind a human being as you'll ever find. The first time I called him, it went straight to voice mail. His recorded greeting was laughter, followed by the brief message, "I hope you find something to smile about today."

IN THE WORLD OF GROUP RESEARCH, THERE ARE DIFFERENT ways of looking at how we behave. Social psychologists look at *what* we do and how the mind works now. Evolutionary biologists and evolutionary psychologists look at *why* we do it and where those workings might have come from. The two fields don't necessarily agree on any unifying answers about groups and what makes them go, and in this chapter and the next we'll cover the wide range of their disagreement as it pertains to sports fans.

However it happened, it's clear from psychology, we humans are programmed to rapidly divide the world into groups. Our entire perception system is set up for instant categorization, down to the most basic level. As German psychologists started to argue in the early 1900s, it would be difficult for us to make sense of anything coming through our eyes as a pure mosaic pattern of individual atoms reflecting light. We must, they argued, sort things into grouped objects instantaneously, somewhere between the light hitting the retina and the brain reading the input.

What we do, modern researchers argue, is stereotype people that we see based on any obvious categories we can apply to them. This allows us to use experience and long-term memory to make quick decisions about the rest of the world. It allows us, in particular, to find people who are like us and to stereotype them positively and to find people who are not like us and stereotype them negatively. You would think it has to be something obvious like race to sort out us-and-them, but a series of groundbreaking psychology studies in the 1970s showed that it doesn't matter whether you're sorting white from black or ukulele fans from mandolin fans—the mental process is exactly the same, as are the cognitive consequences. We sort subconsciously and instantly and then change our behavior accordingly. The Harvard psychologist Gordon Allport, who pioneered the field of social categorization and prejudice, wrote in 1954, "We cannot possibly avoid this process. Orderly living depends on it."

WANDERING AROUND THE MARRIOT CONVENTION CENTER, I was repeatedly struck by the way various Raider fans greeted each other. They hugged—emotionally. They slapped each other on the back, they asked about each other's kids. They beamed like long-lost cousins. An adorable fourteen-month-old in a black RUN DMC* shirt toddled around the exhibition floor to unanimous coos and giggles; the Raider Nation loves Raider kids. Once you're in the family, it's an unbreakable bond no matter where you find yourself.

Stereotype and prejudice are negative words, but at the most basic they're a way of finding friends in a hostile universe. In this crowd of men and women, young and old, blacks, whites, and Latinos (plus one gorilla), the only category that mattered was Silver and Black. It's worth keep-

---

*DMC is Raider shorthand for Darren McFadden, the team's talented and usually injured running back. Run DMC, of course, is a play on the awesome old-school hip-hop group.

ing in mind, when you think of sports fans, that fan tribes welcome diversity in a way we often don't, and that the study of groups has as much to say about love and friends as it does about conflict and enemies.

HENRI TAJFEL, A POLISH JEW, ESCAPED POLAND JUST BEFORE World War II, joined the French army, and was captured in battle by the Nazis. He survived a prisoner-of-war camp, but most of his friends and family died in the Holocaust. Tajfel had studied chemistry before the war, but he moved to England afterward to study psychology, fixated on questions of prejudice, group identity, and the way individual psychology plays out in group contexts. In 1967, he took a professorship at Bristol University, where he led the famous studies now known as the "minimal group" experiments. Tajfel reasoned that although the depth of feeling between two groups changes with history and experience, people pretty much all draw from the same well of discrimination. In an article in *Scientific American* in 1970 he related anecdotal proof: he had a Slovenian friend list all the stereotypes that Slovenians applied to Bosnians, then took the list and asked a group of students at Oxford who they thought it applied to. Almost unanimously, Tajfel wrote, they thought it applied to nonwhite immigrants to England. "Whenever we are confronted with a situation to which some form of intergroup categorization appears directly relevant," he wrote, "we are likely to act in a manner that discriminates against the outgroup and favors the ingroup." Tajfel's interest was to see just how much of an ingrained behavior that process was, and just how arbitrary he could make that categorization.

Tajfel brought several dozen school-age boys into his lab and divided them into two groups based on something ridiculous: a fake score on a dot-counting test. Then, telling them that he also wanted to learn more about decision making, he sent each boy off to a cubicle to fill out a form. On the form a boy could choose to give real money to anonymous members of his own dot-counting group and to simultaneously take money from anonymous members of the other dot-counting group. The important point is that the reward and penalty went together, so by choosing the maximum reward for your group member you'd also choose the maximum penalty for the boy from the other group. By choosing the middle ground, the boys could reward or gain nothing for the boy in their own group but minimize the penalty for the out-group boy.

Since all the boys in both the arbitrarily created "in" and "out" groups knew each other well before the experiment, the practical thing for them to do would be to maximize the total amount of money that everyone took home. They could select the midpoint, the largest amount they could get for their own group without penalizing the other group, and at the end everyone would cash out.

But of course they did not. Even though they'd been split up arbitrarily by a fake performance score on a dot-counting test, the boys rewarded in-group members significantly more than out-group members. When Tajfel repeated the experiment again, this time sorting the boys even more meaninglessly by identifying them with a particular painting, he found the same result. "When the subjects had a choice between maximizing profit for all and maximizing the profit for members of their own group, they acted on behalf of their

own group," Tajfel wrote. "When they had a choice between profit for all and for their own group combined, as
against their own group's winning more than the outgroup
at the sacrifice of both of these utilitarian advantages, it was
the maximization of *difference* that seemed more important
to them."

This work has since become the basis of how many psychologists view groups. People sort instantly and then make
decisions—including decisions about rewarding and punishing other people—based on those "minimal" groups. It
matters tremendously that you're in the Raider Nation, in
other words, because it informs your entire perception of
the world. In the same way your individual loyalty to a team
or your relationship with that team can affect the way you
see events, your loyalty to people in your own group affects
how you see other people. You do this unconsciously, but
it's something like the way you could unconsciously become
more aggressive following a testosterone-increasing victory.
Stereotyping is not taking over your free will, and instantaneous applied bias is not destiny. Self-control, as always,
matters.

IF THE CLEVELANDER'S PRIDE DERIVES FROM LOYALTY TO A
losing team and individual pride in the city, the Raider Nation's
pride comes in large part from the oneness of the family.
The Raiders have a widely distributed fan base. Through its
inception in Oakland, and mid-1980s move to Los Angeles,
and then mid-1990s return, the Raiders somehow kept fans
in both cities. Guys like Pete Gutierrez—a lifelong Southern
Californian who as the child of two first-generation Mexi-

can immigrant soccer fans started rooting for the Raiders because they were the local team—abound. The Raiders' most intense rivalry might be with the San Diego Chargers because the game in San Diego every year, being closer to Los Angeles than to Oakland, inspires a Nation reunion.

Lisa Williams's early work established a potential evolutionary motive for pride as an emotion that keeps individuals working on tedious tasks. But from that evolutionary perspective *vicarious* pride makes less sense, since you're proud of the accomplishments or persistence of a group even if you contributed nothing to its achievement. Williams told the story of her own parents, who were born in San Diego and rooted for the Chargers for years. They moved to Hawaii when Williams was growing up and when she went back for a visit after her first year in Australia, it was to find that her parents had abandoned the Chargers for the Green Bay Packers.

"I was like, 'What? What tie do you possibly have to Green Bay?'" she said. It turned out that her parents liked the story of the NFL's only fan-owned team. They were proud of what the Packers represented. "So now they're sitting in Hawaii cheering for Green Bay, and I'm like, 'How do you do that? You're in your sixties, you can't just give up on your teams!' They say, 'Well, we hope the Chargers do well, but Green Bay is where it's at.' They haven't even been within four states of Green Bay!"

This identification with a group, even when you don't really belong or participate, reminds me of the search for identity highlighted by Orrin Klapp. It's not just that you can base your individual identity on being a fan of the Green Bay Packers—it's that you can base your identity on belonging to the group "Packers fans." Arsenal fandom really sank in for Mark Barbeau of the Bay Area Gooners when he met a stranger and they didn't even have to sniff each other out, just went straight to the bonding. Bill Morgan and Steve Winfield became lifelong friends because they happened to be members of the exclusive group "sports fans" in a place where most people weren't.

This is the benefit of our instant categorization, that when you're walking down a street in a strange world and wearing your Packers jersey, and a stranger walks the other way in his Packers jersey, you are no longer strangers. And following the self-expansion ideas of Art Aron, the more the group's behavior and principles line up with your own personal ones, the stronger that identity source becomes. These are two separate things, called in the social sciences self-concept (your personal identity) and social identity (the part of your identity based on groups). It's an interesting question, actually, that continues to intrigue social scientists: Which one is more important? For Oakland-born Raiders fans, say, is it more important to support the local team, or is it more important to belong to the Raider Nation?

I'm not sure that's a question you could ask of a Clevelander; separating the Browns from Cleveland doesn't make any sense. The Cleveland professional football team, of course, did separate from Cleveland, when owner Art Modell took them away in the mid-1990s. The city sued and ultimately reached an agreement with the NFL that the owner and his employees could leave—but only if Cleveland got an expansion Browns team. Same name, same colors, same history. The settlement showed that Art Modell was free, and he could take Vinny Testaverde with him, but that no one could take the Browns, their color scheme, or their history out of Cleveland. Compare that to Oakland, where there are still rumors that the team might move back to Los Angeles after already having done one ten-year stint there. The city might be irritated (especially since it forked over a ton of cash to "upgrade" the Coliseum to lure the Raiders back), but the Raider Nation would just ride on to the next rally point—as so many of the Los Angeles members already did when the team moved north.

In each NFL team's fan base, I'd guess, there's some level of conflict between self-concept and social identity, between being a fan of the city and being a member of the fan base. The tension seems almost isolated in the dual nature of American team names: it is always the region plus the nickname, each with its own weight, tradition, and history. It's an interesting contrast with European club football, where teams occasionally have nicknames but the identity is almost entirely with the region. Given the vast number of leagues each village seems to have its own team,* and the idea of taking PSV Eindhoven out of Eindhoven is ridiculous. But the tension may just lie elsewhere: in who owns the right to call themselves an Eindhoven fan and what the team and fan base represent. As with the Browns, ownership of a European football team is a sacred community trust, and you see increasing conflict with the fans and owners, particularly in England, as wealthy foreigners buy teams as status symbols or moneymakers.

---

*One of the proudest moments of my life is taking the practice field with the fine lads of Dosko '32, who represent the Dutch village of Duizel and play in the sixth tier of Dutch football. I stuck around to watch them play the next day and it was a village event that drew about a thousand people. They lost.

Steve Busfield, the sports blogs editor for the *Guardian*, suggested I look at the example of Manchester City. The joke in England, he said, is that if you live in Manchester you support City, if you live anywhere else you support United. In its own way, though, Manchester City had created a strong fan identity. They were the lovable losers, "joyous in their misery," Busfield said, famous for introducing to English football a tradition of giant inflatable bananas in the stadium grounds at a time when hooliganism and the post-Heysel European ban overshadowed almost everything else. Having not heard of this, I immediately had to go look it up, and (a) it's true and (b) there's video: a news report from 1988 that I found on YouTube that explains the origins. In it, a sky-blue-clad Manchester shop owner lists his inventory of inflatables and says, "Anything just to bring a bit of fun back to the game, you know. I do watch all the fighting at the game and the punching and beating people up. Why not bring a bit of fun back for when we get back into Europe?"

In 2008 an investment group run by a member of the royal family of Abu Dhabi purchased the team and started spending to produce a winner. They brought in incredible talent and three years later won the Premier League for the first time in more than forty years. If you were an individual fan of Manchester City, the sky-blue shirts won, you won with them, and who cares how it happened. But if you identified more with Manchester City fans, with the traditions and culture of joyous misery and silly non sequitur handed down through four decades of lack of success, the team's success would come almost as a challenge. A part of your personal identity would sing, while a part of your social identity would wilt. Depending on where you fall on the scale, victory could be almost Pyrrhic.*

As a person, and not just a sports fan, I'm probably far on the social concept end of that scale. I'm much more comfortable in isolation, much less comfortable in groups. Self-concept matters to me, and clearly I derive a significant part of my identity from being a fan of certain teams just as I derive a significant part of my self-esteem from their success. I don't get much satisfaction from belonging to a group of fans. I might identify myself as a Raiders fan—lapsed—but not a member of the Raider Nation. Which is one reason I was so particularly interested in following up with the guys for whom life was entirely the other way around.

THE FIRST GUY THAT I CAUGHT UP WITH AFTER THE FAN CONvention was Pete Gutierrez. Pete also goes by Hi Roller Raider, and he has a truck that he has turned into a temple to the tribe. In the same way that the sheer awe-inspiring hugeness of Notre Dame moves the spirit within to religious expression, you will, I think, be impressed by Pete's truck.

I was interested in watching members of the Raider Nation at their numerous public appearances, since many of them told me that, after all, they don't really consider themselves mere "fans." The sixteen games in a National Football League season are just gathering points, important

---

*When I wrote this chapter in late 2012, the Wikipedia page for Manchester City F.C. Supporters had three paragraphs on the inflatables tradition, a long paragraph on "City humor," and row upon row of celebrity supporters. It did not mention the Premier League title or anything after the 2010 season.

but not as big as the cosmic significance of the family. So Pete and I had arranged to meet a week before Christmas at a VFW post in Rancho Cucamonga, where he was bringing the truck as part of a holiday charity event for foster children. It was a blustery gray day, and I stood in the parking lot in the shadow of the San Gabriel Mountains and watched volunteers unloading tacos while kids flitted in and out of the hall wearing Santa hats.

The low growl of the truck precedes it by a block or so. I had the advantage over the foster kids in that I'd seen the thing once at the Raider Fan Convention, but still it is somewhat like watching an alien spaceship gliding in for landing. The truck is enormous, the length of a bus and almost as tall as the single-story concrete VFW building. The wheels are waist-high, deep-treaded like a bulldozer's and so immaculately clean that the rubber gleams black. The body is raised up another two or three feet and the base of the driver's side door comes up to Pete's chest. A step runs out the side like a plank and allows him to get in and out, and he tells me later that the height of the truck is "hard." It's one of two things that make him paranoid about driving it, along with, he said, "stopping." He has installed $3,000 brakes.

The body of this truck is a 2002 Ford Excursion, a truck that the car review site Edmunds.com says is "too much truck for too many people," a truck that Motor Trend calls "a bus of the first order," a truck that has a curb weight exceeding three tons.* The base is an ivory white that has been fanatically detailed in silver-and-black Raiders iconography. A kind of flame pattern along the sides swirls with skulls

---

*Possibly, however, it is a truck that could climb a flaming corkscrew in the Mojave Desert.

and the familiar faces of prominent members of the Nation. The hood features a take on the Raider logo, a skull in a football helmet with bony finger outstretched, emerging from a black shield. On the tailgate is a lovingly detailed portrait, designed by Pete's wife, Silvia, of a Raider taking off its mask to reveal the skull beneath. The porcelain-white wheel spokes are custom-painted with more skulls and images of notorious Raider fans—the Violator, Señor, Gorilla Rilla, Pete, and Silvia. The paint job took almost seven months. The entire awe-inspiring thing—so far—has cost around $150,000. Pete would consider selling it, but only to a player—and he said the former Raiders wide receiver Javon Walker was interested.

The truck rumbled alongside the VFW post and stopped in the red "no parking" zone near the open entryway. Pete hopped out of the truck's driver's side door in a NATION FOR LIFE black T-shirt, shorts, and black Nike tennis shoes with skull images on the toe. Silvia crawled out of the backseat behind him. A man dressed in a silver-and-black Santa outfit—in standard Santa beard, skull necklace, and Raider belt buckle—stepped down from the passenger side. "That's my elf," he said of Pete, who was also wearing a Santa hat.

A harried event organizer greeted Pete and asked almost immediately if he could turn on the car stereo, as the DJ hadn't arrived yet.

Why yes, as a matter of fact. You think you spend five years fixing up a truck and neglect the sound system? The monster stereo setup features Raider Nation touches all its own, with music-and-video "For the Nation, by the Nation" that you just kind of knew was going to blow these kids' minds. Pete disappeared into the cab to fiddle with things.

He popped the hood, the better to display the skull and shield. The back of the truck slowly yawned open to reveal speakers, subwoofers, and three video screens. Then he turned on the music.

AT THIS POINT PERHAPS YOU ARE WONDERING ABOUT THE OTHER side to the Raider Nation. The fearsome, loathsome, Hunter S. Thompson–approved hive of scum and villainy that throws batteries at rival players and showers beer (and worse) on rival fans. We'll talk much more in the next chapter about war and conflict, but regarding these Raiders fans, what if I were to tell you that's all just an unfortunate misunderstanding?

Marilynn Brewer, who is one of the international leaders in the psychology of groups, does not deny that conflict happens or that groups dislike other groups in the heat of competition. People who mainly just love others in their own group react to a challenge, particularly a winner-take-all challenge like a football game, with fierce denigration of out-groups. The question is whether you retain the out-group hate when you remove the competition. Because if not, Brewer says, you could argue a lot more convincingly that the main characteristic of human groups is that people just want to love other people like themselves.

Brewer, a psychologist at the University of New South Wales and professor emerita at the Ohio State University, has spent her career researching intergroup relations and has proposed that loving people from your own group is more important and more relevant to us than hating people in other groups. Evidence from psychologists' lab experiments and anthropologists' field studies hasn't shown a strong connection between in-group positivity and out-group derogation, Brewer says. In a study she conducted in the late 1960s of thirty ethnic groups in East Africa, for example, Brewer found strong evidence of in-group love—group members all rated their own group higher for trustworthiness, obedience, friendliness, and honesty. But there was no relation between how much they liked their fellows and how much they disliked anyone else. More recent work shows that children display similar biases toward their in-group, but no signs of out-group hate.

In another project, Brewer showed two examples of discrimination, one where it was clear the discrimination came from favoring in-group members, one where the discrimination appeared random. She asked people to judge the discriminators, to assess their prejudice. She found that when it was clear that it was just in-group favoritism, people were very reluctant to criticize. That, they seemed to say, is what we all do. So Brewer extends the idea: maybe most of what we think of as out-group discrimination in the world is just misunderstood favoritism. Not that there's no out-group hate in the world, because obviously there is. But just that there's a lot more in-group love than you'd think. One reason the Raider Nation is so interesting is that its purpose goes so far beyond providing individuals a chance to better root for their favorite sports team. It goes beyond a typical fan-team relationship entirely. The Raider Nation is as much about the Nation as about the Raiders, something that Brewer highlighted. The result, though, is that the obvious team rivalries for the Raiders football team don't have an analog in the fan groups. Arsenal fan clubs provide fanatic

Arsenal loyalists an opportunity to unify around their hatred of Tottenham. The Raider Nation essentially has no archrivals because it exists only for itself.

"Much of the work on sports fanship has assumed it is identification with the team," Brewer said. "But really it's the other supporters. The team is just the focal point or the symbol. The identification is with those of us who remain loyal to this particular cause through thick and thin."

A FEW YEARS AGO AN OAKLAND-BASED TRUCK DRIVER WHO goes by the hip-hop moniker Don't Even checked his manifest and realized he was carrying a cocktail of the most explosive stuff known to man. Any kind of leak in the back and: Boom. Paranoid out of his mind, he made the harrowing drive to Los Angeles checking his mirrors and inching along well below the speed limit. He dropped the load off in L.A., where his stupendous relief gave way to epiphany. He was visiting his occasional partner-in-rapping Raider Raspect and thought, you know, we spit toxic lyrics. I've just been driving toxic stuff around. Who do you call when the toxic stuff spills?

Thus was born the Hazmat Boyz' two-song debut album, *Fixin' to Clean Up*, and a partnership that would create the official Raider Nation sound track for Pete Gutierrez's charity events. We met for a drink in Oakland and both rappers made it clear, straightaway, they don't think of themselves as fans.

"See, I don't like the word *fan*," Don't Even told me. "Fans come and go. The Raider Nation, it's family. When we see people around us, that's family."

"It's something you feel," Raider Raspect added. "If you're not part of the family, you don't understand. It's a culture."

In the early 2000s Raspect and Don't Even had the idea to write some lyrics about the Raiders. Those were halcyon years, years when a Raiders team could reliably carry a cancer victim to the Super Bowl. Under the name Dem Raider Boyz, they started wandering around the Coliseum before home games, rapping over the beats of a band called Raiderhead. Their act gradually grew as more and more Raiders fans recognized them. They started performing at Ricky's, the San Leandro sports bar that's the unofficial home to the Nation. Then came a string of Raider-themed hits including "Raider Nation," "Total Eclipse," "Thank You, Al," and "Black Sunday."

Through the miserable years following the 2003 Super Bowl, as the on-field product strung together a decade without a winning record, Dem Raider Boyz still inspired. "People were coming up to us, like, that's the feeling when we're winning," Raspect said. "It still gave people hope."

They started to toy with the idea of writing something to reinforce the message of the Raider Nation. They wrote some lyrics and went on Facebook to survey their fans for a name. Someone suggested the word *solidarity*. It clicked.

"We thought about what we were trying to achieve," Raspect said. "Total solidarity of everyone coming into the Coliseum. Create a song to let them know. If we can get everyone on the same page, we can create solidarity."

"Solidarity" would be a song to unite the occasionally bickering family members under a pirate banner and an easy dress code. In the YouTube video, after an opening montage of Raider greats and denizens of the Black Hole (the nickname of the notorious south end zone section of the Oakland Coliseum), the lyrics begin with "Black hat, black shirt, black pants, black toes, football's most notorious so meet us in the Black Hole," with the Black Hole, in this case, reaching out to encompass the entire stadium and spread the love to the entire Nation.

The five-minute video features shout outs to the great Nation superfans like Pete ("Black and silver love to Hi Roller") and references the car clubs, tailgate grill masters, and young Raiders that make the Nation great. To max the inclusion, to show that in this Nation, at least, group identity matters more than self-concept, Don't Even carefully constructed the geographic references. In writing the lyrics he arrived at essentially a fill-in-the-blank: "This is how we do it," his line goes, "here in ____-____, California." Da-dum. Two syllables, descriptive of where in California they are . . .

In the video, Don't Even delivers this line while walking the train tracks just behind the Oakland–Alameda County Coliseum, a stadium complex owned by the city and built in the 1960s as a celebration of Oakland pride. The word he picked? "This is how we do it here in *Raider*, California." The point, this lifelong Oakland resident said, was that the Raider Nation is bigger than just Oakland. When times get rough, the song says, you remember that you're part of something bigger and more meaningful than just this fleeting, temporal game.

"That's what we hold on to," Don't Even said. "We know we love each other. We know we're family."

SOLIDARITY IN THE FAMILY IS ACTUALLY A NEAT DEMONSTRATION of Henri Tajfel's social identity in action: the more fans in the Raider Nation, the more intimidating it looks, the higher the benefit to each group member from belonging. The more you identify with the group, the more benefits accrue, the closer your own success gets tied with the team's success. A highly identified member of the Raider Nation has a lot to gain by inspiring renewed loyalty.

The team losing creates a problem, then. Social scientists call it a social dilemma or public goods dilemma: other fans can leave the Raider Nation at any time. It's a real threat, because the smaller the Nation, the less benefit to each group member. This explains the hardcore fan's loathing for bandwagoners or fair-weather fans. If you've sacrificed some amount over a great deal of time for the team, you're wired to deeply resent newbies coming in and claiming the benefits of victory and then bailing without sharing the costs of defeat. Humans, it turns out, have an incredible ability to suspect others of lacking sufficient loyalty to the group. We spend a fair amount of brainpower trying to discern who's a real fan and who's not because in groups, knowing who's going to sacrifice for the group and who's free riding matters.

"For the sake of the Nation it's a bad thing to have these interlopers come in," Marilynn Brewer said.

Lowercase nations get around the free-rider problem and force contributions from everyone in the group by appointing leaders with the power to punish non-contributors or wavering group members. In the lawless Raider Nation, rules and rulers don't apply. So they turn to a second method of preventing free riders: group leaders demonstrably sticking with the group even when they could get better results elsewhere.

Mark van Vugt, a researcher at the University of Amsterdam, calls this the social glue hypothesis of social identity. Part of the way Brewer defines social identity is that the more your personal self-esteem gets tied up in the group, the more you're willing to make personal sacrifices on the group's behalf. Van Vugt wanted to test whether increasing social identity makes a person more willing to ignore an enticing option to leave the group. He brought sixty undergraduates into his lab (then at the University of Southampton), divided them into groups of six, and gave each of them £2. Then he gave them a choice to make in isolation: give £2 to the group or keep your money. If four of the six people chose to give, everyone would get £4. If the group failed to raise £8, no one would get anything—and the people who had invested in the group would lose their money. Then he added the manipulations. Half of the students were told they were being tested on how well they would act individually. The other half were told they were being tested on how well they would act compared to other universities. In some cases, he promised individual students extra bonus money if they acted individually, raising the attractiveness of leaving the group. What he found was what you'd expect: the more you're identified with the group, the more you'll stick around even when leaving promises individual financial gain. The finding basically illustrates the difference between a Raiders fan like me and a member of the Raider Nation. The Raiders have gone nine years in a row without a winning season and I bailed from whatever group loyalty I had a long time ago. I'm not willing to spend time or money on Raider fan group events because the group has no value for me. Leaving, for me, had no cost. For a member of the Nation, though, it would be much, much harder.

If you're deeply involved in the group and you know you're going to stick with it, then how do you compel loyalty in others? One of van Vugt's findings is that when their group is challenged, men respond by increasing their identification with it. Belonging, cooperation, and fellowship are most important when the game gets rough because that's when the appeal of leaving becomes strongest. When your team has had several losing seasons in a row, what you need is, in a word, solidarity. That's why everyone rallies around Dem Raider Boyz.

Once your identity becomes mixed up with the group's, you make public demonstrations of loyalty to reassure other group members and to prove your own loyalty. The most invested group members will make the greatest personal sacrifices to the group—like spending six figures on a truck to honor a losing group when you could just go become a Packers fan instead. It is, van Vugt said, a form of signaling device. I had asked him specifically about what the Cleveland sportswriter Scott Sargent told me, that you can't grow up rooting for the teams that are good because that would be silly, which I understand emotionally but not rationally. Van Vugt answered in Cleveland terms.

"One could see this as a manifestation of group-selected tribal psychology: if the group goes down, then I'll go down as well," he said. "But that also means that loyalty is a commitment device. It's signaling to your fellow Clevelandians that you are a trustworthy, loyal person. That the city of Cleveland, your mates, and friends you grew up with, they can still be around, you will support them."

Todd Dery proudly relating the story of his post–World Series vomiting in the shower, it turns out, helps him burnish his no-freeloaders-here street cred. Building a Raider-themed truck in a losing season could be a beacon to the rest of the Raider Nation in an especially timely way. A slick hip-hop video that confirms the mystique of the Black Hole, and grooving rap beats to inspire solidarity, help reward group conformity at a time of potential defection. All of which, I should add, would be pretty subliminal. These are the processes underlying, "I don't know, that's just the way I feel about it," but they're not exactly obvious, conscious decisions.

Still, you only need to see "Solidarity" blasting from the back of Pete's truck to know there's something compelling there. At the VFW post one of the foster kids turned, wide-eyed, to his friend. "You hear that bass?" he said. The bass thundered across the parking lot with rib-unmooring, Dumpster-rattling power. Raider Santa head-bobbed and held up a single white-gloved finger at me to show off a Raiders ring. I wandered around to the tailgate televisions—three of, I should say, twelve that I counted in the truck—to watch the looped Raider anthem.

There, in exactly the context they hoped to be in when they created the video, Don't Even and Raider Raspect stood in front of a mob of Raider-jerseyed friends, signaling loud and clear: this Nation is so strong it doesn't matter what happens on the field.

Football's most notorious fans
It's a Raider thang, you wouldn't understand, man
Unless you're part of the fam
La Familia, we worldwide
So welcome to the dark side
of silver and black poise and pride in this Raider World

Hundreds of millions of the Raider boys and Raider girls
dressed in solidarity the Raider Nation the next generation
diehards and players be in.
Black shirt black pants black toes
Football's most notorious
So meet us in the Black Hole
Where we go crazy with the Raider ladies
A new breed of warrior
Just Win Baby

Aaron Ahuvia, the marketing researcher, suggested you could measure sports fan love by looking at the degree to which they act toward the team as they act toward themselves. If you see sports fans exhibiting the kind of cognitive biases toward their team that you see them exhibiting toward themselves, he said, then you know they've expanded their self and thus are in love. There are a number of ways of thinking about that, but one is minor acts of self-sacrifice on behalf of the team. Giving is common among the Raider Nation, and that's why you find someone like Pete Gutierrez at a VFW post in Rancho Cucamonga a few days before Christmas.

"Not that it doesn't happen, but it's fairly unusual for people to behave in an altruistic way toward a brand," Ahuvia said. "But people are altruistic toward their sports teams all the time. If the sports team is doing something for charity, all the fans are like, 'Of course we can help you out.'"

Ahuvia sees that as the ultimate proof that fans love their teams, or their fan groups. Pete exemplifies the love and the Raider Nation's altruistic principles. I met him at this particular foster kid charity event, for which he had raised more than fifteen hundred toys, but it was just one of more than fifty charity events a year for Pete and his truck.

"My passion is all year," he said. "It's not just a Sunday thing."

I'm not sure Pete himself can fully explain the origin of his passion. It's just what he does, he said. He's always liked fixing up cars, and so he had a chance to do a grand fixer-upper on a giant truck and things just kind of went from there. Each step was a logical one from the previous place. He's Hi Roller Raider and one of the kings of the Nation's superfans, but like a lot of the Raider Nation, it doesn't feel to him like anything particularly extraordinary—it's just the way he lives.

Why does he do it? He's a fan who watches every game, but the truck and the fund-raisers—the rest of his life—is much more an extension beyond the team. "It's my own thing," he said, and he sounded the solidarity note. "It's my passion. I built my truck in a losing season, I didn't jump on the bandwagon."

THERE'S ONE FINAL THING THAT REINFORCES PETE'S ALTRUISTIC behavior, and it has to do with the way we respond to challenges. Faced with a threat or even a competition from an outsider, men in a group tend to rally to in-group charity. The Raider Nation, for all its talk of love, lives in a permanent state of challenge. Not just rival fan groups: broadcasters, moralizers, public safety officials, they all take their shots at the Nation, and the Nation, let's be clear, can be pretty hypersensitive to criticism. For a good time, call Al Davis a bad name on the Internet.

Mark van Vugt's lab explored men's and women's responses to criticism of their group by running a test similar to the social glue experiments. Undergraduates at the University of Southampton came to the lab and were given money to either keep or donate to the group. Once again, the catch was that if at least four of six chose to donate, they'd all get a bigger reward. This time, van Vugt added a competitive note. He looked up the other universities that Southampton students regularly applied to before choosing Southampton, then told half the participants that they were part of a nationwide survey on college campuses. He specifically named the rival universities.

Competition changes men. When they were told they were being measured on individual performance, men chose to keep the money. When they were told they were being compared to the other universities, men decided to give the money to the group. Women were pretty consistent no matter the condition. The results, van Vugt wrote in a 2007 paper in *Psychological Science*, "demonstrate that men become more altruistic when their group is competing with other groups."*

Lisa Williams, the pride researcher—who happens to be in the same department as Marilynn Brewer at the University of New South Wales—has recently started to study pride at a group level on a parallel track. People who are proud of belonging to a group, she guessed, would be more likely to lash out when the group was threatened. In a series of experiments presented at the 2012 Society for Personality and Social Psychology conference, Williams showed that

---

*This explains in part why the most effective political fund-raising to get money from men mentions a shadowy and nefarious opponent—the presence of the challenge inspires increased giving.

Americans confronted with a threat by al-Qaeda or North Korea responded more aggressively when they were feeling proud. "Group-level pride," Williams wrote, "can indeed promote a warrior mindset."

The Raider Nation bristles at provocation, in part because when the competition's not there they're mostly harmless—and so they see themselves as utterly blameless in most confrontations. It offends someone like Pete when people stereotype Raiders fans as crazy, or violent, or dumb. "Some of us, we've got our things together," he said. "Got college degrees, got our head on our shoulders."

It also motivates him. "I couldn't do this if I didn't make a hundred thousand dollars a year," he said. Pete runs several small businesses—a manufacturing shop that makes the envelopes for commercial mailers, a liquor store. He's organized and fully functional. He's happily married and has three kids. His passion just happens to involve spending his money adding skull décor to his three-ton truck—and then using that truck for charity.

One of the foster kids walked by as Pete and I talked.

"It's cool," he said, "but I like the Steelers."

Pete, challenged, merely smiled. "I hear that all the time, bro," he said.

THE DESCRIPTION, OF COURSE, IS ALWAYS "US AND THEM." IN many theories, liking members of your own group necessitates disliking anyone who's not in that group. The problem is that there just doesn't seem to be any other way, evolutionarily, to explain the competing human urges for self-interest and cooperation.

But some intriguing work in anthropology and psychology right now says that you might actually be able to uncouple those two pronouns. "Us" doesn't have to be defined in opposition to "them," and "them" might be a readily identified enemy without any "us" around to provide backup. Every researcher seems to have a different take on it, but the idea is that allies and enemies not only exist independently, we might have learned to identify one of them first and then necessarily developed the ability to identify the opposite. As a question about sports fans you could phrase it like this: What's going on in our social brains when we go to the game? Is it love for our fellow fans, hate for opposing fans, or some mix of the two?

That it's mostly in-group love except in cases of heated competition makes sense from an evolutionary standpoint, Marilynn Brewer argues. There's no evidence in the archaeological record that there was pervasive war or hostility during the time period in which people evolved—somewhere around two to three million years ago. It's likewise easy to imagine early humans coming together in groups not for war but to survive in a tough landscape. Other people would help you hunt, gather plants, cook, thwart dinosaur attacks, pack your stuff, and haul it somewhere dinosaur-free*—all useful, obvious purposes that would select for people who worked well in groups. If a group of people is better at staying alive than individuals, then the individuals in the group will also do better, and the individuals that are most adapted to living in groups will do the best. Brewer talked to me by Skype from her new home in Australia and pronounced her-

---

*This is a joke, obviously. There was nowhere that was dinosaur-free.

self delighted at the family nature of the Raider Nation. She's followed the theme of in-group love's importance in her work for forty years but has started to gain traction among the evolution-studying crowd only recently.

"I don't even understand why evolutionary psychologists think competition is necessary, when you think of all the benefits of cooperation, the survival issues, why people would only assume that cooperation was selected for competition with others," Brewer told me. "How could you have intergroup competition if you don't already have groups?"

Anyone searching for an explanation for group living has to make the argument about how group membership benefits individuals or, even more appropriately, that the benefits of being good at cooperation are so important that those who are social have more children and are able to keep those children alive to have their own children, and so on. War and violence create obvious selection pressures: if you're killed in a raid you're not sticking around to have children. The challenge for psychologists like Brewer—entering into evolutionary psychology, which is a different field that's slightly hostile to social psychologists to begin with—is to explain both the absence of conflict as a selection pressure and the presence of a strong selection pressure for group living.

The benefits (the dinosaur-thwarting previously mentioned, etc.) are legion and obvious, the absence of conflict less so. Brewer's argument is simply about personal space. A 1981 estimate by the renowned archaeologist Fekri Hassan puts the total human population during the Middle Paleolithic—say roughly three hundred thousand years ago—at 1.5 million. At that time we were already living in groups, implying that our brains had already developed the ability to recognize and deal preferentially with in-group members. But if there were only 1.5 million people in the world, Brewer argues, there was no competition for resources and there were no neighbors to be mad at. "In light of both paleoanthropological and archaeological evidence," Brewer wrote in one 2007 paper, "it makes little sense to see conflict as the source of in-group formation."

Haters gonna hate, as the members of the Raider Nation will tell you, but that doesn't concern a true member of the Nation. All that matters, all that's real, is the love for the silver-and-black family.

EVOLUTIONARILY, GROUP RECOGNITION SEEMS TO BE QUITE NEW. It's different from pure social living, which of course tons of animals do—recognition requires recognizing "self" and then recognizing that "self" belongs to "group." That's serious cognition happening right there, making it provocative to consider the example of our closest relatives. Humans, chimpanzees, and bonobos have basically 97 to 99 percent of the same genes and share a common ancestor that lived five to six million years ago. Chimpanzees and bonobos are even more closely related; they appear to have split from each other only one million years ago, while our ancestor *Homo erectus* was already mucking about using stone tools and taming fire. Something very interesting happened in that chimpanzee-bonobo split, though. Chimpanzees are widely known to form groups and then go to war. It's mainly male chimps that conduct raids, ambushes, and skirmishes. They are one of the only animals that will intentionally murder—not predation in the way that a shark hunts and kills a seal, but murder. Bonobos, meanwhile, don't. Their brains are wired in incredibly similar ways to chimpanzees; their genetic code is nearly identical; they, too, recognize self as well as in- and out-groups. We're still not sure exactly what they do to resolve conflicts or group competitions—sex does seem to play a major role— but they haven't been seen having wars.

In June 2012 scientists succeeded in fully sequencing the bonobo genome. They've already done chimpanzees and humans. The love-versus-war question was the first one that occurred to John Hawks, a Wisconsin anthropologist. If there is a genetic predisposition to violence in our lineage, this might be how and where we'll find it.

"What branch do humans come from?" Hawks told the *Los Angeles Times*. "Is it 'Make love, not war,' or 'Make war, not love'?"

Why not, I thought, turn to a primate superfan to answer the question?

IF THERE IS SUCH A THING AS AN INDIVIDUAL THAT MAKES THE Raider Nation go, it is the man in the gorilla suit. "Gorilla Rilla," Raider Raspect told me, "is the beating heart of the Raider Nation."

I met the Gorilla and his fiancée, who goes by Jungle Jane, at a diner an hour east of Oakland, in the sprawling suburbs of the Sacramento River Delta. He rolled up in a truck with the official superfan "Gorilla Rilla" logo on the side. He had just come from his job at a small landscaping company, and he shook my hand with the assured grip of a physical laborer. He was not wearing his suit but had on a Raiders jersey.

"Bro," he said repeatedly, "I have so much to tell you." We had talked on the phone earlier in the week, and after I had briefly sketched out the idea of the book, the Gorilla said, "I have so many ideas for you, bro. I've been thinking about this for sixteen years."

Since I really only had variations on one question—*why?*—I decided to let the Gorilla talk. The waitress interrupted us three times for our order before he'd finished.

Mark Acasio was not born into fortune. His mom had a drug problem; his dad ran with the wrong crowd. They put him up for adoption and he was raised by a foster family. His father, he said, was murdered. His mom died around the same time. His foster mother died of breast cancer. The situation with his foster family was tough. Young Mark sometimes slept in the garage. "For real, bro!" he said. And then one day when he was nine or ten years old he walked out of the garage and was hit with a thunderbolt: "There's something special about me." He always made himself laugh, he thought, and given everything in his life, that was pretty incredible. He started to think about the world as a place where he could make his mark just by doing right by other people, just by making himself and others laugh. When he first donned the gorilla suit sixteen years ago, it was purely about spreading the love. When Marilynn Brewer talks about decoupling in-group love and out-group hate, and how as soon as the competition ends you can once again separate the two, it's almost like she has the Gorilla in mind.

"Don't get me wrong," he said. "There's times it gets heated in the stands. But I don't get violent. I've had that in my life. Don't work. I'm there for my team. I'm there for my family."

These guys—Dem Raider Boyz, Hi Roller Raider—they're the family. When Gorilla Rilla and Jungle Jane tied the knot, Pete Gutierrez was there with his truck. Don't Even and Raider Raspect performed "Solidarity" live as the Gorilla, in sparkling white tuxedo with GORILLA RILLA printed across his chest, walked down the aisle. The Violator, another Black Hole regular famous for his spiked shoulder pads and tiger-striped silver-and-black face paint, stood in full costume as best man. Armando Leon, pastor of Raiders for Christ ("One Nation. One God."), officiated. The bride looked resplendent in traditional white dress and gleaming silver "Gorilla Rilla–Jungle Jane" bling. After the ceremony the happy couple posed for photos with the Raiderettes.

For Gorilla Rilla, the Raiders love certainly came first. Conflict happens, in the form of heated exchanges at games, but that happens only in the presence of competition. I wondered a bit more about uncoupling love and hate and taking it from an individual to the world. If the Raider Nation can exist for three hundred and forty-nine days a year without the haters, does it mean that we could live without conflict except in culturally sponsored competitions?

ONE ANTHROPOLOGIST, AT LEAST, THINKS IT COULD. DOUGLAS Fry, a researcher at the Abo Akademi University in Finland, wrote a 2012 review paper in *Science* arguing that "nature and human nature are less 'red in tooth and claw' than generally acknowledged by a competition-based view of the biological world."

Fry argues that new evolutionary theories show less conflict and more cooperation. He says you can't base everything on chimpanzees because some human fossil ancestors like *Ardipithecus ramidus* have more bonobo-like physical appearances. One of the lines of evidence for figuring out human evolutionary behavior is looking at modern tribal societies; in these war is not unanimous but sharing and cooperating are. Fry highlights a number of "peace systems," groups or nations that don't do the war thing.

Fry focuses on three societies in particular to assess the conditions that make a peace society work. The first condition, he writes, is to expand the common identity. You make everyone part of the "us," you disregard the "them," and you live in peace—as did the tribes of the Upper Xingu River basin in China, the six nations of the Iroquois League of Peace, and the twenty-seven member nations of the European Union. "Expanding the us is a powerful force in the service of peace," Fry wrote. Other conditions include better intergroup ties— the Mardu of Australia have diverse connections linking all the various tribes together and don't even have words for *feud* or *war*; interdependence—several tribal groups that live in desert areas share water, and having a war in such a situation "would be suicidal"; having peaceful values, morals, and symbols—the tribes of the Upper Xingu shun macho types as amoral; and creating institutions that can peacefully mediate conflicts—like the EU's European Court of Justice.

I managed to reach Fry by phone as he worked a summer archaeological study in the foothills of California's Sierra Nevada. He suggested an entirely different way of thinking about groups and conflict, something like the way the testosterone researcher Allan Mazur has noted how "quietly" humans sort into dominance hierarchies. Pay attention, Fry said, to how many hunter-gatherer groups in the world use ritual competition to avoid violence. Watch how we pull our punches.

"I would think the first sports would have been in these hunter-gatherer groups," he said. "Not all of them but some of them have had these ways to make the serious not so serious. It's a competition but it doesn't have to have consequences."

In the paper in *Science*, Fry had mentioned a study of caribou showing that the overwhelming majority of caribou-on-caribou fights were ritual sparring that never escalated into real violence. How much, I asked, could you learn about people from watching caribou exercise restraint?

"My approach on this is to look most significantly at these nomadic hunter-gatherer groups," he said. "They're not pristine, perfect examples of our ancestors, but taken as a group they're the best way to get information. This is the way the human species has existed for ninety-nine percent of our time on the planet. And you see a lot of self-restraint."

Humans are at heart a nonviolent species, Fry said. We don't like violence, we go to great lengths to avoid it, and we invented a number of ways of punishing those who engage in it, from early tribes ostracizing violent members to modern nations sending criminals to courts. The Raider Nation—in this way like a great many loyal, cohesive fan bases around the world—polices its own. When violence does happen, when one or two people get out of control, highly identified fans are usually the first to say, "That guy's not one of *us*."

Whether you believe that reflects our true nonviolent nature, or whether you think that's a load of self-deceiving bullshit spun by mobs of little haters trying to cover their own embarrassment, you can probably find some science to back you up. Human co-operation and in-group love have their scientific advocates, but there are a whole lot of researchers who wouldn't consider themselves quite so starry-eyed about human nature.

"Evolution can not only foster self-interest but also promote the generous and ethical behaviors that help us escape the prisoner's dilemma and avert the tragedy of the commons, and that permit us to sustain the hope for a society committed to freedom and justice for all," the economists Samuel Bowles and Herbert Gintis wrote in *A Cooperative Species: Human Reciprocity and Its Evolution*. But the rosy note stops there. "However," they concluded, "we will see that this is true not despite, but in important measure because, evolutionary processes are 'red in tooth and claw,' in Alfred, Lord Tennyson's famous words."

While Marilynn Brewer promotes the primacy of in-group love—apparently in coordination with the Raider Nation—more researchers seem to take a middle ground between love and war, following an idea coined by the political economist Bowles that's called "parochial altruism." The explanation is that in-group love makes sense evolutionarily only if it's coupled with out-group dislike. Parochialism means denigrating the out-group; altruism means favoring the in-group despite a personal cost. While Marilynn Brewer argues that what appears to be parochialism is often just in-group favoritism, Bowles argues that the two are actually distinct and inextricably commingled.

"Neither parochialism nor altruism would seem likely to survive any selection process that favors traits with higher payoffs," Bowles and Jung-Kyoo Choi wrote in a 2007 paper in *Science* to introduce the idea. "But parochial altruism could have emerged and proliferated among early humans because our ancestors lived in environments in which competition for resources favored groups with substantial numbers of parochial altruists willing to engage in hostile conflict with outsiders on behalf of their fellow group members."

If you assume a large enough population you can model evolution statistically. The fewer the number of genetic "alleles"—regions of DNA that code for any particular characteristic—the easier it is to model. Bowles and Choi assumed two hypothetical alleles: one for parochialism and one for altruism. They built an extremely elaborate computer model that takes into account various selection pressures, random violence, mutation, random mating, immigration, groups, and resource scarcity. They ran the model ten times, each time for five thousand "generations" of humans. The numbers were quite clear: parochial altruism is a winning combination. In fact, they could tweak the model to raise the rate of random violence, which initially occurred at a relatively low rate; the more violence, the more parochial altruists survived at the expense of others.

There's of course no such thing as a single gene or even set of genes for altruism or parochialism and this isn't an argument that we have a gene for war. These are complex behaviors powerfully influenced by genetics, environment, and culture. But the importance of Bowles and Choi's work is to show that if there is a genetic component to parochialism, it is likely it came paired with a genetic component for altruism, and vice versa.

In the sporting sense, parochial altruism fits neatly. It is difficult to argue that the Raider Nation is a purely inward-facing group, because you see them on game day shrieking insults, throwing beer, and wearing spiked shoulder pads. It is just as difficult to argue that they are evidence of inherent conflict, though, especially when you see them outside the stadium. The members of the Nation bond in common defense against an out-group, but they also cooperate fiercely. Parochial altruism is a necessary idea, Bowles argues, because traditional biological arguments that humans were merely self-interested weren't cutting it anymore. There's just too much evidence that at a fundamental level we are a cooperative species.

There's something appealing to me in the idea that there's a deeply evolved dual nature at the heart of every sports fan. The game really does bring out the best and the worst in human nature and the Raider Nation puts it all on display. The puzzle, the researchers would say, is not so much that humans occasionally succeed in acts of great cooperation, because clearly we're wired for them. The puzzle is how we got that way.

JUNGLE JANE HAD BEEN WRITING DOWN MY QUESTIONS AS I asked them. She interrupted the Gorilla in the midst of a lengthy story. "Yes," she said, "but his question was, 'Why do you love people who aren't blood family?'"

I explained, very generally, that scientists have a lot of trouble figuring out why people do nice things for other people. What do you get out of it?

"It's just the way I was raised," he said. "I'm going to root my team on. But I'm not going to spill beer on you."

Gorilla Rilla pulled out a newspaper from his stash of clips, a copy of the *Porterville Recorder* from the day after a recent trip to visit kids on an Indian reservation. "Gorilla Rilla Spreads the Love," the headline said, and there was a picture of the Gorilla and a host of smiling children.

"There's the psychology," the Gorilla said, and he jabbed at each of the words in the headline. "Spreads. The. Love."

9
War:
Man Law

I WAS SITTING IN A BAR ONCE AND TALKING WITH SOME friends about why people watch sports. It was one of those places where the tables are six inches too close to each other, and there was a guy sitting at the next table over who was eavesdropping a little too easily on our conversation. Just as we got to the point where I was talking about the list of motivations that Daniel Wann had suggested, the neighbor leaned over and whispered, very solemnly, "Dude. It's a big war metaphor, bro." Then he sat back, pleased, and resumed coloring in psychedelic greeting cards with crayons. Needless to say, this happened in San Francisco.

So, bro, here is your chapter. I hope at this point that I've convinced you that sports is not merely a big war metaphor, unless you look (plausibly, I suppose) at war as a life metaphor involving love, empathy, pride, relationships, addiction, and so on (Dude. Mind blown, bro.)

But we've also hinted quite a bit at the nature and origins of out-group conflict, the yin to in-group love's yang.

(The chimpanzee to its bonobo?) Marilynn Brewer argues that all you need is love. Samuel Bowles makes the yin-yang argument that you can't have parochialism without altruism. Some researchers, meanwhile, including most of the ones who taught me as an undergraduate, are chasing door number three. You not only wouldn't have altruism without parochialism, they argue, the conflict came first. We are a murderous species and our adaptations to deal with it have shaped not only our view of outsiders but ultimately our view of our own friends and family. War, beyond teaching Americans geography, could be one of the great shapers of the human mind.

Maybe it's not the only thing going on, but there's no doubt that sports often looks pretty murderous. Fans, particularly when they start to taunt each other or when they get into clashes outside the stadium, seem to behave like mobs of soldiers running off to battle. I remember going to a soccer game once in the famous Bombonera stadium in Buenos Aires and there was a half-mile maze of crowd control to navigate before we could enter the stadium. Inside a cement wall topped by a thick Plexiglas shield topped by what looked like concertina wire separated home from visiting fans. When Boca Juniors (the home team) scored a goal a tidal rush of home fans crashed into the wall, screaming and jeering and hissing like waves on a breakwater. After the third or fourth goal I remember watching a boy, maybe sixteen or eighteen, scream past me, veins bulging on a forearm held aloft in a warrior pose, mouth stretched in a exultant snarl as he stormed the wall yelling for the visiting fans to applaud the skill that had produced the goal.

Marilynn Brewer and others have argued that low population densities in the human evolutionary period would have generally precluded war or conflict and that coalitions are probably more formed for their usefulness in staying alive in a harsh environment. People in the Raider Nation cooperate because there are benefits purely to group membership. Now let's consider the idea that this young man in the Bombonera is just one archetypal member of a permanent class of warrior males, programmed for out-group hate, looking for a fight and finding it in the stadium.

Mark van Vugt has proposed what he calls the "male warrior hypothesis," the idea that men are evolved to want to form groups and then work with those allies to go fight other men. The familiar background for the argument, a widely supported one in anthropology and evolutionary psychology, is based on parental investment. A woman has to carry a kid for nine months and only gets one shot at it in that time period, so women have a strong selection pressure to select carefully for optimal genetics or strong likelihood that the dad will put a lot of effort into raising the child. Men are reproductively limited only by access to fertile women, so men have strong selection pressure for improving and consolidating their access to women. It makes more sense in this scenario for men not only to compete with other men but to risk death by warfare if that would lead to decreasing the number of other men and increasing the number of available women.

Biology is not destiny; the argument doesn't consider the role of culture and individual variation, both of which can make any individual man more pacific or more aggressive. But the basics hold: men are generally programmed for competition with each other, which seems also to mean that men are programmed for conflict with each other. Men are the ones with high levels of the aggression hormone, men are the ones who kill each other in the vast majority of homicides, men are the ones who after a goal in a soccer game crash into a ten-foot-tall Plexiglas wall to scream tribal insults at members of the visiting fan base. If we men didn't have such a strong need to organize for more effective violence, we might never organize at all.

"To be honest," van Vugt told me, "I think that's the only way you can have such strong intragroup cooperation."

The male warrior hypothesis is not only an argument that competition has shaped our in-group and out-group behavior, it's a hypothesis to suggest that the competition has shaped men and women differently. In an article published in 2011 in the *Philosophical Transactions of the Royal Society*, van Vugt and Michigan State psychology researcher Melissa McDonald reviewed the scientific literature for evidence of men and women behaving differently and found four major lines of support for the male warrior hypothesis. These sound something like a reformulation of the Miller Lite Man Laws—in fact, some of the stereotypes fit with our manly Man Council. But again, just because these have been beneficial traits in our evolutionary past does not mean that they are how we should or must behave. Van Vugt sounded the exact same line that Marco Iacoboni did. "We have these biological tendencies," he said, "and they can be overruled." Culture can provide a buffer against any of this stuff—or it can reinforce it. Perhaps this is why I find the Man Laws so frustrating: they're lazily reinforcing values I think we ought to fight against.

There's little argument, though, that this stuff appears.

First in McDonald and van Vugt's review was men's views of out-groups: no matter where or when they live, men are more xenophobic and more ethnocentric than women. Men are more likely to find out-group members dangerous if you put them in a vaguely threatening situation—as the University of British Columbia researcher Mark Schaller cleverly did by simply turning out the lights on an experiment. Schaller asked his participants to look at photos of black men and make judgments about stereotypes—with half of the participants in a well-lit room and half in a dark room. The participants in the dark room were more likely to find the photos threatening and to engage in prejudicial stereotyping. Men are also more likely to "dehumanize" out-group members—possibly, van Vugt and McDonald write, as a way to make themselves feel better about physically hurting them. And when given a task in which they get an opportunity to punish an out-group, men are more likely than women to take on sacrifice themselves in order to secure the maximum punishment for the out-group—but only if the out-group is made up of other men.

Men also just care more about group hierarchy. Men identify more strongly with groups, want group divisions to exist, and want the groups ranked. In the psychological literature this is called "social dominance orientation," and there's kind of a standard set of questions for determining your SDO preference. Men consistently score higher. Across genders higher scores on SDO questions are linked to racism, social conservatism, patriotism, and support for wars of aggression.

As we've already seen, men also are more likely to behave altruistically toward their in-group when a competing out-group is mentioned. This was van Vugt's original line of support for the male warrior hypothesis: his male university students throwing their money into the collective pool as soon as a rival was mentioned, while the women fairly steadily donated to the group regardless of whether or not it was a competitive situation.

The final line of evidence in support of the male warrior hypothesis comes from studies of competition and aggression. In a wide range of experiments men are more competitive and more aggressive than women. One of my favorite studies, conducted by Lei Chang at the Chinese University of Hong Kong, showed men pictures of attractive or unattractive women and then asked them a series of questions about war. Men who'd seen an attractive woman were far more aggressive on the subsequent questionnaires. Chang titled his paper with a reference to Helen of Troy and the "face that launched a thousand ships."

All this sounds pretty remarkably parallel to the behavior of sports fans. Men are more likely than women to be fans. I'd guess but have no evidence that they are more likely to care more about the other team, and more likely to flood Internet comment boards with dehumanizing comments. Rarely do you see a female name attached to a comment like (perusing the Internet briefly), say, this fairly typical one, in a letter to the editor of *Deadspin*: "when you mention Al Davis or the Raiders make sure to wipe your mouth dick, as a matter of fact i dont think your even worthy enough..go to oakland mf and talk all that mess, dont hide beind a computer and talk shit you fucken coward . . . RAIDER NATION TILL I DIE MF!!"

There are thousands and thousands of these on the Internet, and they paint a depressing picture of my fellow sports fans.* But note to the Man Law Council: it doesn't have to be that way. Note to my bro in the bar: tribalism can be part of being a sports fan, but it just as easily can be avoided entirely. Remember Daniel Wann's sports fan motivations—you don't have to hit eight out of eight to call yourself a serious fan. Mark van Vugt calls himself evidence that you don't have to engage in the tribal aspect at all.

"Definitely I think, if I look at myself, I'm a soccer player, but I'm also a soccer fan," van Vugt told me. "But I'm not tribal in a sense that I have a favorite team. Yes, I'd like Holland to do well and maybe Ajax Amsterdam. But I moved a lot, lived in the UK for fifteen years, and these tribal loyalties seem to disappear."

Van Vugt considers himself more of an aesthetic fan of the game, someone like Iacoboni (who plays tennis) or like me—someone who plays the same sports he watches and so has extremely active mirror neurons and reacts very strongly to the action.

"I'm an addict but I do it for other reasons," van Vugt said. "I want to know what is going on on the pitch, I want to know about strategies and tactics. I look at it as a psychologist and I see an interesting group dynamic. How does Barcelona work, how do they pass the ball around? You can be a fan of the game and it's not necessarily instigated by tribalism.'"

---

*The thousands and thousands who are motivated to write this kind of stuff for publication on the World Wide Web are probably not representative of the millions and millions of sports fans in the country. I remember hearing once that only 10 percent of the world leaves comments, while 90 percent are content to read the 10 percent's oddly fascinating work.

ALL THIS TALK OF AGGRESSION AND MEN MIGHT REMIND YOU of testosterone. Testosterone, though, is not the only thing going on in a group setting. The entire adaptive value of the way testosterone pulses in our bodies, remember, was to *prevent* us from needless aggression. Testosterone rises when a fight is valuable, but it doesn't cause us to see the world any differently. That, it seems, is the role of another hormone that we haven't really mentioned yet: oxytocin, the famous hormone of love, which turns out to be not quite all it's hyped to be.

As with testosterone, scientists are rapidly learning more about what oxytocin does. Researchers have suggested it plays a role in players reading each other's body language for encouragement, and that it might also encourage both players and fans to gloat. Carsten De Dreu, a colleague of van Vugt's at the University of Amsterdam, ran an experiment in which men were dosed with oxytocin or with placebo and then asked to make financial decisions affecting their group and an out-group. (The nice thing about oxytocin is that you can squirt it up your nose—no injections needed.)

De Dreu worked off what he calls the "pivotal implication" of parochial altruism, "that the human brain evolved to sustain motivated cognition and behavior critical to the survival of one's own group, to facilitate contributions to in-group welfare, and to defend against outside threats, including competing groups." His investigation, he wrote in a 2010 paper in *Science*, was to find out whether oxytocin could be the biological basis for parochial altruism. He made four predictions: men dosed with oxytocin would show more in-group trust, more in-group love, more out-group hate, and more out-group aggression.

Somewhat to his surprise, only two of the predictions came true. Oxytocin did influence the men's allocation strategy—but only toward cooperation. Men dosed with oxytocin were significantly more likely to choose to benefit the in-group but didn't do anything differently about the out-group. "Oxytocin led people away from shortsighted self-ishness to in-group love," De Dreu wrote, "but did not affect spiteful out-group hate."

Maybe, he thought, oxytocin acts more on people who are inclined to cooperate. He ran the same experiment again, this time with more participants and a lengthy preexperiment assessment of disposition. But when all the euros had been sorted, he found the same thing. Oxytocin increased in-group love whether the person was a cooperator by nature or not, and it likewise had no effect on out-group spite.

De Dreu had one more idea. Maybe oxytocin doesn't inspire out-group spite but increases aggressive responses to an out-group challenge. He ran another experiment in which seventy-five men were split into small groups and again asked to make financial decisions. They had to make the decision privately but in concert with a member from another group, and the results were contingent on what both partners had decided. If both decided to cooperate, both were rewarded with the full value of what they had risked. If both decided not to cooperate, both were rewarded with a fraction of what they had risked. If one decided to cooperate and one decided not to cooperate, the non-cooperator received more than what they had risked while the cooperator—referred to in the scientific literature as the "sucker"—received an even smaller fraction.

The strong incentive, then, is not to cooperate—this hedges your bets in case the other person decides not to cooperate, too, and maximizes the return in case the other group does decide to cooperate. But by tweaking the amount of the reward and making it more or less risky to be greedy or to be fearful, De Dreu could look for links between oxytocin doses and greed or fear. He found nothing when he looked at greed, but a significant effect when participants were afraid of what the other group might do. In other words, when the out-group presented much more of a financial threat, participants taking oxytocin were much less likely to cooperate. In a follow-up survey, De Dreu asked whether the participants had acted to try to protect their own group, whether they expected their own in-group members to also not cooperate with the out-group to protect the group, and whether they expected out-group members not to cooperate. He found, again, that the men given oxytocin were more motivated by protectionism and more trusting of the rest of their group—but not any more likely to distrust the out-group.

The overwhelming message from all three studies, De Dreu wrote, was to consider oxytocin very much an in-group love sort of hormone. Compared to men who snorted placebo, men given oxytocin were more likely to trust and love their in-groups, and more likely to act defensively when the out-group presented a threat, but not any more or less likely to hate or distrust the out-group.

I saw De Dreu present his findings at a conference, where he concluded his presentation with a nod to what—if you'll remember—was the same enormous open question with which we concluded the first chapter. Work on oxytocin is barely in its infancy and almost nothing is known about the "cross talk" between it and other hormones—in particular testosterone. Somewhere in there, it seems, is one more part of the puzzle that the Spanish researcher Alicia Salvador identified: the root causes of testosterone surges and aggression are incredibly varied and individual. You can't generalize behavior or hormonal changes onto one person, you can't predict the way a person will respond to a game without understanding all the ways the game matters to them.

It is an odd quirk of history that the legend of the "Guerra de Fútbol" starts with a girl. In June 1969 the soccer teams of El Salvador and Honduras played each other as part of World Cup qualifying. The first game between the teams took place in Tegucigalpa, Honduras, on June 8. Honduras won 1–0, and then things, according to the now-famous account by Polish journalist Ryszard Kapuściński, got crazy. An eighteen-year-old Salvadoran named Amelia Bolanios watched the game-winning goal on television, then "got up and ran to the desk which contained her father's pistol in a drawer," Kapuściński wrote. "She then shot herself in the heart. 'The young girl could not bear to see her fatherland brought to its knees,' wrote the Salvadoran newspaper *El Nacional* the next day."

Bolanios was celebrated throughout the capital, and according to Kapuściński's story "the president of the republic and his ministers walked behind the flag-draped coffin," with the soccer team just behind them. The next game of the cup qualifying took place a few weeks later in San Salvador, where Salvadoran fans gathered in an unstable, revenge-minded mob. Kapuściński reported the Honduran players being driven to the game by armored cars and the burning of the Honduran flag. El Salvador won the game 3–0 and the Honduran players were driven back to the airport with their armored car escort, but the few hundred Honduran fans were not so lucky. Two were killed and many more were hospitalized. Within a few hours of the end of the game, the two countries had closed their border, Kapuściński wrote. El Salvador started bombing the Honduran capital the following night. Kapuściński was the only foreign correspondent in the city and his breathless typewritten dispatch reported both countries bombing each other, and the El Salvadoran army crossing into Honduras. Kapuściński reported that the war lasted four days and resulted in six thousand dead and more than twelve thousand wounded. Kapuściński didn't blame soccer, although he did note that in Latin America, politics and soccer are often the same thing.

The problem with Kapuściński's account is that it's extremely alluringly written, and he probably made some of it up. Kapuściński was famous and celebrated—in certain circles—for his "magical realism." He wrote beautiful prose and often combined people and moved events in order to do it. In this case, he moved the timing of the war to happen after the second game. But the 3–0 game in El Salvador actually took place June 15, according to William H. Durham's *Scarcity and Survival in Central America: Ecological Origins of the Soccer War*. Another tiebreaker game took place in Mexico City on June 29. The war didn't start until July 14.

Researchers who have studied the war sniff at the idea it had anything to do with soccer.

"If there is one thing that all sensitive observers agree on, it is that the war was not over something as trivial as football," wrote Thomas P. Anderson in *The War of the Dispossessed: Honduras and El Salvador, 1969.* "Indeed, the squabbles during the games were the product of existing tensions, not the source of the hostility."

Durham, a Stanford anthropology professor, wrote his dissertation on what he termed the "ecological" sources of the war. The tension extended back to long before the soccer games, he wrote, and basically this was a war of scarce resources. El Salvador was badly overpopulated, so much so that Salvadorans had started to immigrate en masse across the border into Honduras. Some three hundred thousand Salvadorans were living in Honduras at the time of the war, raising further tensions. Both countries were struggling economically, with high poverty rates, and both were run by military dictatorships. Both countries were irked at the results of a 1960 trade agreement, and the border had been in dispute since they had won independence from Spain.

In June 1969, with the soccer games in the background, Honduras decided it was no longer going to tolerate the Salvadorans living in the border regions. The Honduran government started to deport them by the thousands, and El Salvador responded by closing its border to try to deny them reentry. That action, Durham wrote, was the war's major cause. In the late 1970s, El Salvador was the most densely populated country on the planet. It was, he declared, truly a straightforward case of a war caused by too many people and too few resources.

There is something, though, to the way the World Cup qualifiers inflamed tensions on both sides of the border. Remember Daniel Wann's finding: sports fans absent a sporting event aren't any more violent or aggressive than anyone else, but sports can act to temporarily cause increased aggression. Hooking into truth that's deeper than surface data is the whole point of Kapuściński's magical realism. It might not be strictly literally accurate in the way date-and-time-obsessed North Americans think. But by compressing the events together, he might have got more to the heart of what happened than a strict accounting would allow. Dispassionate ecological analysis sounds much more reasonable, but if you were on the ground in Honduras listening to the bombs fall, were you thinking about immigration and poverty, or were you thinking about how much that soccer game left you hating your rivals?

For individuals—soccer hooligans, for example—the venue and expectations of violence can provide the cover for people who need only the excuse. For the governments of Honduras and El Salvador, the World Cup qualifiers might have provided the appropriate cover for something they had already intended to do. The important part in anything of this nature, it seems to me, is the role of mass opinion and crowd behavior. You've got to get the crowd to provide the cover or to tolerate the violence for it to succeed or spread, whether you're looking to break windows at Occupy Oakland or in the Manchester train station.

Or for that matter, the Tuileries Palace. In 1898 an influential French philosopher named Gustave Le Bon looked back to try to understand what had happened to French mobs at the end of the eighteenth century to inflame them into revolution. Although much of it is no longer in favor academically, Le Bon's subsequent work, *The Crowd: A Study of the Popular Mind*, has been extraordinarily influential in shaping the way we think about crowds and about the way we think about what happens when an in-group expands into a mob. "While all our ancient beliefs are tottering and disappearing, while the old pillars of society are giving way one by one, the power of the crowd is the only force that nothing menaces, and of which the prestige is continually on the increase," Le Bon wrote in his introduction. "The age we are about to enter will in truth be the ERA OF CROWDS."

Le Bon's basic argument was that once an individual joins a crowd—a "psychological crowd," actually, to imply some unity and separate the idea from just a bunch of random people in the same place at the same time—he entirely loses his individual identity. A crowd, Le Bon argued, will always be mentally inferior to the brightest individuals among it. It will always be a barbarian with no power except destruction. This fallen individual will then be subject to contagion—the rampant spread of ideas or information, accurate or not—and suggestibility—the hypnotic but overwhelming suggestion that he act in a certain way.

"By the mere fact that he forms part of an organized crowd, a man descends several rungs in the ladder of civilization," Le Bon wrote. "He possesses the spontaneity, the violence, the ferocity, and also the enthusiasm and heroism of primitive beings, whom he further tends to resemble by the facility with which he allows himself to be impressed by words and images."

Le Bon smartly guessed that most people running

around in everyday life had only the thinnest veneer of conscious individuality. It was the style at the time; Sigmund Freud had just invented psychoanalysis and published his account of dream interpretation, and Carl Jung was just about to propose his own theory of the collective unconscious. Le Bon compared what we could know about ourselves to the waves on the surface of the ocean, each one the product of "deep-lying disturbances of which we know nothing." What this allowed, though, was for everyone in a crowd, despite their veneer of individuality, to have a vast ocean of commonality. When they joined the crowd, the common parts took over. It sounds almost like a structural argument about the brain and self-control (and sports): we humans alone have this prefrontal cortex growing on the top of our brains that allows us reason and self-control, but under the right circumstances we can cede the control of it to the mid- or even hindbrain structures, the deep reptilian side of us that makes us go crazy in crowds.

Which, modern crowd researchers say, is almost but not quite correct. The problem with Le Bon is that his is a narrative of loss, says Stephen Reicher, a professor at the University of St. Andrews and one of the world's leading scholars on crowd behavior. Individuals in a crowd aren't actually losing anything, Reicher told me—they're just shifting the way they think about themselves from individual identity to social identity. The result is that control switches more to the beliefs of the group.

Just as important, Reicher says, Le Bon failed to look at context. What turns out to strongly influence crowd behavior is the same thing that most psychologists think influences in-group behavior: the actions of the out-group. If the police—usually the out-group—understand a protest as a Le Bon–like mob, lacking individuality, contagious, suggestible to wild ideas, then there's no surprise they show up in riot gear thinking the crowd needs to be controlled. But that, Reicher says, is where they make a mistake. His research, much of it on the policing of football matches, shows that crowds respond to police strategy. A strategy that involves facilitation, communication, and "differentiation" works. When the police show up and start trying to physically control the crowd, Reicher says, they unwittingly augment the crowd's perception of the police action as illegitimate. Think about how in-groups respond to a challenge, of the Raider Nation in and out of the stadium. Pleasant people can become decidedly un-so in the presence of competition. People who showed up having no intention of resisting the police or becoming violent themselves will join in supporting or even working with the people who showed up intending violence.

"One of the core aspects of classic crowd models is that they explain violence in terms of the nature of the crowd itself," Reicher wrote to me in an e-mail. "This is profoundly ideological for it misses the point that violence always arises out of interactions between groups."

Reicher's team has spent years examining the types of interaction that lead to conflict. He's famous for coordinating a BBC reality TV show (*The Experiment*) as a vehicle to study the way people behave in groups and deal with inequality. His conclusion is that individuals in a crowd are keenly attuned to the legitimacy of actions by both in- and out-groups. "To be more precise, the issue is generally not why is there violence (a few people may well desire and intend to be violent) but rather why does violence escalate to the extent that it becomes genuinely collective and capable of overwhelming forces of order," Reicher wrote. "That happens precisely where fear of violence amongst some in the crowd leads to action against all in the crowd and hence to a generalised sense of illegitimacy (and hence to generalised violence)."

Reicher's work has inspired a number of crowd control reports in the UK, including a chapter in a two-hundred-page report by Her Majesty's Inspectorate of Constabulary on adapting police techniques to modern protest movements. Much of what the HMIC report concludes is based on experience controlling football crowds.

Crowds, importantly, almost always follow some larger set of rules. Sports fans pull and stretch and twist as they can, but they still accept the rules of the game they're watching. Reicher said transitions can happen quickly, and he gave an example. In 2012, the stadium at White Hart Lane in London was filled with a Tottenham crowd and a Bolton crowd for a highly charged FA Cup match. Midway through the game the Bolton player Fabrice Muamba collapsed of a heart attack. In thirty seconds it turned from two crowds into one crowd of soccer fans. The home Tottenham fans chanted the visiting Muamba's name. Many of them, the *Daily Telegraph* reported the next day, were in tears. That's the thing Le Bon never appreciated, Reicher reminded me. Crowds are deeply context dependent.

If crowds are not inherently destructive, then maybe individuals aren't either. As with hormones, any analysis of group behavior or even individual behavior has to take context into account—personality, culture, mood, circumstance. Looking back at the "soccer war" in this way, actually, the conflict becomes a compelling anecdote in favor of the idea that people aren't inherently warlike and that sports are not an expression of that inherent violence. There was going to be a war anyway, and the war's cause lay in resource scarcity, the researchers would say. It goes, oddly, to Marilynn Brewer's argument about the primacy of in-group love: if population density is low and resources are plentiful, it makes a lot more sense for people to cooperate to survive in nature than it does for them to go to war. To establish that humans are selected for war, and that sports fans are having mini-wars, you'd first need to find a case study in which there was lots of violence *and* ample resources.

A LITTLE MORE THAN A DECADE AGO, I SIGNED UP FOR MY FIRST undergraduate anthropology course, "Introduction to Cultural Anthropology," with a professor named Napoleon Chagnon. UC Santa Barbara had an honors program in which students who maintained a half-decent GPA could take small sections with the course instructor in addition to the regular section taught by a graduate student teaching assistant. I showed up for this class as an eighteen-year-old with no particular notion of anthropology and no idea at all about Chagnon, and then got an epic introduction to both.

In 1964 this same Napoleon, then a mid-twenties graduate student at the University of Michigan, arrived in the Amazon basin. For the last fourteen years a missionary named James Barker had been traveling into the deep reaches of the jungle along the Orinoco River in Venezuela to contact the Yanomamo, a tribe of Stone Age Indians who had been almost completely isolated from the rest of the world. It was a three-day boat journey from the then small Venezuelan outpost of Puerto Ayacucho to the mission, where Chagnon met Barker, and then several more hours from there to the village. Chagnon and Barker walked into the village around two in the afternoon and, by Chagnon's account in *Yanomamö: The Last Days of Eden*, were greeted at arrow point by "a dozen burly, naked, sweaty hideous men." Expecting to find Rousseau's noble savages—"I had visions of entering the village and seeing 125 social facts running about altruistically, calling to each other in kinship terms and sharing food, each waiting anxiously for me to collect his genealogy"—Chagnon was instead greeted with the "fierce people."

We've been talking generally about how people in the modern era behave tribally. I wondered how much groups of sports fans look like the tribal groups that marked our past. Douglas Fry argued that modern hunter-gatherer societies show the way people pull their punches to avoid real violence. Chagnon's Yanomamo, though, might be as authentic a "tribe" as you can find. And they did not pull their punches.

He lived in the village for the next eighteen months, gradually adjusting to the ways and culture of the Yanomamo. Relatively quickly he noticed, wow, there's a lot of war going on here. It was constant and pervasive, he later wrote, and perhaps even the dominant feature in their lives. It's what they talked about and what shaped their decisions about where to live. Chagnon thought this tribe might offer a chance to draw some conclusions about the nature of warfare. The investigation of violence among the Yanomamo would occupy Chagnon for the next thirty years, until we crossed paths in 1999 in what would turn out to be the final class he ever taught.

As you might guess, this was great stuff to an impressionable undergraduate. Chagnon, who always lectured in an utterly straight-from-the-explorer's-catalog cargo field vest, told amazing stories about his time with the Yanomamo; about violence, ritual, hallucinogenic drugs. I've long been fascinated by Charles Darwin and the way he set out to explore a seemingly unexplored world; listening to Chagnon was listening to a great explorer who had ventured out into a seemingly unexplored world. He had hacked through jungle, fended off bugs, slept in hammocks, interacted with chiefs and missionaries, been threatened at club and arrow point—all in romantic pursuit of some bigger truth about human nature. Now, bearded and wrinkled and sporting only the cargo vest as a reminder of past glories, he spoke to us as if he were giving a presentation to the Royal Society.

The contention of anthropologists for a long time, Chagnon argued, had been that war and conflict were purely over scarce resources. This is one of the planks of Marilynn Brewer's logic that there was no need for war in the time when humans evolved: population density wasn't high enough to require it. But Chagnon found that the Yanomamo, living in the same way that our ancient ancestors did, had all the resources they required and killed each other anyway. Maybe, he concluded, violence is just part of the human condition.

He laid this out carefully in a notorious paper published in *Science* in 1988 titled "Life Histories, Blood Revenge, and Warfare in a Tribal Population." Over twenty years of study,

Chagnon wrote, 44 percent of males aged twenty-five and older had participated in killing someone, 30 percent of male deaths were due to violence, and nearly 70 percent of all adults over the age of forty had lost a close genetic relative to violence. With these levels of violence there's almost undoubtedly a strong pressure on warrior men who can survive battles, and that's where Chagnon's decades of careful recording of family histories came in. He found that men who had killed had more wives and more offspring than men who had not.

"Violence," Chagnon wrote, "is a potent force in human society and may be the principal driving force behind the evolution of culture."

If we consider sports to be a cultural construct that's making use of our paramount brain and body functions, you might then conclude from Chagnon's work that we have sports—that we play in them and watch them—because we are inherently violent.

Chagnon's data has been challenged pretty much from the day he published it. Other anthropologists have studied the Yanomamo and not found the killing rate to be as high, while more recently some have gone over Chagnon's own data and declared it to be less sound than it looks: men who have killed are generally older than men who have not, so of course they have more children.

Chagnon has never suggested that violence is the only shaper of human culture, but he's long argued that most anthropologists underestimate its role. It wasn't just the violence that he reported that shocked. It was the origin of it. The Yanomamo were not fighting over access to scarce food items, Chagnon wrote, they were fighting over women.

One of his favorite stories, cited in the paper in *Science* and repeated in greater detail in *Yanomamö: Last Days of Eden*, is about a presentation by a French anthropologist in Venezuela that was attended by an Indian who had grown up in a village that was half-Yanomamo. The presentation was about the causes of war among the Yanomamo and, according to Chagnon, at the end the Indian raised his hand and said "something like, 'I was very impressed with all of Lizot's sophisticated words and sayings, but he missed the most important thing. What he forgot to say is that the Yanomamo fight over sex and women.'"

Chagnon has always engaged in what you might call defensive aggression against his critics, many of whom have suggested that revenge killings over women are irrelevant to the human narrative. He seemed particularly incensed at critics who suggested that the Yanomamo were actually fighting over a protein scarcity—that they didn't get enough meat to eat and so killed each other over access to food.

"Some Saturday night just visit a hard-hat bar where fights are frequent," Chagnon wrote in *Yanomamo*. "What are the fights usually about? Are they about the amount of meat in someone's hamburger? Or study the words of a dozen country-and-western songs. Do any of them say, 'Don't take your cow to town'?"

Chagnon's work is now considered, depending on your perspective, as a more-or-less valuable case study. Many other researchers, including Chagnon's UC Santa Barbara colleague John Tooby (also one of my former instructors), have proposed more elaborate theories of the way an inherent proclivity for violence has shaped our minds. In a chapter in a recent textbook entitled *Human Morality and*

Sociality: Evolutionary and Comparative Perspectives, Tooby and his wife, the evolutionary psychologist Leda Cosmides, argue that warfare is so inherent and so important that we are deeply evolved to form coalitions to better survive the constant battles. The opening to this chapter is worth quoting at length, because it's so contrary to some of the earlier arguments we've discussed:

> War is older than the human species. It is found in every region of the world, among all the branches of humankind. It is found throughout human history, deeply and densely woven into its causal tapestry. It is found in all eras, and in earlier periods no less than later. There is no evidence of it having originated in one place, and spread by contact to others. War is reflected in the most fundamental features of human social life. When indigenous histories are composed, their authors invariably view wars—unlike almost all other kinds of events—as preeminently worth recording. The foundational works of human literature—the *Iliad*, the *Bhagavada-Gita*, the *Tanakh*, the *Quran*, the *Tale of the Heike*—whether oral or written, sacred or secular—reflect societies in which war was a pervasive feature.

Given such evidence and in such a condition, they argue, humans cannot help but be shaped by war. The result is that we have brains evolved for all the coalitional behaviors we've already described. But they go further than this. The strong selection pressure explains why we have self-expanding relationships—it is a "useful delusion" to be able to better deal with groups as we deal with individuals. It helped midwife our inherent understanding of morality—without the need to keep groups tightly knit for warfare, there would be no pressure to punish moral outliers. Sports in this sense, whether played or watched, isn't just a metaphor for war, it's tapping into this critical evolutionary adaptation for coalitions and providing us with another arena for making allies.

Tooby and Cosmides are well respected and essentially cited in any paper on the subject of war, evolution, and group behavior, but they work at one end of the spectrum on understanding groups. Whether our coalitional nature evolved through war or through love, though, it is certainly present today. We are also today a species with a giant prefrontal cortex for overriding our own nature. What happens in our genes and in our brains and how we choose to act are separate, it's worth noting again. Testosterone does not mandate aggression; dopamine reward does not mandate addiction. Conflict in our genes is not conflict in our destiny.

MARK VAN VUGT AND I WERE TALKING ABOUT VIOLENT FANS, and he asked me a question: Where do sports actually come from? How has culture shaped sports through time?

The answer, of course, is that sports have arisen separately in all sorts of human cultures, as you would expect from anything that so powerfully hooks into our evolutionary behaviors. Egyptian soldiers wrestled with each other, but so far as I can tell the first people in the Western world to have spectator sports and write a lot about them were the ancient Greeks.

What's great about the Greeks is that, as in philosophy and politics, their sports sound so much like ours. In *Combat Sports in the Ancient World*, the classical historian

Michael Poliakoff relates story after story that sounds utterly modern. A comedian on the stage twisted the vocabulary of wrestling into fart jokes (Man Law!). Academics like the sixth-century BC philosopher Xenophanes "complained bitterly about the free meals, treasures, and other benefits athletes reaped" while Plato "maintained that contemporary athletes were overtrained and overspecialized and would be ineffective citizens in his ideal state." Referees, according to one decree, could beat Olympic wrestlers with sticks for trying to break each other's fingers, showing, Poliakoff wrote, that "Olympic foul play started early." Popular literature at the time was crammed with the technical jargon of wrestling, showing widespread appreciation for strategy and minutiae.

Poliakoff, though, also separates out war from athletic competition, arguing that the Greeks prove more that humans have an inherent need to compete that's separate from any inherent warlike tendencies. The Greeks chose culturally to emphasize competition and as a result had the most significant sports scene, while the Romans sneered at the Greeks for their games and gloried in Colosseum violence. The Egyptians enjoyed wrestling but didn't emphasize winners or losers; some modern African tribes similarly admire the skill and determination of individuals without any attempt at a zero-sum winner. Poliakoff argues in some sense that different societies choose to emphasize different parts of our genetic wiring. Competition elicits a powerful instinctive response in us but some cultures choose to control that and shun it while others celebrate it. All men might have testosterone that responds to social challenges, but not all cultures choose to celebrate those challenges.

This is kind of why I keep returning to the theme of self-control. Ultimately sports is one of the deepest and most profound expressions of culture that we have. But we control that culture. We can choose who we want to be. The question is: If we have all this wiring, do we have to choose to use it for something?

FROM MY PERSPECTIVE, THE WARRIOR SPORTS FAN IS THE MOST interesting case study out there. I sometimes feel incredible hostility toward players on other teams, and I sometimes behave more aggressively following games. But there's something in the tribal nature of groups of sports fans—crowds of sports fans—that's foreign to me. Like I said about testing my own testosterone in a group setting, I'm generally content to watch from home because the belonging aspect means little to me. I've traveled to occasional Cal football games, but always avoided interaction with the other teams' fans. I don't usually wear team gear and I have an actual visceral fear of even casual pregame trash talk. I watch other fans do that and find it mystifying—something, I think, about the risk-reward ratio. "What if they lose?" "But you'll never see this person again!" "But *I would know I was wrong!*" Whereas I think a lot of people just say something silly and then forget entirely that they'd said it. Did I talk some trash before the game and then we lost 52–0? Oh well, just part of the game. The fun part, in fact. *At least we won the tailgate party!*

That Boca Juniors game where the male warrior went screaming by me toward the shield separating him from the visiting fans—those very same visiting fans got louder after every goal. The further behind they fell, the more dementedly insistent their bloodthirsty cries became. It's like when my daughter misses her bedtime and instead of going to sleep she just cries louder and harder, screaming utterly in the face of reason and accountability. Then again, she has the brain of a two-month-old. There is probably no aspect of sports fan culture that to me is less understandable.

When I was in Kentucky for the Sports Psychology Forum, something interesting occurred. A calendar coincidence had the San Jose Sharks flying in to Nashville the same day to play the Predators. Rick Grieve, the cohost of the forum with Daniel Wann, is a Predators season ticket holder. (Bowling Green, Kentucky, is about ninety minutes' drive from Nashville.) We had actually talked about hockey and the Predators on the phone six months before the forum, well before he'd scheduled it for the same night as a Sharks-Predators game. But by miracle, I now had the chance not only to attend my first-ever Sharks road game— I was going to bring a psychologist from the out-group with me.

"I don't do evaluations," Grieve said as he picked me up at my hotel for the drive to Nashville.

Instead we talked about our lives as sports fans. Grieve grew up in northern Michigan, a fan mainly of the Detroit teams. A football player through college, he had always wanted to be a sports psychologist, to work with athletes. But it didn't quite happen. Instead, while he was in graduate school at the University of Memphis, he received a packet of reprinted sports fan studies authored by Daniel Wann. Every six months or so, he'd get another packet, and he'd read it and think it was cool. His first teaching job happened to be at Austin Peay State University in Clarksville, Tennessee, only an hour from Wann at Murray State. Grieve e-mailed Wann, and they struck up a research partnership. "With Dan being the kind of person that he is and being nice enough to include me on things, I just kind of continued," Grieve said.

Grieve had also met his wife at Memphis, and although he'd always thought about moving back to Michigan, the professorship offer from Western Kentucky was good. He had an offer from Eastern Michigan University, too, and thought he would take it, but he tore a knee ligament playing basketball a few days before his scheduled visit and he knew his wife wanted to stay in the South. He never went on the visit.

He's been in Kentucky ever since, a hybrid Detroit/Nashville fan who follows the Tigers, Lions, Predators, and Titans. His two boys have grown up in Bowling Green and root for the Nashville teams; he splits his two Predators season tickets between them.

I suppose I kept prodding him with biographical questions as a way of avoiding the elephant in his Honda CR-V: the fact that we both care too much about our sports teams, and that those sports teams were about to play each other and one of us was about to be quite happy at the other's expense. (I had a good idea which way this was going to work out.) The intimate details of our lives became, for me at least, a kind of reflexive refuge from what I was actually thinking about.

The drive from Bowling Green to Nashville is good for conversation: straight, mostly flat, just a few low trees and ranch houses off the road for visual interest. There was a long sunset, pinks and oranges and reds that faded as we drove into a kind of mellow rust ringing the Nashville skyline. At 6:30 Grieve switched on the Predators pregame show and asked who the Sharks goalie was this year. "Antti Niemi," I said, "but he's having a terrible stretch right now."

A few hours later, I remembered that moment in particular.

We stopped in Nashville to pick up Jason Lanter, a psychologist from Kutztown University in Pennsylvania who'd presented earlier in the day on fan reactions to the Joe Paterno firing at Penn State. Lanter wrote his dissertation on celebratory fan violence, and so in some sense he was as well positioned as anyone to make sense of the riots that followed Paterno's dismissal. He'd been able to get two hundred Penn State students to fill out a questionnaire about perception and identification, and confirmed what you might expect: the more identified you were with Penn State football, the more you felt Paterno should have kept his job and Penn State employees acted appropriately. He summarized his work in a quote from an undergraduate, who wrote on the survey, "But . . . it's JoePa!"

Lanter's work on celebratory violence was published in excerpts in a few different journals. So far, he said, he's only found one major takeaway. "The thing that really prevents celebratory violence, the thing that solves it, is to have your team suck," he said. "It only does happen when there's a big contest of some sort, where it's really meaningful. Maryland had a ton of fan violence in the early 2000s; it's not happening now. How are their football and basketball teams now?"

They are lousy.

"There's your answer," he said.

Grieve parked underneath the railway tracks at the Frist Center for the Visual Arts and we walked a few blocks to the arena in a bitter cold. Grieve and Lanter chatted about student evaluations. Inside the arena, we split up: because I'd bought a late ticket, I was a few sections away. I sat down and had a pizza. Nine college-aged boys sat down immediately behind me.

They made jokes like, "Miller Lite? I'm gonna have a Miller Heavy." They laughed in bulleted staccato: *Huhuhuhuhuhu.*

"I don't often drink beer," one of them said, "but when I do, I don't drink beer."

"Dude, I hate the Sharks," another said.

I felt a bit of a reflexive twitch, a desire to turn around and say something back. I could feel a familiar rage building inside of me. The monster within me visualized my witty rejoinders, driving them insane with jealousy, leading to a fistfight in which I stomped among them in righteous Thor-like wrath. Because part of my brain also knows better, I leaned forward, rested my chin on my hands, chewed a bit on my molars, and focused on the ice.

A SIMILAR SORT OF EXPERIENCE LED TO THE DEVELOPMENT OF a clever series of experiments on schadenfreude. Mina Cikara, then a graduate student at Princeton, went to a Yankees–Red Sox game at Yankee Stadium with her boyfriend. The boyfriend had gone to school in Boston and wore a Red Sox hat. The abuse rained down on them, and after everyone had had a few beers Cikara started to worry about things escalating. So she had an idea. She took the hat from her boyfriend and wore it herself, figuring, she said, "They won't be as bad to me as they were to him because he's a guy."

Cikara learned something about sports fans that day, and she reported the results of her hat-switching gender theory to me over the phone in what were definitely all-caps.

"TOTALLY NOT TRUE," she said. "I was getting called names I've never even heard of before. They were insulting my mother. The subway ride home was maybe the most uncomfortable forty-five minutes of my life."

A few months later she and the boyfriend were at the graduate student pub at Princeton and the boyfriend was talking happily to a friend and colleague of Cikara's. Until the friend turned his backward hat forward to reveal a Yankee logo. "All of a sudden it was like two cats hissing at each other," Cikara told me. "'So you're a Yankees fan? What's that all about?' 'What, you're a Red Sox fan?' What was perfectly normal turned into this chest-puffing display of intergroup competitiveness. I was like, this is amazing."

Out of it Cikara had a research idea that would become a large part of her dissertation. What would happen in the brains of Red Sox and Yankees fans when you provoked them with the success or failure of their rival team?

When we divide the world into us and them, two things can exacerbate the division. One is simply making it a group of us versus a group of them. When researchers run those prisoner's dilemma money experiments with people facing off individually, the participants are far more likely to decide just to split the money fifty-fifty. Put them in groups—even, as Tajfel showed, those minimal totally arbitrary groups—

and suddenly they want to maximize not just the amount the in-group gets, but the suffering of the out-group.

The other thing you can do, as Marilynn Brewer suggested, is turn it into a competition. "Circumstances matter," Cikara said. "What happens in sports in particular, it's not just groups, it's competitive groups fighting for a zero-sum resource. Unless it's preseason or something, there's always high stakes. Any time you start to mess with the group dynamics, competition is going to make things a lot hairier."

Cikara invited Yankees and Red Sox fans to come into her lab for an experiment. To make sure they were actually Yankees or Red Sox fans, or at least slightly knowledgeable baseball fans, she gave them a lengthy survey followed by a photo identification: each fan had to identify three players from each team based solely on a picture. Then she put them in an fMRI scanner and showed them an ESPN Gamecast. The Gamecast, for those who didn't spend half their twenties staring at one, is a live and close-to-real-time-updated box score. To make it more appealing, it has all the information arranged on a baseball diamond, so, for example, you can see the pitcher's name, photo, and stats over the pitcher's mound, and the batter's name, photo, and stats in the batter's box. When the pitcher throws a pitch, a little cartoon baseball travels from the mound to home plate, and if it gets hit it rebounds and travels out into the field slowly but roughly on the trajectory of the real ball. So you can see, basically live, how the game is going.

The idea was to have everyone experience success and misfortune. The fans watched one of six different plays— their team succeeded against the rival, the rival failed against their team, their team failed against the rival, the rival succeeded against their team, the rival team failed against a neutral team, or, for the control condition, a neutral team failed or succeeded against another neutral team. The main neutral team was played by the hapless Baltimore Orioles, and for the neutral-against-neutral condition Cikara added the equally inoffensive Toronto Blue Jays.

After each play the fans scored the result on a scale of 1 to 4 for anger, pain, and pleasure. Cikara then was able to compare what they said they were feeling with how active their brains had been.

The Gamecast was rigged, of course, which the fans knew in advance. It didn't matter. When Red Sox fans watched Baltimore hit a home run against the Yankees, they exulted. Remember the reward region of the brain? The ventral striatum, one of the chief components of the area, glowed with pleasure. When Red Sox fans watched a Yankees player hit a home run against Baltimore, though, the opposite happened. The brain centers for pain, especially the anterior cingulate cortex, activated.

The theory behind our understanding of schadenfreude—which can also be called an empathy gap since you are choosing not to empathize with someone in pain—is that not only does the competition context matter, the actual circumstance of the teams matters. In a roundabout way we're back at the empathy gap between the UCLA researcher Marco Iacoboni and me, when the two of us watched the Zidane head-butt with dramatically different reactions. Cikara thought that to maximize the empathy gap you'd have to have two teams that were hotly competitive—in other words, they both would have to be a real threat to activate the outgroup hate. But that turned out not to be the case at all.

In a recent study Cikara tried to have a competition in which there was no schadenfreude. The easy idea was that you'd just reduce the threat from the out-group, and then watch the schadenfreude disappear. But when she told participants that the out-group was now trailing in points, the bias got worse. Okay, she thought, we need to reduce the threat even further. She told the participants that the out-group had lost the competition. No threat at all and now no competitive situation. The out-group bias got worse again. It turned out, she said, that there's something to the concept of a rival worthy of your respect. When you envy a rival that's much better, or disdain a rival that's much worse, that's when the schadenfreude maxes out. You want to avoid blowouts. If Nashville beats the Sharks 3–2, it may not be any more immediately palatable to me than if Nashville beats the Sharks 7–0, but the score will change the way I think about Nashville when I think about them again.

"That's what's really interesting about sports," Cikara said. "It's not like when you get crushed the losing fans walk out like, 'Well, sorry, you whipped our butts.'"

HOCKEY GAMES OFTEN HAVE A BIT OF UNCERTAIN BACK-AND-forth at the beginning as the two teams find their rhythm. The 2012 Sharks, in defiance of this trend, liked to give up early goals. Two minutes into the game in Nashville, with the Sharks zipping around looking pretty good, one of their players made a stupid pass back to his own defenseman. The defenseman muffed it and the puck caught under his skates, causing me to think, "Uh-oh." A Nashville player pushed the puck past the defenseman and carried it in two-on-one. He passed. Most times in hockey, if the pass gets through on the two-on-one, it ends up in the net. The pass went through. "Shit," I thought. Two seconds later, the puck was in the net. The arena erupted. Everyone around me jumped up screaming. The country music hit, "I Like It, I Love It, I Want Some More of It" blared over the sound system, with Tim McGraw wearing a Predators jersey and singing on the Jumbotron.

In Nashville, when the home team scores, they follow up McGraw with the traditional da-da-da-DA-da-da-HEY music, except that everyone shouts, "HEY, YOU SUCK, ASS-HOLE!" (Or at least, everyone in section 303 and the next section over did this.) This is followed by an enthusiastic ser-enade of the goalie, "Niiiiieeeeemmmmmi, Nieeeeeemmmmmii, YOU SUCK, ASSHOLE!" Then they chanted, "It's all your fault! It's all your fault!"

"Dude, this is the best team in their division?" one of the kids behind me said, mockingly. *Huhuhuhuhuhuhuhuhuhu.*

I agonized at the unfairness of it all. The Sharks looked good for two minutes, they made one mistake, and some-how it was 1–0. It wasn't fair, or right, or justified. My team was better; I should be the one quietly celebrating—on the inside, mind you—while I listened to them complain. And what did they even know about hockey? Nothing. The score was just an excuse for them to feel superior and make stu-pid comments and broadcast their hockey ignorance and it was all *undeserved.* Luck, fluke, the flapping of the wings of a fucking butterfly in some fucking country where they don't even have ice. The Sharks were going to score and tie the game and *then* those innocent bastards would have some serious worldview adjusting to do while they were forced to watch a real fan's dignified reaction. Screw what Dan Kahan says about cultural cognition—cold data *would* make this out-group see reason.

Less than a minute later, Nashville scored again.

After the game, the Sharks coach, Todd McLellan, told the media, "Two shots, two goals, two mistakes. Game over."

McLellan had had this thing all year about the Sharks that boiled down to "first team to three wins." The season statistics really bore him out.

It was 3–1 at the first intermission.

In other words: game, with forty minutes of hockey left to play, over. Nothing to do for the next two hours but squirm, listen to the catcalls of the kids behind me, and try to adjust to the psychological reality of my life as a fan of a loser.

I went to see Rick and Jason.

Grieve continued to be polite, to not gloat. He said we had to walk around the rink to his lucky water fountain. Several years ago one of his kids stopped there—the water fountain on the opposite side of the arena from his seats— and he told him it was lucky and that the Predators would come back and win the game. They did; he's gone there at intermissions ever since. Also, he said, he liked the walk. "This is my exercise," he said, chuckling.

It must have been a lucky water fountain, because Nashville scored three more times. Antti Niemi, the Sharks goalie on a terrible stretch who Grieve and I had chatted about in the car, was pulled by the coach in the first period for sucking, which was the only mildly satisfying wrinkle to the game: the fans didn't know the name of the Sharks backup goalie, so the "It's all your fault" chants slackened. Plus two single girls arrived late at the game and sat next to me, distracting the college kids, who eventually moved into my seat while I went to the bathroom between the second and third periods. I quietly took an empty seat a few rows down.

After the game, as we drove out of the parking lot, Lanter asked if I'd found anything useful.

"Well," I said, "you saw that game. Evaluate me."

Grieve looked over, in a very kindly way. "We're not going to evaluate you, Eric," he said again. There was a kind of odd pity in his eyes, not even the gloating kind. For whatever reason, I felt a little better.

I decided to drop some jargon.

"I don't think I'm CORFing," I said.

Sports fans can react to winning and losing in a variety of ways. The obvious one is the BIRG, short for "basking in reflected glory." Researchers in the 1980s noticed this by studying pronoun use by college undergraduates: when the college team won, use of the pronoun "we" increased dramatically and significantly. (As did rocking the school colors.) When the team lost, the team was "they," which is the second common behavior, CORFing, or "cutting off reflected failure." Pretty easy theory to grasp: if your self-esteem is tied to the outcome of the game, you have to have a strategy to deal with winning and losing. Basking is a way of consolidating your self-esteem gains following a win; disassociating yourself from the team is how you prevent a loss from damaging your ego.

But now for the kick in the teeth that invested fans so richly deserve. Remember that spectator identification scale that Daniel Wann came up with? Apparently, fans with high team identification—people who score above a 35 or so—can't CORF. They can't pretend not to care, and they can't pretend the loss doesn't sting. This irritates me to no end. All fans, no matter the investment level, can bask in the glory. There's no barrier to entry for enjoying a win, so newly minted fans in pink Red Sox hats can enjoy the first World Series in eighty-six years just like someone who's suffered through every moment of exquisite failure for decades. But only the ones who care suffer a self-esteem blow after a loss. This is, once again, why we have such a strongly selected disgust for fair-weather fans. Our evolutionary altruism detectors ring out when they're not making the shared sacrifice.

Since they're stuck in the coalition, highly identified fans have had to develop an alternate strategy to dealing with losses. There are two: blasting and denigrating, both forms of out-group hate. They are, basically, what I was doing to the kids sitting behind me. You call fans of the other team idiots because it makes you feel better about yourself. When the Visigoths are crushing your furniture and trampling your flower beds, it's always nice to remember that after all, they're only barbarians.

But I couldn't really enthusiastically blast or denigrate Grieve, even though he was wearing his yellow Shea Weber Predators jersey and even though the bearded giant Weber has more than a passing resemblance to the Rome-sacking barbarian Alaric. Instead the conversation drifted off into other sports fan behaviors.

ARTHUR ARON HAS RECENTLY STARTED TO BROADEN HIS RELA-
tionship self-expansion work to groups. We treat groups the
same way we treat individuals, he's found, and when we expand ourselves by joining a group, we adopt the characteristics of that group as our own. It turns out that expansion can
be remarkably powerful in reducing our fear of out-groups.

When you expand your self in a relationship with another person, Aron said in a presentation to the Psychology
Department at UC Berkeley, you also adopt the characteristics of any groups to which that person belongs. Having
friends in different groups reduces out-group bias in all of
those groups. But it extends beyond that to something incredible: merely having a relationship with someone *who
knows someone* in a rival group is enough to reduce prejudice and out-group bias. He studied this in a very sports-
appropriate context, with rival universities.

"If you had a friend at the other university, you were
more positive toward the people of that university," Aron
said. "If you knew someone who had a friend, it made you
more positive toward them."

I'm more tolerant of even the kids sitting behind me, in
other words, because of my relationship with a psychologist I met yesterday.

We dropped Lanter off at his hotel. "Sorry about your
Sharks, Eric," he said.

Grieve and I drove north. I told him about my friend Bill
Morgan who runs the Buddhist meditation refuge, and Bill's
inability to conquer the anger associated with painful sports
losses.

"It usually takes me about ten or twenty minutes after
the game," Grieve said, acknowledging that his wife can

sometimes disagree with his assessment of that time frame. We passed a water tower marking some town on the outskirts of Nashville. "Usually by about here I think of all the things I've got that are good, and it's over with," Grieve said. "You have to let it go."

TWO WEEKS AFTER SHE'D HAD THEM ALL IN THE BRAIN SCANNER, Mina Cikara ran the second part of her experiment. She asked her participants to complete a Web survey rating the likelihood that they would act aggressively toward a rival fan or an Orioles fan.

Here was where it got really interesting. Fans who had greater reward-area activation in the scanner when watching the rival fail were more likely to say they'd harm a rival team's fans. But the brain seemed to be signaling something that even their self-reported pleasure didn't. Although it lined up in the proper direction, self-reported pleasure wasn't significantly correlated with likelihood of harm. Only the brain activation accurately predicted it. In other words, Cikara said, the evidence is that "even when explicitly allowed to report emotions like *schadenfreude*—even then people are underreporting."

There's generally societal pressure against announcing how happy you are about someone else's misfortune. Sports is one area where that's not the case—Cikara likes to trot out the Red Sox T-shirt that says, MY FAVORITE TWO TEAMS ARE THE RED SOX AND WHOEVER IS PLAYING THE YANKEES. But even sports fans appear to have some reservations about announcing how happy they really are at a rival's misfortune.

There's something concerning about the idea that fans

who are more likely to act aggressively look exactly the same as everyone else on surveys, and that only a brain scan betrays how they truly feel. But, it seems to me, there also is an upside. It indicates that even in the heads of the most aggressive Yankees and Sox fans, the brain—again—is performing some top-down control. These fans are having a reflex pleasure response in the brain, and then when it comes time to say how much they enjoyed it, they're exerting some awareness. Possibly it's awareness that schadenfreude is not attractive in society. More likely, I think—given that there's no real societal downside to telling a brain researcher that you really enjoyed watching the Yankees give up a home run to the Orioles—is that they're unaware of the depth of their own passion. Maybe it's a hopeful sign about the control the newer brain regions can exercise over the older reward area. Somewhere in this experiment the midbrain reward area on a Yankees fan screamed "*Woohoo!*" and the prefrontal cortex took that data and said, "Okay, it was cool. But it wasn't *that* cool."

THREE MONTHS AFTER MY TRIP TO NASHVILLE, I WATCHED THE best Nashville team in franchise history lose meekly in the playoffs to the unheralded Phoenix Coyotes. The Sharks had already been eliminated, my testosterone had no doubt resumed its normal rhythms, and I was just watching hockey because I enjoy the game . . . or because I wanted to watch Nashville burn. An interesting tug-of-war now took place inside me. The experience of sitting there with the taunting Nashville fans had wounded and scarred. But I liked Rick Grieve as a person and wished the team well for the sake of his kids and him. In Art Aron's relationship world, I had extended myself ever so slightly in his direction. In another world, though, I'd been derogated and attacked by an outgroup and so identified a hateful new rival. And the question was: How much schadenfreude would there be when they lost?

Ultimately, I regret to report, a fair amount. It was the "Hey, you suck" chants that did it; I happened to turn on one of the playoff games and when Nashville scored I heard the chant ringing around the arena again. When I talked to Antonello Bonci from the National Institute on Drug Abuse, he mentioned the way addicts associate intense activity in the dopamine reward system with particular cues. Like Pavlov's dogs, the brain on cocaine pays attention to everything happening around it when it gets that reward. Months or even years later—in the case of an addict, this could be post-jail, post-rehab—a color, or particular street, or name will flash back and reignite the drug craving. If the opposite is true, I'd had a powerful cue linked to my pain. And the instant I heard the chant again, after not having thought about the Predators for three months, the old trauma and emotion awakened. When a few days later they were eliminated, I made a conscious decision to underreport my schadenfreude. The rational part of my brain thought, and I might have even said this out loud, "Oh, too bad for Rick Grieve." The pleasure center went, "*Huhuhuhuhuhu. Hey, you suck!*"

OBVIOUSLY THERE'S NO REAL WAY TO WRAP UP THE ANTHROpological argument about conflict and human nature from a few studies of sports fans. But I did have one more area to explore. Group theory depends so much on context, and one of the major contentions is that there's a difference between unprovoked wars of aggression and defensive wars. Groups that are threatened by another group might act defensively, but this in itself isn't a proof that humans are inherently driven to conflict. To show that, you'd need to show that we go out of our way to engage in unprovoked group violence. I wondered if there was any sporting parallel, any rivalry that started entirely one-sidedly.

In *Among the Thugs*, the classic account of English hooliganism, the American writer Bill Buford joins the Manchester United "firm"—the unofficial, "bad supporters"—on a trip to Turin. The team happens to be playing there, but that's almost a side note. The English supporters' plane is met by the Italian army. Four buses convey the supporters to the town's central plaza, and something about that bus ride stuck in my memory. Buford describes a scene of nonviolent provocation: the fat boy behind him with his naked butt hanging out of his pants, people urinating out the window, people screaming profanities at women and children. Then someone throws a bottle from the bus, a "significant escalation," Buford writes. There's a pause for a moment, and then no repercussions and suddenly all four buses start spitting bottles. When an Italian boy finally responds and throws a stone back, the shocked reaction on the bus is fascinating: *he started it!*

"The incredulity was immense," Buford writes. "'Those bastards,' one of the supporters exclaimed, 'are throwing stones at the windows,' and the look on his face conveyed such urgent dismay that you could only agree that a stone-throwing Italian was a very bad person indeed. The pre-sumption—after all a window could get broken and some-one might get hurt—was deeply offensive, and everyone became very, very angry."

Buford wonders what the citizens of Turin must have thought. You would be living an ordinary day, having done nothing aggressive at all, and suddenly here came police sirens and then four buses full of crazed, demonic English-men screaming insults and obscenities. How could anyone objectively watching the day's action think this had not been defensive aggression on the part of the Italian boy?

But every Englishman Buford talked to went out of his way to emphasize that he was a football supporter, not a hooligan. The English hadn't started it. They had acted de-fensively, not offensively.

In the afternoon, when the English supporters went to the stadium, the same thing happened in reverse. Now the English were herded into a single, unprotected area while the Italian fans greeted them with a hail of bottles. The Ital-ians could argue, of course, that the English had started it by trashing the city's plaza, but there is every suggestion that they would have greeted the Manchester supporters that way no matter what.

Here's what I think is the critical part: the culture of hooliganism at the time let both sides get away with elabo-rate self-deception. The progress in reducing hooliganism in Europe, especially in England, in the last twenty years, shows how important culture is in moderating war—whether we're inherently warlike or not. (That overwhelm-ing majorities of Americans go to watch sports live without battling like proxy armies should make that clear, anyway.)

Buford had, in some sense, the same question about offensive and defensive aggression. As he stood among the English supporters in the stadium and tried to dodge the missiles raining down from above, he noticed the television cameramen and journalists watching calmly from the home supporters side.

"I remember thinking," he wrote, "if the day becomes more violent, who do you blame? The English, whose behavior on the square could be said to have been so provocative that they deserved whatever they got? The Italians, whose welcome consisted in inflicting injuries on their visitors? Or can you place some of the blame on these men with their television equipment and their cameras, whose misrepresentative images served only to reinforce what everyone had come to expect?"

The English and Italians haven't changed their essential human nature in the last two decades. They've just been forced, by self-policing, by regulation, and by changing news coverage, to stop lying to themselves about who started what.

ONE OF THE PRESENTERS AT THE WESTERN KENTUCKY SPORTS Psychology Forum was a young professor from the University of Memphis named Cody Havard. Havard got his undergraduate degree at the University of Texas and one of the things that stuck with him, as a sports fan, was the incredible intensity of the football rivalry with the University of Oklahoma. In the year that Texas beat Oklahoma but suffered a late-season loss that allowed Oklahoma into the national championship game, Havard remembers rooting fervently for Florida to trounce his rival for the title. Which

Florida did, led by Tim Tebow. For Havard the interest in Florida was one-and-done. No residual loyalty to the school or to Tebow, not even residual interest. He just wanted Oklahoma to lose to anyone they encountered and he wondered why. Based on everything we've learned, it makes a lot of sense why your own team winning or losing matters so much. But why, Havard wondered, does it matter so much when your team isn't even involved? Especially, in the case of the 2008 college football championship, when rationally, at least, Oklahoma winning would probably have reflected better on Havard's team?

Havard and I talked a few weeks after the forum and he told me that he was studying the creation of rivalry. College realignment meant that several schools were moving into new divisions in which they had no real history. They were leaving behind rivals with almost a century of history. A new rivalry, I thought, seemed like the best form of unprovoked aggression I could find in sports fans. So I called Havard to ask: Who hated whom first, and why?

Havard and Daniel Wann had recently surveyed more than 150 sports fans from the various teams that were switching divisions. He asked them to identify their traditional rival and who they thought the new rival would be, then asked about aggression: How likely are you to act aggressively toward your old rival versus the new one? He found, unsurprisingly, that fans hate their old rivals more than they hate their prospective new ones. They were more likely to say that if granted anonymity, they'd interfere with or even hurt star players on the other team when asked about the traditional rival versus the anticipated rival. But in the general comments to his survey, he also found something interesting: many fans were excited to switch conferences and generally viewed all the new teams in their division with some level of tolerance. Texas A&M, in fact, had taken out an advertisement to show its excitement at joining the powerful Southeastern Conference featuring Texas A&M fans doing the cheers for each of the SEC teams.

This seemed, to me, like a suggestion that it takes an actual act of aggression to start a rivalry. Over the years, as Arkansas and Texas A&M slug away at each other, fear and loathing will develop. But for now, even though Texas A&M fans anticipated that Arkansas would be the key rival, there just wasn't as much hatred.

"There's this level of anticipation that, 'Oh, we're leaving the bad guys behind,'" Havard said. "'When we join this new conference it's a fresh start where everyone in the conference is going to get along.' Obviously that's not going to happen, but it's occurring a little bit now for a lot of fans."

The traditional rivalries were full of classic parochial altruism. One study that Havard cited showed that fans simultaneously say they know nothing about the rival's academics but are equally positive it can't be as good as their own. Fans of one traditional basketball powerhouse said they couldn't wait to finally get rid of their classic rivals, who had been unworthy of their rivalry for so long.

The anticipated rivalries, meanwhile, remained in what Marilynn Brewer might call purely in-group favoritism. The teams that fans picked as their anticipated rival were generally the ones geographically closest—the ones, you might say, most threatening to the success of the in-group. In some cases, there was even considerable disagreement in whom the anticipated rival would be.

"One thing Dan [Wann] and I have talked about is how interesting it would be to redo this study in three years, after teams have played their anticipated rival, and ask them to compare anticipated and former rival," Havard said. "The rivalries that most of these schools are leaving now date over a hundred years. In a matter of two or three years, are these people going to forget a hundred years of history, aggression toward other teams?"

Implicit in Havard's study, though, is the idea that a rivalry eventually will form. He didn't ask why fans had picked the team that they anticipated would be the rival, but whether it forms in an act of collective unprovoked aggression—hey, now that they're available, let's go beat up on Arkansas!—or in an act of defensiveness—hey, Arkansas beat us, let's attack them back!—it will form.

Which leads to one final question about sports fans, the one raised by Michael Poliakoff's study of the diversity of fan cultures. Do we need rivalry? If we have the wiring for competition, do we have to make the choice to celebrate it?

Conclusion:
Do We Need Sports?

Jason Wigand tells the story of his first Cal football game with particular relish. It was a game against USC and he attended with his friend, a USC graduate. He remembers walking up to the stadium in the horde of people in blue and gold, little kids in Cal sweaters, tailgate aromas, face paint. He remembers how exciting it felt to join that group of Cal fans, and it reminds him of the energy of sports, how easy it is to pore over the new issues of college football magazines when they arrive on the newsstands, or to throw confetti in a victory parade. The question, which he poses as a challenge to the congregation of Redwood Chapel: Am I more excited about this than I am about what's actually meaningful in life?

"Am I more excited," he says, "about the Bears kicking off in August than the God I believe in?"

Jason is the youth pastor at Redwood Chapel, a small evangelical Protestant church in my hometown of Castro Valley. Jason and I went to high school together, and when at some point I started to wonder about an evangelical's take on sports, I turned to him as someone I liked and could trust for a thoughtful answer. We met in his office at the church, literally across the street from my high school. I hadn't been down that street in years, hadn't been inside Redwood Chapel in more than a decade. In the time since I last walked into a Christian religious ceremony I've been to Sikh Gurdwaras, Sufi shrines, and Candomblé rituals. Walking into Jason's surfboard-bedecked office steps from the school I attended almost every day for four years felt dizzyingly foreign.

Religion is one way of categorizing the world, so most of the lessons of group behavior apply equally well to religious behavior. When people compare sports and religion, or sports and politics, it's usually based on the tribal aspects that we've talked about. What I was more interested in asking Jason was about whether as a sports fan and youth pastor he ever felt as if sports somehow became competitive with his faith. He observed, as many others have, that on the surface there's plenty in common—a weekly observance steeped in ritual and promising spiritual ecstasy, with a certain behavioral code, a strong sense of belonging, and a stable foundation for identity. So, I asked, given that, how do you compare the two?

"Anyone who finds their ultimate meaning in God, there's always that tension," he said. "The Giants are on, I want to go surfing. The tension is, I just went to a place where they talked about the ultimate reality of the universe. And I agreed with that. Then I go home, and what do I do next?"

Jason framed it as, in some sense, a competition for his attention, but also a choice that he has to make as an individual. Humans, he said, are worshippers by nature. We'll find something and elevate it above other things, and that can be sports or family or religion.

"I'm a Christian," he said. "The ultimate, for me, is God, Jesus Christ. As much as I love those other things, I don't want to find my identity in the A's or the Bears. Because they're going to move. Or shut down. As much as I enjoy them, if I try to find my identity in these things that are temporary, I'm going to be left unfulfilled."

The tension in his life, then, is in remembering what's ultimate and what's fun but ultimately not as meaningful. "Am I more excited about things that will pass away and be meaningless in one hundred years than something I believe will last all eternity?" he said. "To be honest, that's a constant tension."

When we finished chatting it was late in the afternoon, and Jason walked me to the door. Since he was a Cal fan, I told him I was telling the story, in the book, of the famous Kevin Riley game. (Every Cal fan remains traumatized by this one.) "You talk about tension," Jason said. "That was like being punched in the soul."

Whether it's an "ultimate" thing or not—and in that formulation I don't think sports is an "ultimate" thing for me, either, necessarily—it's something we both enjoy. I left the church thinking about connection, and thinking that at a more basic level Jason the youth pastor was reemphasizing the same lesson I'd heard from testosterone researchers, neuroscientists, and psychologists.

This is one of the major themes of everything we've talked about so far: despite all those behaviors buried deep in our nature, in our hormones, neurons, and psychological processes: with culture, choice, and control you can raise and elevate anything. You can choose, as the Greeks did, to prioritize competition, or as the Romans did, to shun it. You can choose, as Jason does, to prioritize Jesus. You can choose to temper your sports enthusiasm, or to amplify it. But the point is that you can choose.

I WONDER ABOUT THE CONSEQUENCES OF THAT CHOICE. JASON contends that humans have a need to worship something, that if we're not worshipping Jesus we'll worship something else. Whatever it is, we'll find something. Can you broaden that to cover some of the different behaviors we've talked about in this book? If something like violence is pro-grammed into our genetic code, does that mean we have to slake our bloodlust from time to time, whether vicariously or not? For someone like me, leading a generally unemo-tional life, do I need the hormonal swings provided by sports?

Aristotle approved of the theater because he thought it allowed people a healthy emotional release. When Germany played Greece in soccer in the 2012 European Champi-onships, plenty of commentators suggested the game would allow Greeks and Germans to express their cultural differ-ences in a healthy forum. We have the same conversation about soap-opera drama on reality TV and artistic violence in video games.

This is the "hydraulic theory of violence," Steven Pinker wrote in *The Better Angels of Our Nature*. "Many people implicitly believe in the Hydraulic Theory of Violence: that humans harbor an inner drive toward aggression (a death instinct or thirst for blood), which builds up inside us and must periodically be discharged," he wrote. "Nothing could be further from a contemporary scientific understanding of the psychology of violence."

I think this is the confusion: we have a tendency to assume that things that come easily to us are things that are inherent to us. This is my Barcalounger theory of behavior. Our brains are set up to categorize others and form groups, so that when we divide the world into us-and-them and act aggressively, we can defensively claim to being victims of natural human response. We form relationships and map our biases onto in-group members because that's just what we do.

But it is not. We have control. We have this giant reasoning machine in our forehead that can overrule what's easy to us. Almost every scientist I talked to for this book— testosterone researchers, neuroscientists, addiction specialists, evolutionary psychologists—spoke about our ability to override our nature. These scientists aren't coordinating their outfits and their message before they talk to me; control and overriding our nature *are*, in fact, our nature. "An ability to hold our instincts up to the light, rather than naively accepting their products in our consciousness as just the way things are, is the first step in discounting them when they lead to harmful ends," Pinker concluded.

You can choose. It's clear that a lot of sports fans choose poorly. But oddly enough, I think the vast majority of sports fans make pretty decent choices. Pete Gutierrez and Gorilla Rilla choose to sacrifice their own time and money to help out, even when the people they're helping are wearing Steelers jerseys. Todd Dery chooses to sacrifice the happiness of following a winner for the meaning that comes with generations of Indians pride. Jason Wigand chooses to subdue his passion for sports in favor of more important eternal truths. Bill Morgan chooses not to watch live sports to maintain emotional equilibrium. The Tottenham fans that cheered Fabrice Muamba chose to overrule their instant out-group categorization and recognize a player in desperate circumstances as a fellow human being in need of aid.

It gets plenty of publicity when it happens, but sports fan dysfunction turns out to be remarkably rare because the vast majority of people are better than we give them credit for at making humane choices.

IT'S NOW BEEN ALMOST A CENTURY SINCE UPTON SINCLAIR railed against the plutocracy running the University of California and the "mobs of haters" the university presidents had encouraged. In that time the price tag on the stadium that Sinclair decried has grown from $1 million to $350 million. Cal and Stanford still play the Big Game in football, still fight over the possession of a battle-axe, still train their sons and daughters to recognize blue and gold or Cardinal and white as enemy colors. The plutocracy still has deep roots in California government and among the University of California Board of Regents. And Cal remains the top-ranked public university in the world while Stanford remains among the top two or three universities of any kind in the world. Together the two universities have played more than one hundred football games—and together they have accounted for more than one hundred Nobel Prizes. Generations of men and women have cheered at the Big Game and then gone on to incredible individual careers.

On October 7, 2006, almost a year to the day before I had my heart broken in those ruthless ten seconds against Oregon State, I stood in the same familiar place high in Memorial Stadium. My dad was there. The neighboring student section was a frenzied mob of blue-and-gold chaos on a glorious fall Saturday. It was midway through a season that would turn out to be the most successful Cal football season of my adult life, and Cal was ranked seventeenth in the country. The day's opponent, the University of Oregon, was ranked eleventh. Standing there, moments before kickoff, the stadium yet again crackled with electricity. There is nowhere I've ever been that's more exciting than Memorial Stadium in those few moments.

At the fifty-yard line the referees summon the dignitaries for the ceremonial coin toss. Today's dignitary is extra-awesome: it is George Smoot, a physics professor who four days earlier was awarded the Nobel Prize. As the white-haired Smoot walks onto the field, the dancing, leaping students notice him. And then, as the man who helped discover anisotropies in the cosmic microwave background flips the coin, the students chant, "No-bel Prize! No-bel Prize!" Smoot responds by climbing onto the dais separating the field from the stands and leading the students in a cheer of "Go Bears!"

When I set out to write a book about sports fans, I was not in a particularly tolerant frame of mind. It was following a bitter loss and the recrimination led mainly to questions about why billions of people around the world passionately follow something so stupid and psychopathic. I didn't understand why I cared, I wasn't sure I wanted to care, and I felt that I didn't have a choice either way. But the more I researched and reported, the more I started to appreciate being a fan. Sports fans really aren't any better or worse than anyone else, and all the reflexes and cognitive turbulence happening inside us makes this whole spectator thing pretty remarkable. Sports fans exist in every human society in every time period because evolution has given us brain and body systems that respond easily to vicarious competition, and pretty much every culture has figured out some way to celebrate the way we're made. I've come to think of it as a noble endeavor in human culture, the best and worst and greatest hits of *Homo sapiens*. We've evolved for competition and possibly conflict, our hormones spike our aggression, our identification blinds us to bias, prejudice, and violence—but the little gray cells ride through it all masterfully with some level of rational clarity and a good deal of empathetic love.

We are not just warring chimpanzees. We are not beholden to Man Laws. We are not reducible to barbarians at play. We are not even subject to any kind of fan nature; we are more complex than that. We sports fan are glorious expressions of all the wondrous quirks and oddities in human nature.

Index